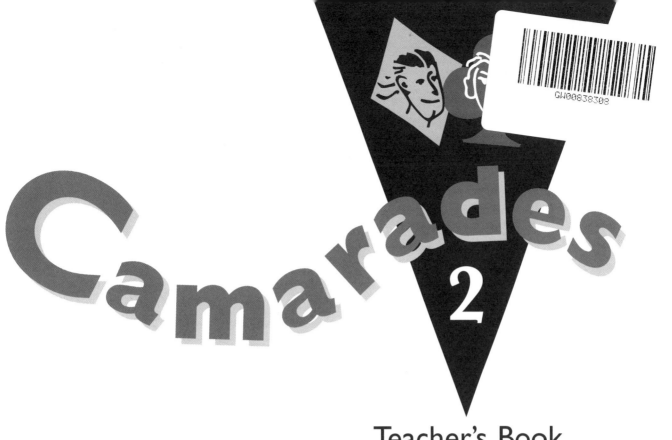

Camarades

2

Teacher's Book

Martine Pillette
with IT opportunities by
David Buckland

MGP INTERNATIONAL

Camarades 2

Pupil's Book
Teacher's Resource File
Flashcards
Teacher's Book
Cassettes (5)

Edited and typeset by Gaafar & Wightwick, 47a High Street, Chinnor, Oxfordshire, OX9 4DJ
The author and publishers would like to thank the following:
Caroline Woods and Steven Crossland for writing the Assessment sections.
David Buckland for writing the IT sections.

First published 1997
ISBN 0 7487 2343 9

Note: The rights of Martine Pillette, Caroline Woods, Stephen Crossland and David
Buckland to be identified as authors of this work has abeen asserted by them in
accordance with the Copyright Designs and Patents Act 1988.

98 99 00 01 / 10 9 8 7 6 5 4 3 2

Mary Glasgow Publications
An imprint of Stanley Thornes (Publishers) Ltd
Ellenborough House
Wellington Street
CHELTENHAM
GL50 1YW

Printed and bound in Great Britain
By Ashford Colour Press, Gosport. Hants.

Contents

Introduction:

    General   3

    Course Structure   3

    IT opportunities   6

    Assessment   7

    Presentation Copymasters   8

    Flashcards   9

Unité 1   10

Unité 2   30

Epreuve 1   51

Unité 3   54

Unité 4   76

Epreuve 2   95

Unité 5   98

Unité 6   120

Epreuve 3   139

Epreuve finale   142

INTRODUCTION

Camarades is a four-stage course designed to motivate your pupils and help them achieve success in learning French. The methodology was carefully devised after two years of extensive research into teachers' needs, and the **Camarades 1** materials have been thoroughly trialled and tested in the classroom.

- **Camarades** has been created for the National Curriculum at KS3/4, 5–14 Guidelines and the Standard Grade Curriculum.

- It is characterised by steady, spiralling progression across all stages.

- It offers a unique differentiation scheme that caters for pupils of mixed ability, with higher- and lower-ability Pupils' Books at Years 9 and 10/11 (S2, 3, and 4).

- It fully supports assessment for the revised National Curriculum and examination requirements (SCAA, GCSE, Standard Grade).

Course structure

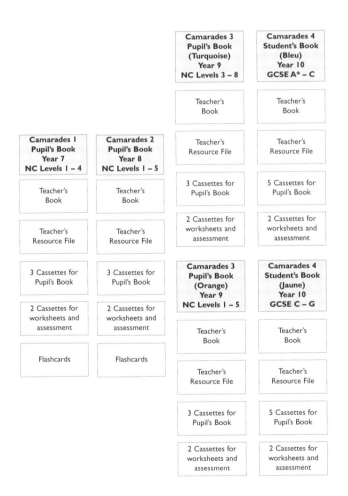

Camarades 2

Camarades 2 provides a full course for the second year of learning French. It equips learners with real language appropriate to their age, and presents and practises the language within authentic and relevant contexts. The components are:

- **Pupil's Book**
  Unit 1 Une visite de la Martinique
  Unit 2 On fait du shopping
  Unit 3 Une invitée idéale?
  Unit 4 On va à Paris?
  Unit 5 Les aventures de Grégory
  Unit 6 L'école est finie!

- **Teacher's Book**

- **Teacher's Resource File** (worksheets and assessment on copymasters)

- **5 cassettes**

- **Flashcards**

Pupil's Book

To increase interest and motivation, a scenario is developed throughout each unit and appears at the beginning of each teaching spread as a *bande dessinée* (*BD*) or presentation.

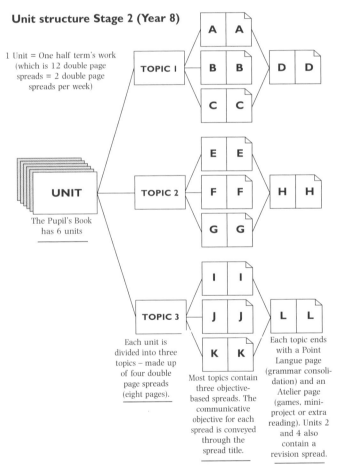

Cassettes

- 3 for the Pupil's Book – one unit per side.

- 1 for the worksheets.

- 1 for the assessment.

Teacher's Resource File

Contains 160 photocopiable copymasters including presentation, vocabulary, worksheets and assessment.

- Assessment materials (see page 7)
- Worksheets for each unit:

  On écoute / On lit /On parle / On écrit Two differentiated copymasters for each skill area.

  Grammaire Differentiated grammar activities that supplement the Pupil's Book **Point Langue** pages.

  On s'amuse Games and creative activities.

  Plaisir de lire Reading for pleasure.

  Que sais-tu? Consolidation activities for each topic.

  Glossaire Bilingual vocabulary list of the key language of the unit.

- Other copymasters:

  Présentation Clear black and white visuals which can be made into OHP transparencies or photocopied and cut up to use in games.

  On communique A reminder of key classroom language (Unit 1).

  On révise Units 5/6 revision activities.

  Grilles Grids to assist pupils with some of the Pupil's Book activities.

  Réponses Answers to worksheet activities.

Teacher's Book contents

- An overview of each unit
- Clear, concise teaching notes
- Teaching notes and mark schemes for the four assessment sections
- Answers to Pupil's Book exercises
- Tapescripts in sequence
- Information and guidance on key aspects of the course
- IT opportunities (see page 6)

Presenting the new language

The teacher's notes for each Pupil's Book spread offer detailed suggestions on how to introduce the new language through:

- flashcards
- presentation copymasters
- *bande dessinée (BD)*
- mime, use of realia, etc.

Additional suggestions using the flashcards or the presentation copymasters:

- *Répétez au choix* Selective repetition (*Répétez seulement si vous aimez ça/vous avez ça/vous préférez ça*, etc.)
- *Vrai ou faux?* Pupils repeat only accurate descriptions.
- *Devinez* Pupils predict the picture you are hiding.
- *Classez* Pupils classify the pictures you describe accordingly.
- *Jeu de Kim* Pupils name the pictures from memory.
- *Jeu de mime* One pupil mimes a picture for others to guess its nature.

- *Contre la montre* Use a stop watch. Individual pupils describe all the pictures displayed against the clock.
- *Loto* Pupils cut out presentation pictures for a game of bingo.
- *Bons réflexes* Pupils use presentation pictures to play snap. When two identical cards show, the first pupil to describe the card accurately is the winner.
- *On épèle* Start spelling a word. Pupils must show the matching picture as quickly as possible and spell the word in full.
- *Le jeu de l'alphabet* Disclose the written words from the presentation copymasters a little at a time. Pupils try to spell them from memory.
- *Faites des phrases* Pupils say as much as they can about a picture.

Additional suggestions, combining pictures from several topics for revision purposes:

- *Catégories* Mix transport/souvenirs/leisure pictures, etc. Pupils first guess the category, then the exact card.
- *Télépathie* Show one picture only from each of a series of topics (eg. a food, a means of transport, etc.). Say something loosely related to the picture without naming the word on the picture (eg. *Je n'ai pas faim, merci; C'est assez cher mais très rapide.*) Pupils identify and name the picture.
- *Ecoutez mon histoire* Mix several topics for revision purposes. Cut out and number presentation pictures, and put them on the OHP. Tell a story based on some of the pictures. Pupils must identify the relevant pictures.
- *Inventez une histoire* Same set up as above, but present fewer pictures and ask pupils to make up a story based on them.

Songs, Rap and Poems

	Pupil's Book	Copymasters
Unité 1	p 7	
Unité 2	p 29, 38	*Feuille 11*
Unité 3	p 57	
Unité 4	p 89	*Feuille 16*
Unité 5		*Feuille 11*
Unité 6		*Feuille 6*

The songs, raps and poems in **Camarades 2** help reinforce vocabulary, structures and pronunciation in an enjoyable and relaxing way. In line with language development, some of the songs, raps and poems in **Camarades 2** contain concrete language while others are of a more abstract nature. Most of the language is familiar to pupils or consists of words very similar to English. Here are some suggestions for presentation, before tackling the activities suggested in the Pupil's Book or on copymasters:

- Where appropriate, invent actions to accompany the songs.
- Allow pupils to hum the tune or clap the rhythm as they listen.
- Give groups of pupils a different key word to listen for: they wave both hands in the air or show the relevant flashcard when they hear their word.

Progression

Extensive research has shown that pupils' progress can be hampered by a lack of structured progression in their learning. **Camarades 2** ensures steady progression through a variety of approaches:

- Spiralling progression in the teaching of language and skills.

- Gradual progression on each teaching spread from the receptive to the productive.

- Regular *A toi!* activities to enable pupils to use the language for their own purposes.

- Revision activities in the Pupil's Book or on copymasters.

- *Que sais-tu?* copymasters for consolidation.

Camarades 2 provides activities at levels 1–5 in every unit. Many activities can be carried out at a variety of levels thanks to the differentiated ♦/♣ tasks, the open-ended tasks and the extra suggestions for differentiation contained in the teacher's notes.

Apart from the assessment materials, specific National Curriculum levels are not indicated for each activity in **Camarades 2**. NC documents stress that a picture of a pupil's performance should be built up across a range of work, and in a variety of contexts, rather than by assessing individual pieces of work. They underline the importance of the teacher's professional judgement regarding the level at which a pupil is operating. Specific guidelines regarding levels can be found in the Assessment introduction below.

Differentiation

Camarades 2 facilitates positive achievement among all pupils through a carefully devised system of differentiation:

- ♦ and ♣ tasks in the Pupil's Book. Less able pupils follow the ♦ rubric while more able pupils follow the ♣ rubric. In some instances, pupils can first follow the ♦ rubric, then the ♣ rubric as an extra.

- ♦ and ♣ single-skill copymasters. Depending on the nature of these copymasters, pupils can either do either the ♦ or the ♣ tasks, or both. Advice is given where necessary in the teacher's notes to organise pupils so that they can work independently.

- ♦ and ♣ tasks on the *Point Langue* pages and the grammar copymasters.

- Open-ended tasks towards the end of spreads, topics and units. These enable different pupils to work on the same tasks, but at varying levels of ability.

- Extra suggestions in the teacher's notes to extend tasks or make them more accessible to less able pupils.

Grammar

The four-way approach to grammar in **Camarades 2** is based on the premise that grammar should be taught, not caught.

- *Grammar boxes* Highlight the new grammar in context on the teaching spreads and encourage pupils to identify the new patterns.

- *Point Langue* One Pupil's Book page at the end of each topic consolidates the work on the key grammar point introduced in the topic. ♦ activities focus on recognition and manipulation while ♣ activities focus on productive use of the new grammar.

- *Grammar summary* Detailed explanations, with examples, at the back of the Pupils' Book.

- *Copymasters* One worksheet per topic to supplement the Pupil's Book activities on key grammar points or provide practice on smaller grammar points.

Language learning strategies

Camarades facilitates language acquisition through systematic teaching of language-learning skills. In **Camarades 2**, strategy boxes give advice to help pupils develop transferable skills in listening, speaking, reading and writing. Each box has a specific focus:

- study skills

- memorisation skills

- organisational skills

- dictionary skills

- reference skills

- improving performance

- logic

Target language

Maximum use of French can only be achieved through a structured, progressive approach. In **Camarades**, every effort has been put into encouraging and facilitating the use of French by all.

- The rubrics are kept as short and simple as possible, and are illustrated with examples wherever necessary.

- Most of the grammar and strategy boxes are in French, but use words sparingly and rely extensively on familiar language, cognates and near cognates.

- In the few instances where English is used, it is kept to a minimum.

- Page 155 of the Pupil's Book provides a bilingual list of the key language of rubrics and teacher instructions as well as pupil-to-teacher phrases.

- The *On communique* copymaster in *Unité 1* provides a reminder of key phrases for pair and group work.

IT opportunities

IT and the National Curriculum

The appropriate use of Information Technology (IT) is referred to in the National Curriculum Orders for Modern Foreign Languages. Reference is also made to the use of IT in the opportunities listed in the Programme of Study, part 1.

'Appropriate' should be understood as the use of IT to support teaching and learning in ways that would have been impossible or harder to achieve using alternative resources.

The activities

IT opportunities are listed at the beginning of each unit. In this way, a teacher using **Camarades 2** can see at a glance what sort of preparations need to be made e.g. booking IT rooms, obtaining software etc.

 There is also this reminder symbol in the summary box at the top of the pages of teaching notes for the spreads that have IT opportunities.

The activities proposed for **Camarades 2** can be classed as either 'core' or 'additional'.

Core activities feature in each unit. They consist of:

- **Text manipulation**
  The teacher creates and saves, in a text manipulation programme, a 'model' of a good quality piece of writing (relating to the themes, vocabulary and structures of the unit) that pupils should be capable of restoring to its original form and, at a later stage, emulating.
  If the programme provides all or some of the features listed below, pupils will be able to access and exploit the text in a range of ways that will demand accuracy while at the same time developing understanding of language systems and structures.

    – The text is presented with the first letter of each word visible.

    – The text is presented in a gapped or "cloze" format.

    – The text can be previewed if required.

    – There are appropriate "help" options (e.g. see the text, reveal a letter, reveal a word).

- **Word processing – guided writing**
  The teacher creates and saves a text with certain words or phrases highlighted. Pupils are asked to substitute these words and phrases for others that would be appropriate.

- **Presentation**
  Pupils produce a presentation using available and appropriate software. Depending on the task suggested, this could be anything from a word processor incorporating clipart to a full multi-media authoring package.

The core activities themselves, along with further guidance, are included in the teacher's notes for each unit.

Additional activities feature in some, but not all, of the units. They consist of:

- **Word processing – extended writing**
  This involves either free writing or activities in which pupils expand a simple text or set of notes, for example by including new vocabulary or previously learnt elements of grammar and structure.

- **Data handling**
  These activities are intended to produce interesting and possibly controversial information that will stimulate the teaching and learning of a wide range of language.

- **The Internet**
  Pupils are given strategies for searching the World Wide Web in order to find appropriate and useful information.

These additional activities, along with further guidance, are included in the teacher's notes for the units in which they occur.

Timetable considerations

The inclusion of core activity-types in each unit will give teachers the best possible opportunity to provide entitlement to all pupils in situations where access to IT resources might be limited.

For example, if it is not possible to get all classes in the year group into a computer room to use a wordprocessor during the time allocated to Unit 1 of the book, one or two classes could use the facilities at this stage, while others could have the opportunity to work on similar word processing tasks in any of the later units.

Similarly, if computers are used in the classroom, a third of the class could work on the text manipulation activities in Units 1 and 4, a third in Units 2 and 5, and a third in Units 3 and 6.

Thoughtful planning of the additional activities can also support entitlement. For example, half the year group could take part in the first of the two data handling activities, while the remaining half year could take part in the second.

Differentiation

Differentiation is possible in a number of the above activities. For example:

- The teacher can create texts of different length and complexity for text manipulation and word processing activities.

- The text manipulation package used may provide a variety of options (e.g. preview the text – or not) that will support a differentiated approach.

- Presentation and free writing tasks have been designed to achieve differentiation by outcome.

- Presentation software can range from the comparatively simple to the very complex.

- A database can be interrogated with simple or complex searches, depending on the information required.

- The language used by pupils to explain/follow up a database activity can extend from the simple to the advanced.

Practicalities

Teachers are frequently asked to write and save files for pupils to work on whether these are for text manipulation, word processing or data handling. A backup of the files should always be kept in case pupils overwrite them.

Pupils should be reminded that when they amend a teacher file in any way, they must save it under a different file name in order to preserve the master file for others to use.

Assessment

Epreuves

These are all photocopyable and can be found in the **Teacher's Resource File**. Each assessment consists of four separate tests, in Listening, Speaking, Reading and Writing, to match the National Curriculum Attainment Targets.

Epreuve 1
Revision and testing for Units 1 & 2   pp 42–50

Epreuve 2
Revision and testing for Units 3 & 4   pp 91–98

Epreuve 3
Revision and testing for Units 5 & 6   pp 143–151

Epreuve finale
Final testing covering all six units   page 152–160

Assessment of levels

- The separate exercises are graded according to difficulty, in order to cater for various levels of ability. With more able pupils, teachers may decide to leave out tests designed to elicit performance at lower levels.

- The assessment criteria referred to in the mark schemes for each test are referenced against the NC Level descriptions (Levels 1–5).

- Each test has been written to provide pupils with opportunities to display characteristics of performance across a range of contexts, and through a variety of activities and inputs, which feature in the level descriptions.

- It should be remembered that "the level descriptions are not intended to be used to level individual pieces of work" (S.C.A.A. – Teacher's Handbook Key Stage 3 Optional Tests and Tasks – *Modern Foreign Languages*).

Differentiation

Speaking and Writing – tasks feature assessment techniques which generally differentiate by outcome. A common stimulus may elicit different performances from pupils of different abilities.

Listening and Reading – differentiation by task is carried out using different:

- levels of difficulty of input materials
- density and speed of delivery of taped materials
- types of task (e.g. identifying main points, points of view, specific details etc.).

Aims of summative testing

These summative assessments, provided at intervals throughout the course, are designed to:

- help teachers obtain a rounded judgement about each pupil's attainment
- assess how well pupils can tackle material from a range of topics (this especially applies to the final assessment, though each test provides some revision of material presented in the preceding units)

- pinpoint areas that may require revision on an individual or class basis, and thus assist future planning

- supplement, but in no way supplant, teacher's on-going or formative assessment of his/her pupils by giving opportunities to build up a profile of each pupil's performance in the four language skills

- help departments work together to achieve consistency in assessment methods.

Points to note

- All listening assessment has been recorded twice, with a 'beep' for you to pause the tape. You will need to decide on the length of timing of the pause to allow your pupils adequate time to write their answers. Before each repetition, you will hear the words: *Ecoute encore une fois*.

- **Dictionaries** – teachers may or may not want to give access to dictionaries. As a general guideline, it is suggested that pupils have access to dictionaries in Reading and Writing tests and in the preparation time for Speaking tests (i.e. in situations in which the context makes it likely that a dictionary could be used) but not in Listening tests.

- **Scene-setting/explanation of tasks** – target language rubrics have been kept to a minimum and reflect the wordings used in the Pupil's Book. However, before commencing a test, teachers may feel it necessary to give extra support in terms of scene-setting or checking that target language rubrics are fully understood. This extra support should be borne in mind when judging attainment, particularly across a group or several parallel teaching groups.

- **Speaking** – Pupils may work in pairs or teachers may prefer to interview individual pupils. The Speaking tests have been devised so that a variety of activities can be usefully tackled while allowing the teacher to circulate if necessary. Preparation time for such tests, could either be at home or in class.

- **Timing of the tests** – although the tests have been designed to take place after particular units of work have been covered, the timing can be varied. A department may choose not to use all the tests, but may prefer to select tasks, as appropriate. The time allowed to complete a test may also vary.

- **Marking for comprehension** – unless otherwise stated in the marking schemes (e.g. some of the Writing tests at the higher levels), pupils' written French should be assessed for **communication**. The marking schemes give guidance in terms of utterances produced and a system of bonus marks can be used which enables communication/accuracy and the amount of teacher help needed to be assessed.

- **Recording the outcomes** – Each department can, of course, adopt its own method for recording progress through the levels for individual pupils. A notional total of 25 marks per test, per skill has, however, been retained. Although not referred to directly in the marking schemes, this notional total may help departments to allocate marks according to the curriculum model which they may be following under their own notional system, as it clearly reflects the equal weightings of the four skills across the tests.

Presentation copymasters

Unit 1, spread B
J'ai les cheveux…
… noirs / … blonds / … bruns / … roux
J'ai les yeux…
… bleus / … verts / … gris / … marron

Unit 1, spread F
Allemagne / Angleterre / Belgique / Ecosse / Espagne / France /
Grande Bretagne / Grèce / Irlande / Italie / Pays de Galles

Unit 1, spread J
Est-ce que vous faites des voyages?

Est-ce que vous travaillez le samedi?

Qu'est-ce que vous portez au collège?

Qu'est-ce que vous faites à midi?

Qu'est-ce que vous faites comme sports?

Unit 2, spread C
C'est trop grand / petit

C'est trop long / court

C'est trop large / juste

C'est parfait

Je peux essayer?

C'est là-bas

Unit 2, spread F
Où est…
… le poisson?
… la boucherie?
… la boulangerie?
… la laiterie?
… la pâtisserie?
… l'alimentation générale?
… la caisse?

Où sont…
… les boissons?
… les fruits et légumes?
… les surgelés?

Unit 2, spread G
après / devant / derrière / entre / en face de / à côté de /
à gauche de / à droite de

Unit 3, spread C
Est-ce que je peux…

Est-ce que tu veux…
… prendre un bain?
… prendre une douche?
… téléphoner?
… écouter un CD?
… manger quelque chose?
… boire une limonade?

Unit 3, spread E/F
Il est…
… quatre heures
… quatre heures cinq / dix / et quart / vingt / vingt-cinq / et demie
… cinq heures moins vingt-cinq / moins vingt / moins le quart /
moins dix / moins cinq

Unit 3, spread G
un film

un jeu-télé

un feuilleton

du sport

les informations

des variétés

des dessins animés

Unit 4, spread F
– Je voudrais dix francs en pièces de 1f, s'il vous plaît.
– Oui, voilà dix pièces.
– Je voudrais 100f en billets de 20f, s'il vous plaît.
– Oui, voilà cinq billets.

Unit 4, spread G
Je voudrais deux billets pour adultes, s'il vous plaît.

Je voudrais deux billets pour enfants, s'il vous plaît.

Vous avez un tarif groupes?

C'est une visite guidée?

Vous avez des dépliants?

Où est-ce qu'on peut acheter des souvenirs?

Où sont les vestiaires?

Où sont les toilettes?

Où est la cafétéria?

Où est-ce qu'on peut manger?

Unit 5, spread E
J'ai été…

J'ai visité…

J'ai mangé…

J'ai regardé…

J'ai écouté…

J'ai travaillé…

J'ai acheté…

Unit 5, spread F
J'ai pris des photos

J'ai bu un coca

J'ai fait une promenade

J'ai vu la station spatiale

J'ai perdu ma veste

Unit 5, spread G
C'est tout droit

C'est la première / deuxième / troisième / rue à gauche / droite

C'est sur la gauche

C'est sur la droite

Unit 5, spread K
Tu as…
… voyagé comment?
… pris le car à quelle heure?
… voyagé avec qui?
… visité Paris quand?
… mangé où?
… bu quoi?
… acheté des souvenirs?
… payé combien?

Unit 6, spread B
J'ai… / Je n'ai pas…
… bien travaillé
… beaucoup travaillé
… beaucoup révisé
… bien fait mes devoirs
… beaucoup bavardé
… souvent oublié mes cahiers
… trouvé le travail difficile
… en maths, etc.
Et toi?

Unit 6, spread C
Cette année,...
... j'ai été dans l'équipe de netball
... j'ai été au club de musique
... j'ai fait douze matchs de foot
... j'ai gagné une compétition d'athlétisme
... j'ai aidé à la bibliothèque
... j'ai aidé pour la fête
... j'ai joué dans Bugsy Malone
... je n'ai pas fait d'activités

Flashcards

Unité 1

1 travailleur (-euse)
2 paresseux (-euse)
3 embêtant (e)
4 drôle
5 sympa
6 sportif (-ive)
7 timide
8 bavard (e)
9 industriel(le)
10 calme
11 joli(e)
12 bruyant(e)
13 ancien(ne)
14 moderne
15 un bureau
16 un magasin
17 un grand magasin
18 une usine
19 un hôpital
20 une banque
21 un hôtel
22 une ferme
23 à la maison
24 il / elle ne travaille pas

Unité 2

25 un T-shirt et un short
26 un jean et une chemise
27 une jupe et un pull
28 une veste et un pantalon
29 un demi-litre de lait
30 un kilo de pommes de terre
31 500g de viande hachée
32 100g de fromage
33 une bouteille de limonade
34 une boîte de tomates
35 une tranche de jambon
36 un paquet de beurre
37 un pot de yaourt
38 un tube de dentifrice
39 une tarte aux fraises
40 une baguette

Unité 3

41 un / ton porte-monnaie
42 une / ta télécarte

43 du / ton savon
44 de l' / ton argent
45 une / ta brosse à dents
46 rester à la maison
47 sortir
48 aller à la patinoire
49 aller à la discothèque
50 aller au bowling
51 je fais la vaisselle
52 je fais la cuisine
53 je fais les courses
54 je fais le ménage
55 je fais ma chambre

Unité 4

56 visiter un musée
57 visiter la Tour Eiffel
58 faire du bateau
59 aller au zoo
60 aller au parc
61 aller à Disneyland
62 en avion
63 en bus
64 en train
65 en voiture
66 en car
67 un badge
68 un porte-clés
69 des autocollants
70 des cartes postales
71 un livre sur l'Afrique

Unité 5

72 la librairie
73 le commissariat
74 la pharmacie
75 le marché
76 un aller simple
77 un aller-retour
78 le train part à quelle heure?
79 le train arrive à quelle heure?
80 il y a un wagon-restaurant?
81 c'est quel quai?

Unité 6

82 faire le jardin
83 laver la voiture
84 garder mon petit frère
85 aller en vacances
86 je ne vais pas travailler
87 faire des barbecues
88 nager
89 bronzer
90 aller à la montagne
91 aller à la mer
92 aller à la campagne
93 aller dans un camping
94 aller dans un hôtel
95 aller dans un gîte
96 aller chez mes grands-parents

CAMARADES 2		OVERVIEW – UNITE 1 – UNE VISITE DE LA MARTINIQUE			NATIONAL CURRICULUM	
	Topics/Objectives	Key language	Grammar	Strategies	PoS coverage	AoE
A	**Une visite de la Martinique** Introduction to Martinique	Partial recycling of personal details, house, pets, school subjects and hobbies		Cognates & near cognates as an aid to understanding	1 g, i 2 a, j, n	ABCE
B	**J'ai les cheveux bruns** Saying what someone looks like	*Tu es comment? / Il (elle) est comment, ton frère (ta sœur)? J'ai / Il a / Elle a ... les yeux bleus / gris / verts / marron. ... les cheveux blancs / noirs / blonds / bruns / roux / assez longs / très courts.* Recycling of days of the week	Present tense of *avoir* Recycling of adjectival agreements	Looking up French words in a dictionary	1 a, d, g, i 2 a, j 3 f	B
C	**Ta classe est sympa?** Saying what someone is like (personality)	*Tu es comment? / Il est comment, ton frère (ta sœur)? Je suis... / Je ne suis pas... / Il (Elle) est... / n'est pas... paresseux (euse) / sportif (ive) / travailleur (euse) / bavard(e) / embêtant(e) / sympa / drôle / timide.* Recycling of hobbies and school subjects	Recycling of *être* (present singular) Recycling of adjectival agreements	Pronunciation: *-eux / -euse -eur*	1 a, c, g, h, i, j 2 a, f, j, k 3 a, b	B
D	**Point Langue Atelier**	Recycling of personal details and hobbies	Present tense of *avoir* and *être*	Applying a pattern	1 a, b, c, f, h, i 2 a, h, j, m 3 e	B
E	**Voici ma famille** Introducing your family	*Parle-moi de ta famille. Tu as un frère / un demi-frère / une sœur / une demi-sœur / un(e) cousin(e)? Je n'ai pas de frère. Ton père / beau-père s'appelle comment? Ta mère / belle-mère a quel âge? Ton grand-père / Ta grand-mère habite où?* Recycling of numbers 1–69	Recycling of *avoir*	Learning to spell new words	1 a, c, f, g, i, j, k 2 a, d, j, k 3 a, b	B
F	**Tu es né où?** Saying in which country relatives live or were born	*Tu habites où? / Tu es né(e) où? J'habite / Je suis né(e)* ... *en Allemagne / Angleterre / Belgique / Ecosse / Espagne / France / Grande Bretagne / Grèce / Irlande / Italie / Suisse.* ... *au Pays de Galles.*		Learning to spell new words	1 a, c, g, h, i 2 a, j, n 3 b 4 d	BCE

CAMARADES 2	OVERVIEW – UNITE 1 – UNE VISITE DE LA MARTINIQUE		Cont.	NATIONAL CURRICULUM	
Topics/Objectives	**Key language**	**Grammar**	**Strategies**	**PoS coverage**	**AoE**
G Ils ont quel âge? Saying how old people are	*Ton grand-père a quel âge? Ta grand-mère a quel âge? Il / Elle a* + numbers 60–79 Recycling of numbers	Recycling of *avoir* + age	Pronunciation: *-an / -en / -on*	1 a, c, d, h 2 a, b, f 3 b	B
H Point Langue Atelier	Numbers 50–79 Recycling of alphabet and family		Learning through games	1 a, c, d, i 2 a, b, j 3 d, f	BC
I Ma ville? Pas mal! Describing your town	*C'est comment, ta ville / ton village? Ma ville / Mon village est... / n'est pas... calme / moderne / joli(e) / bruyant(e) / ancien(ne) / industriel(le). J'aimerais bien habiter à... Pourquoi? Parce que...* Recycling of alphabet	*... plus... que... ... moins... que...*	Recognising irregular adjectives in the dictionary	1 a, c, d, f, h, k 2 a, d, e, g, h, n 3 a, b, d, f 4 a	CE
J C'est comment, ton collège? Talking about your school	*Est-ce que vous faites des voyages / vous travaillez le samedi? Qu'est-ce que vous portez au collège / vous faites à midi / vous faites comme sports? Nous portons / faisons / jouons / allons / mangeons...* Recycling of clothes and days of the week	Present tense with *vous* and *nous* (regular *-er* verbs)	Looking up French verbs in the dictionary	1 a, c, h 2 a, d, e 3 d, f, c	AE
K Ta sœur travaille où? Saying where your relatives work	*Ton père / Ta sœur / Tes parents travaille(nt)? Il(s) / Elle(s) travaille(nt)... à la maison;... dans un bureau / hôtel / magasin / hôpital / grand magasin; ... dans une usine / banque / ferme. Il(s) / Elle(s) ne travaille(nt) pas* Recycling of names of family members	Recycling of present tense with *ils* and *elles* (regular *-er* verbs) Recycling of *ne... pas*	Checking gender in the dictionary	1 a, c 2 a, d, n 3 c, d, f	D
L Point Langue Atelier	Recycling of school routine and personal details	Present tense of regular *-er* verbs *On / nous*	Bringing variety into productive work	1 a, c, d, j, k 2 d, e, g 3 c, f, g	ABD

IT Opportunities

CORE ACTIVITIES

Text manipulation

Spreads A–I

Produce a model text in the first person in which a young person writes about some or all of the following:

a his/her name, age, physical description, character and family

b where he/she lives and where he/she was born

c the differences between where he/she lives and where he/she was born

d where he/she would like to live and why

When pupils are using the programme:
- decide whether to give them visual or aural support
- decide whether or not they will need to preview the text
- ensure that they know how to use the "help" options
- plan ways of helping them progress from the text manipulation task towards emulating the model with their own writing

Word processing – guided writing (i)

Spreads A–I

Create and save a simple text, similar to the one below, in which a young person gives details of herself, her family and where she lives. Highlight or underline a number of words that could be substituted. Pupils write about themselves or an imaginary person, replacing the highlighted words with others that would be appropriate.

Salut! Je m'appelle <u>Christine</u>. J'ai <u>quatorze</u> ans, j'ai les yeux <u>bleus</u> et les cheveux <u>blonds</u>. Je suis <u>sportive</u>, <u>bavarde</u> et <u>travailleuse</u>.

J'ai <u>deux</u> frères et une sœur. Mon père travaille dans <u>un hôpital</u> et ma mère travaille dans <u>une usine</u>.

Je suis née à <u>Hythe</u>, une <u>petite</u> ville au bord de la mer dans le <u>sud</u> de l'Angleterre, mais j'habite à <u>Birmingham</u>.

Word processing – guided writing (ii)

Spread A

Exercise 2

Pupils rewrite the letter *Salut Ludivine!* using the alternative picture clues as prompts.

Presentation

Spreads A and F

Pupils produce a presentation, containing at least 25 words of text, about Martinique. The presentation should refer to the island's location, its capital and the language spoken. Other details, such as the weather and the local crops, could be researched and included.

ADDITIONAL ACTIVITIES

The Internet

Type *Martinique* into a search engine. Try to find pictures and maps as well as information in both English and French. For more information and guidance on searching the Internet, see the IT notes at the end of unit 2.

Word processing – extended writing

Spreads A–G and K

Pupils produce an imaginative description, in the third person, of a highly active senior citizen who likes to look and live like someone much younger. The description could include details of name, age, character, appearance, family pastimes and work.

Provide pupils with clear strategies for using support materials, for dictionary use and for checking work prior to possible redrafting.

Copymasters

The *présentation* and the *grilles* copymasters should be used as indicated.
The other copymasters (worksheets and vocabulary lists) should be used with or after the spread indicated.

Pupil's Book Spread	Corresponding Copymaster
A	20–21 *Glossaire*
B	1 *Présentation*
C	4 *On communique; Grilles 1*
D	5 *Grammaire; Grilles 1*
E	6–7 *On parle*
F	2 *Présentation; Grilles 1*
G	8–9 *On écoute*
H	10 *Grammaire; 11 On s'amuse; 12 Que sais-tu?*
I	13 *Grammaire; 14–15 On lit*
J	3 *Présentation; 16 Plaisir de lire*
K	17–18 *On écrit*
L	19 *Que sais-tu?*

Notes to accompany Copymasters (CMs)

Feuille I
Presentation Sheet to teach eye and hair colour.
Refer to **Ways in** section (Spread A notes) for further
details.

Feuille 2
Presentation Sheet to revise *Grande Bretagne /
Ecosse / Pays de Galles / Angleterre / France* and
introduce the new countries. The words at the bottom
can be cut out for placing in the relevant places, for
instance against the clock.

Feuille 3
Presentation Sheet to familiarise pupils with the new
question forms from the key. Focus purely on the
question forms, not the answers. See if pupils can
make out the difference between questions using *Est-ce
que...?* and questions using *Qu'est-ce que...?* Also remind
pupils of the difference between *tu* and *vous*.

Feuille 4 On Communique
Pupils may find this CM useful to remind them of key
phrases for pair or group work.

Ask pupils to keep the CM for reference and revise the
relevant phrases when pupils are about to do
pair/group work.

Feuille 5 Grammaire
This CM provides further practice of the two verb
paradigms. Again, the ♦ task focuses on singular
forms while the ♣ task mixes singular and plural
forms.

♣ For an extra challenge, ask pupils to have a go
without looking at the words in the box.
Answers
Ex 1: **1** C *Tu es / Je suis* **2** B *Tu es / Je suis*
3 E *Tu as / J'ai* **4** D *J'ai* **5** C *Tu es / Je suis* **6** A *j'ai*
Ex 2: *Je suis J'ai Je suis je suis a elle est nous avons
nous sommes Il est il a ont ils sont Tu as Tu es*

Feuilles 6–7 On Parle
These two CMs provide additional speaking practice on
spreads B, C and E.

If you use the two CMs concurrently, first do some
pronunciation practice, asking pupils to repeat each
line from the CM 6, Ex 1 dialogue after you. ♣ Pupils
need not see the dialogue.

Then go through the CM 6 (♦) rubrics with the
weaker pupils while the more able pupils start
preparing CM 7 (♣), Ex 1 in silence.

Feuilles 8–9 On Ecoute
These two CMs provide additional listening practice on
numbers.

Feuille 8 ♦
Ex 1 – **Extra**: Improvise similar practice if necessary.

Numéro 1– a: 66 – b: 69 – c: 64
Numéro 2– a: 66 – b: 67 – c: 62
Numéro 3– a: 67 – b: 69 – c: 68
Numéro 4– a: 66 – b: 68 – c: 65
Numéro 5– a: 72 – b: 70 – c: 62
Numéro 6– a: 70 – b: 75 – c: 76
Numéro 7– a: 77 – b: 76 – c: 74
Numéro 8– a: 78 – b: 75 – c: 77

Answers
1 a **2** c **3** b **4** b **5** a **6** b **7** c **8** c

Ex 2 – **Extra** Pupils can make up some items of their
own for testing their partners and for practising the
alphabet.

Numéro 1: 76 ... 63 ... 68 ... 65 ... 73 ... 63
Numéro 2: 62 ... 75 ... 61 ... 66 ... 65 ... 68
Numéro 3: 67 ... 60 ... 62 ... 72 ... 65 ... 62
Numéro 4: 61 ... 63 ... 72 ... 66 ... 65 ... 68
Numéro 5: 61 ... 72 ... 75 ... 77 ... 63 ... 66 ...
66 ... 63 ... 73

Answers
1 Venise **2** Dublin **3** Madrid **4** Berlin **5** Bruxelles

Ex 3

72 ... 68 ... 66 ... 74 ... 78 ... 60 ... 75 ...
69 ... 71 ... 79 ... 61 ... 70.

Answer
73

Feuille 9 ♣
Ex 1 – When doing the corrections, ask pupils to
explain the purpose of each phone call in French in
full sentences.

1 – *Allô? Ici la chambre 73. Je voudrais un sandwich
au jambon, s'il vous plaît! Oui, le numéro 73.*

2 – *Allô? Ici la chambre 67. J'ai un problème avec le
téléphone. Non, non, chambre 67.*

3 – *Allô? C'est la chambre euh... numéro 79. Il y a
une araignée dans la salle de bains. Chambre 79.
Vous pouvez m'aider?*

4 – *Allô, la réception? Je vous appelle de la chambre
72. Je suis désolé, mais vous pouvez m'apporter
un stylo? J'ai oublié mes stylos. 62? Non, non,
chambre 72... Merci!*

5 – *Allô? Euh, ici c'est la chambre 68. Je voudrais
dîner dans ma chambre. Vous avez un menu?*

6 – *Allô, la réception? J'ai un problème dans la salle
de bains. Les toilettes, euh... ça ne fonctionne
pas. Oui, je suis au numéro 71.... Dans vingt
minutes? Bon, d'accord.*

Answers
1 73, F **2** 67, D **3** 79, E **4** 72, B **5** 68, C **6** 71, A

Ex 2

> 1 – *Allô? Le numéro? Oui, c'est 48 AH 70. Oui, c'est ça: 48 AH 70. C'est une petite voiture rouge.*
>
> 2 – *Oui, j'ai le numéro. C'est 58 KY 57. Non, non, non, 58 KY 57. La voiture est... elle était jaune, très grande.*
>
> 3 – *J'ai le numéro de la voiture. C'est 75 NKD 78. Non, non, NKD. Le chauffeur a les cheveux bruns, très longs.*
>
> 4 – *La voiture responsable de l'accident, c'est le numéro 76 TR 59. C'est une voiture noire. Le chauffeur a... 60, 65 ans.*
>
> 5 – *Le numéro, c'est 77 UW 39. Oui, 39. C'est une voiture marron, le chauffeur a les cheveux blonds.*
>
> 6 – *Je vous donne le numéro de la voiture? C'est 67 PR 49. Oui, oui, j'en suis sûre, 67 PR 49. Le chauffeur? Je ne sais pas. C'est une voiture jaune, jaune et noire.*

Answers
1 e 2 f 3 a 4 d 5 g 6 c

Ex 3 – Point out to pupils that phone numbers are read out in pairs.

> 1 – *Vous avez faim? Pour bien manger, Le Chatrou, c'est le restaurant idéal. Réservations au 76 77 16. Je répète: le 76 77 16.*
>
> 2 – *Pour les informations sur le tourisme, téléphonez au 55 72 74. Je répète, le 55 72 74*
>
> 3 – *Vous cherchez des activités au bord de la mer? Téléphonez vite au Club Méditerranée. C'est le 76 72 72. Je répète, le 76 72 72.*
>
> 4 – *Vous aimez le camping et vous adorez le calme? Essayez le camping de Pointe Marin au 76 72 79. Oui, le 76 72 79.*
>
> 5 – *Vous aimez les promenades en mer? Téléphonez à Locaboats, au 66 07 57. C'est bien ça, le 66 07 57.*
>
> 6 – *Vous cherchez un hôtel sympa, calme, traditionnel? Téléphonez à l'hôtel Saint-Aubin. C'est le 69 34 77. Vous avez bien compris? Le 69 34 77.*

Answers
1 E, 76 77 16 2 F, 55 72 74 3 C, 76 72 72
4 A, 76 72 79 5 B, 66 07 57 6 D, 69 34 77

Feuille 10 Grammaire
Ex 1 – Pupils practise using *je m'appelle... / tu t'appelles... / il/elle s'appelle...* to complement spread E key.
Answers

1 *Je m'appelle*	2 *Elle s'appelle*	3 *Il s'appelle*
4 *Tu t'appelles*	5 *Elle s'appelle*	6 *Je m'appelle*
7 *il s'appelle*	8 *elle s'appelle*	

Ex 2 – Pupils work on positive and negative sentences (*ne... pas*) for ♦ receptive purposes /♣ productive purposes.
♣ Pupils may need help with *Je ne suis pas né(e)*.

Extra – ♣ Pupils can make up their own shield and write sentences to go with it.
Answers
♦ **1** *J'ai un frère.* **2** *Je n'ai pas de sœur.* **6** *Je n'aime pas la musique.* **7** *J'ai des lapins.* **9** *Je n'habite pas dans un appartement.* **12** *Je fais du sport.*

♣ *J'ai un frère.* *Je n'ai pas de sœur.* *Je n'aime pas la musique.* *J'ai des lapins.* *Je n'ai pas de chiens.* *Je ne suis pas né(e) en Espagne.* *Je suis né(e) en France.* *Je ne joue pas au tennis.* *J'habite dans une maison.* *Je n'habite pas dans un appartement.*

Feuille 11 On s'amuse
These reading games provide additional practice of language covered in topics 1–2.

♦ Pupils can do A and B while still looking at 1 and 2 but should, in that case, be given a challenging time limit or be made to keep a record of how long they spent on the tasks. ♣ If pupils find the last task too difficult, they can have a brief look at what to do under C before reading 3 and then doing C.
Answers
A *Mot absent: Allemagne   Mot supplémentaire: Rome*
B *Mot absent: sœurs   Mot supplémentaire: père*
C *Mot absent: maths   Mot supplémentaire: histoire*

Feuille 12 Que-sais tu?
This CM offers some revision of topics 1 and 2. For each task, pupils proceed from *Préparation* to *Que sais-tu?*, then onto *Bilan / Conseil*.

Ex 1 – Pupils can instead look for as many classmates as they can find for each item.

Ex 2 – Point out that *mon / ma* at the beginning of each item helps narrow down the options.
Answers
1 *sœur, travailleuse* **2** *demi-frère, timide* **3** *grand-père, sportif* **4** *cousine, bavarde* **5** *demi-sœur, embêtante*

Ex 3 – Pupils need to be careful about masculine/feminine: *né / née*.
Answers
1 *né, France* **2** *née, Espagne* **2** *né, Italie*
4 *née, Allemagne / Angleterre* **5** *née, Grande Bretagne / Grèce* **6** *né, Allemagne / Angleterre*

Feuille 13 Grammaire
This CM provides additional practice of *plus / moins* (Spread I).

Ex 1
Answers
1 F 2 F 3 V 4 V 5 V 6 F 7 F

Ex 2

> – *Et... le nord de la Martinique, c'est comment?*
>
> – *Le nord est moins touristique que le sud. Les villages sont plus calmes. Mais dans le sud, ils sont plus jolis.*
>
> – *J'aime les promenades...*
>
> – *Dans le nord, la montagne est plus intéressante que la mer.*
>
> – *Super! Mais... ma famille est moins sportive que moi.*
>
> – *Le sud, c'est bien, mais... les touristes! La région est plus bruyante que le nord.*

Answers
1 *moins* 2 *que* 3 *plus* 4 *plus* 5 *plus* 6 *que*
7 *moins* 8 *que* 9 *plus* 10 *que*

Ex 3 See if pupils can guess the meaning of *âgé* from the context.
Answers
*Guillaume: 32 ans   Gonzague: 48 ans   Gaston: 51 ans
Gaëtan: 56 ans   Gustave: 69 ans   Gontrand: 73 ans*

Feuilles 14–15   On lit
These two CMs provide additional reading practice on most spreads covered so far.

The rubrics are short and simple and the two CMs can easily be used concurrently. If necessary, ask the more able pupils to go through the CM 15 (♣) rubrics on their own while you go through the CM 14 (♦) rubrics with the weaker pupils.

Feuille 14 ♦
Ex 1 – **Extra**: for written practice, ask pupils to make up additional items of their own.
Answers
1 *Afrique*   **2** *sympa*   **3** *bleus*   **4** *cinquante-trois*
5 *joli*   **6** *marron*

Ex 2
Answers

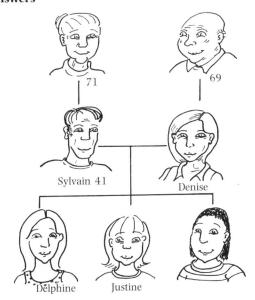

Ex 3
Answers
1 ✔   **2** ✘   **3** ✘   **4** ✘   **5** ✔   **6** ✘   **7** ✘   **8** ✔

Feuille 15 ♣
Ex 1 – Pupils need to watch out for negative sentences.

Extra: for written practice, ask pupils to make up additional items of their own.
Answers
*Bonnes phrases: 1, 3, 5, 9
Phrases stupides: 2, 4, 6, 7, 8*

Ex 2
Answers
1 *Ce n'est pas très grand*   **2** *La ville est (...) au bord de la mer*   **3** *c'est une ville assez bruyante*   **4** *il y a beaucoup de bus et de voitures*   **5** *c'est un peu sale*
6 *la population est très sympa*   **7** *Il y a des hotels petit budget et grand budget*   **8** *Pour le shopping, il y a un choix exceptionnel*

Feuille 16   Plaisir de lire
This CM provides a summary of authentic teenage books on family and relationship issues as well as a reading game that revises the family vocabulary.
Answers
Ex 2 *Marcelle est la <u>mère</u> de Michel et la <u>fille</u> de Marie.*

Feuilles 17–18   On écrit
These CMs provide additional writing practice on a variety of topic areas covered in Unit 1. The rubrics are short and simple and the two CMs can easily be used concurrently. If necessary, ask the more able pupils to go through the CM 18 (♣) rubrics on their own while you go through the CM 17 (♦) rubrics with the weaker pupils.
Answers
CM 17 Ex 1 **1** *Il travaille dans un bureau.*   **2** *Elle travaille dans une ferme.*   **3** *Il travaille dans une banque.*   **4** *Elle travaille dans une usine.*   **5** *Il travaille dans un hôpital.*   **6** *Elle travaille dans un hôtel.*
CM 17 Ex 2 **1** *portons*   **2** *travaillons, travaillons*   **3** *mangeons*   **4** *jouons*   **5** *faisons*   **6** *faisons*

Feuille 19   Que sais-tu?
This CM offers some revision of topic 3. For each task, pupils proceed from *Préparation* to *Que sais-tu?*, then onto *Bilan / Conseil*.

Ex 1 Remind pupils of *mon / ma* as clues to gender.
Answers
1 *jolie*   **2** *ancien*   **3** *que*   **4** *plus industrielle*
5 *parce, plus*

Ex 2
Answers
1 *travaillons*   **2** *joue*   **3** *jouez*   **4** *jouons*   **5** *faites*
6 *faisons*   **7** *mangez*   **8** *allons*

Ex 3
Answers
*mère, 2   père, 5   frère, 3   demi-sœur, 1
cousin, 4   grand-père, 5*

Feuilles 20–21   Glossaire 1–2
These two sheets provide a spread-by-spread bilingual reference list for pupils to refer to at any point during Unit 1. You could distribute them as soon as you start work on the unit. They are particularly useful for setting learning homework and for revising for *Epreuve 1*, so pupils should be encouraged to file them carefully.

Grilles 1
Grids to accompany listening exercises on Spreads C, D, and F.

A Une visite de la Martinique

pp 2–3

Objective
Introduction to Martinique

Resources
Cassette for BD and Ex 3
CM 20–21 for reference throughout Unit 1
OHT – see **Ways in** section
Camarades 1 Flashcards (see Ex 2 notes)

Key language
Partial recycling of personal details, house, pets, school subjects and hobbies

Language learning strategies
Cognates and near cognates as an aid to understanding

Ways in
In this Unit, Carole, a young girl from Martinique, comes over to France to spend a term with Ludivine, a pupil from the class featured throughout **Camarades 2**. On this spread, the geography teacher tells the class (*5ᵉ 2, collège des Acacias, Chartres*) about Carole – due to arrive soon – and about Martinique.

This spread revises some topic areas and introduces the theme for this unit. There is no new key language. You can introduce **Camarades 2** and Spread A like this:
Camarades 2 *présente une classe dans un collège en France. C'est la classe 5ᵉ2 au collège des Acacias. Le collège est dans une ville. La ville s'appelle Chartres* (show on map if possible). *Chartres est à l'ouest de Paris. Il y a six unités dans* **Camarades 2**. *On trouve la classe dans chaque unité. Ici, dans l'Unité 1, on parle d'une visite.*

First, pupils read the BD while they listen to the cassette. Then you can use an OHP transparency of the Caribbean from an atlas to show Martinique. (BD tapescript – see Pupil's Book)

1

When doing the corrections, ask pupils to correct the false statements.
Extra – Ask pupils to do the exercise again with books closed while you read out the statements, or ask them to say as much as they can remember about Martinique. You can then go back to the atlas transparency to point out, or make pupils guess, which other islands speak French. As a reminder, also discuss which other countries pupils know where French is spoken, or ask them to do research.
Answers
1 faux   2 vrai   3 vrai   4 faux   5 vrai

2

Extra
a To train pupils to spot detail quickly, say a key word contained in the letter, for example *frères*, and ask pupils – in two teams – to say the word before. The fastest team gets a point.

b Say a word, for example *maths* and ask pupils to say from memory whether it is in the letter or not.

c Start reading out one of the sentences from the letter and ask pupils to complete it from memory. Ask pupils to change as much detail as they can to the letter:
– as a whole class activity (read out one sentence at a time)
– as a pair/group activity: pupils take it in turn to change one sentence at a time in as many ways as they can, thus revising vocabulary
– individually, in writing.

d You can also use **Camarades 1** Flashcards to revise the topic areas approached in the letter: rooms in the house (58–63), pets (49–57), school subjects (26–35) and leisure activities (36–48).
Answers
1 a   2 a   3 b   4 b   5 b

3

Preparation – Ask pupils to say and write down any words connected with each photo, for example *football*, *maison*. After they have done the task, they can then listen again and tick the words which are on their list.

Extra – Pupils say or write their own commentary for each photo. This need not be a memory activity, as pupils can produce anything relevant to what they see on the photos.

COUNTER

1	*Ça, c'est mon copain Patrick. Il adore le football!*
2	*Ça, c'est un village pour les touristes. Il y a des petites maisons.*
3	*Ça, c'est la mer. On va à la pêche. Et toi, tu aimes la pêche?*
4	*Ça, c'est ma ville, Fort-de-France. J'aime bien ma ville.*
5	*Ça, c'est la fête, en ville. On aime beaucoup les fêtes en Martinique.*
6	*Ça, c'est la mer. Avec une piscine pour les touristes. Et il fait beau!*

Answers
1 c   2 e   3 f   4 b   5 a   6 d

B J'ai les cheveux bruns

pp 4–5

Objective
Saying what someone looks like

Resources
CM1
OHT (see **Ways in** section)
Cassette for BD, Ex 3 and Ex 5
A4 paper optional for task 7 (display)

Key language
Tu es comment? / Il (elle) est comment, ton frère (ta sœur)?

J'ai / Il a / Elle a...
les yeux bleus / gris / verts / marron
les cheveux blancs / noirs / blonds / bruns / roux
les cheveux assez longs / très courts

Grammar
Present tense of *avoir*
Recycling of adjectival agreements

Language learning strategies
Looking up French words in the dictionary

Ways in
Ludivine meets Carole at the airport and shows Carole a photo of one of her classmates. You can introduce the spread like this: *Carole arrive en France. Ludivine dit bonjour. Dans la voiture* (explain *voiture* through action) *Ludivine parle de ses copains.*

Revise the colours (*bleu, vert, jaune, noir, gris, blanc, brun, rouge*) using classroom objects. To teach eye colour with *je*, use faces and colour pens/chalk before asking pupils to describe themselves. Pupils can then colour in the eyes on CM1. Teach hair colour/length using pupils in the class. Pupils then colour in CM1.

Instead you can colour in CM1 yourself on an OHT. Choose a picture for pupils to describe. Alternatively, describe – or ask a pupil to describe – one of the pictures and ask the rest of the class to guess which face it is. You can then practise in pairs.

Point out that 'hair' in French is plural. Give a reminder about the plural of adjectives and point out the invariable *marron* and *roux*.

1 Pupils can hear the cassette as they read the BD before doing the task. (BD tapescript – see Pupil's Book)
Answer 3

2 *Extra* – Pupils hide the speech bubbles and practise speaking and listening in pairs. Pupil A reads out a speech bubble. Pupil B identifies the correct picture. Remember that so far pupils have only practised using *je*. These pictures are used again in Ex 4.
Answers 1 f **2** d **3** e **4** a **5** c **6** b

3 *Preparation* – Revise the days of the week. You can also revise school subjects at the same time: name a subject and ask pupils to say on which days it figures on their timetable.

COUNTER

1	*Le mardi, j'ai les yeux verts.*
2	*Le dimanche, j'ai les yeux bleus.*
3	*Le samedi, j'ai les yeux... marron!*
4	*Le jeudi, en général, j'ai les yeux gris... oui, les yeux gris.*
5	*Et puis... euh... le mercredi... verts! J'aime bien avoir les yeux verts le mercredi aussi.*
6	*Alors, le vendredi, j'ai toujours les yeux marron!*
7	*Le lundi? Ah, le lundi, j'ai les yeux noirs!*

Answers
1 a, mardi **2** c, dimanche **3** b, samedi **4** e, jeudi
5 a, mecredi **6** b, vendredi **7** d, lundi

4 *Preparation* – Practise describing eyes and hair using *il / elle*. For example, test how well pupils know their classmates' or famous peoples' eye colour.

Extra – Pupil A names one of the characters from the pictures. Pupil B describes the character from memory.

5 *Preparation*
a Train pupils to listen out for key words (*les yeux, les cheveux*). Say the words *les cheveux* and *les yeux* quickly, again and again, in any order, and ask pupils to point at their hair or their eyes as you speak.
b Ask pupils to describe pictures **a–e** in speaking.

COUNTER

1	–	*Mon cousin Frédéric a les yeux marron. Il a les cheveux assez courts. Il a 14 ans.*
2	–	*Mon cousin Jérémy? Il a les cheveux noirs. Il a les yeux marron. Ah, il a les cheveux très courts. Il a sept ans.*
3	–	*Alors... et il y a mon cousin Fiz. Fiz a les yeux marron, et il a les cheveux bruns, assez longs. Il a... euh... 17 ans. Oui, c'est ça. Il a 17 ans.*
4	–	*Et ton cousin Freddie?*
	–	*Alors, Freddie a les cheveux longs... roux et noirs. Et les yeux? Alors, la... verts, parce qu'il a des lentilles de contact.*
	–	*C'est bizarre!*
	–	*Ah, oui, il est bizarre.*
	–	*Il a quel âge?*
	–	*Freddie? Il a quinze ans.*

Answers
1 d, *14 ans* **2** c, *7 ans* **3** e, *17 ans* **4** a, *15 ans*

6 Alert pupils to the use of *ne/n'... pas.*
♣ Encourage pupils to learn these new words.
Answers
♦ **1** e **2** c **3** b
♣ *frisés* = curly   *frange (f)* = fringe
   foncés = dark   *bouche (f)* = mouth
   Picture = e

7 Pupils work on A4 paper for a class display. They can work individually or in pairs. Suggest a minimum number of sentences. ♦ Pupils can present their work in individual sentences. ♣ Pupils write a paragraph.
♣ Encourage pupils to reuse the new words from Ex 6.

17

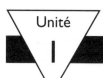

C Ta classe est sympa?

pp 6–7

Objective
Saying what someone is like (personality)

Resources
Flashcards 1–8
CM4
Card for task 1
Grilles 1 CM (optional for Ex 2)
OHT (optional for Ex 2)
Dictionaries for Ex 1 and 6
Cassette for BD and Ex 2, 4 and 5

Key language
Tu es comment? / Il est comment, ton frère (ta sœur)?
Je suis... / Je ne suis pas... / Il(Elle) est... / n'est pas...
... paresseux, euse / sportif, ive / travailleur, euse / bavard(e) /
embêtant(e) / sympa / drôle / timide
Recycling of hobbies and school subjects

Grammar
Recycling of *être*
Recycling of adjectival agreements

Language learning strategies
Pronunciation: *-eux/-euse, -eur*

Ways in
Carole is in Ludivine's bedroom. Ludivine tells her more about her classmates. You can introduce the spread like this: *Carole est dans la chambre de Carole. Carole va aller au collège avec Ludivine. Mais... la classe de Ludivine est chouette, oui ou non?*

Introduce the key adjectives using the flashcards (see Teacher's Book introduction page 9), mime and facial expression.

Pupils then read the BD while they hear the cassette. Interrupt the cassette after each of the new adjectives to illustrate meaning further through facial impressions and mime if necessary.

To familiarise pupils with the new adjectives, say them and ask pupils to act them out.

To train pupils to spot key words quickly in written text and practise pronunciation of the new adjectives, name one of Ludivine's classmates and ask pupils to find the relevant adjective(s) in the BD.

To train pupils to retain meaning through mental associations and train them to learn through silent activities, say an adjective and ask pupils to think of someone for whom the adjective is relevant.

Pupils can then practise reading the BD in pairs, putting the emphasis on intonation as an aid to conveying feeling. (BD tapescript – see Pupil's Book)

1 This task is meant to reinforce retention of meaning through copying. Because of the introductory work already done, pupils should avoid using the glossary at the end of the book if at all possible.

Extra – Ask questions in the class: *Qui t'intéresse le plus? Pourquoi?* This also revises *Il / Elle est*, first introduced in **Camarades 1**.

Ask pupils to look at the key and explain why many of the adjectives have two forms. Pupils can then make masculine and feminine cards with the adjectives, mix the cards and sort them into masculine and feminine cards as quickly as possible. They can also do pair practice:

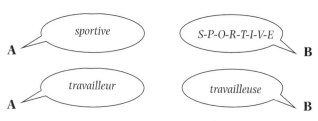

Answers
drôle = funny   *sympa* = friendly   *travailleur* = hard-working   *paresseux* = lazy   *embêtant* = annoying   *bavard* = chatty   *timide* = shy   *sportif* = sporty

Extra – **Part a**: *Ecoute les adjectifs. Ecris M (masculin) ou F (féminin). Exemple: 1 MMF.*
Part b: Divide the class into two. One half repeats the masculine adjectives only, the other half repeats the feminine adjectives only.

COUNTER

Part a

1	*embêtant, embêtant, embêtante*
2	*sportive, sportif, sportive*
3	*paresseux, paresseuse, paresseuse*
4	*bavard, bavarde, bavard*
5	*travailleuse, travailleur, travailleuse*
6	*sportive, embêtant, travailleur*
7	*embêtante, bavard, sportif*

Part b

travailleur sportive drôle bavarde embêtante
sportif timide paresseux sympa embêtant
travailleuse paresseuse bavard

2 A grid is provided on CM.

Preparation – Before pupils hear the cassette, rehearse hobbies and school subjects to facilitate understanding.

◆ You can suggest pupils enter only one item per column for each number. Alternatively, show pupils the completed answers but add one item each time: pupils tick the correct items as they hear them to isolate the 'intruder'.

When checking the answers, ask full questions and ask pupils to answer in full sentences.

1 *Je m'appelle Alicia, A-L-I-C-I-A. Au collège, je suis bavarde. Je suis sportive. J'aime l'athlétisme et je fais du judo. J'aime les maths.*

2 *Je m'appelle Candice, C-A-N-D-I-C-E. Je suis sympa mais timide. J'aime bien la natation et la télé. Au collège, j'aime l'anglais.*

3 *Moi, je m'appelle Mahmoud. Ça s'ecrit M-A-H-M-O-U-D. je suis... travailleur. Je suis drôle, mais... embêtant avec ma sœur. Je joue au tennis. Au collège, j'adore la géographie.*

4 *Moi, c'est Thomas, T-H-O-M-A-S. Je suis sympa avec mes copains. Je suis sportif, mais je suis paresseux! J'adore les ordinateurs. Au collège, j'aime bien la musique!*

Answers

Prénom	Personnalité	Sports/loisirs	Matière
1 Alicia	bavarde sportive	judo athlétisme	maths
2 Candice	sympa timide	natation télé	anglais
3 Mahmoud	travailleur drôle embêtant	tennis	géographie
4 Thomas	sympa sportif paresseux	ordinateurs	musique

On prononce bien

Ecoute: paresseux, travailleur
Répete: les cheveux, les yeux, paresseuse, professeur, ordinateur, ma sœur

Practise further using familiar words, for example:
– *deux, bleu, déjeuner, délicieux, ennuyeux*
– *baladeur, sœur, rétroprojecteur*
Exception: *monsieur*

3
Start as a whole class activity with two teams. The first one to give the correct answer gets the points.
Pupils may find CM 4 (*On communique*) useful to remind them of key phrases for pair or group work.

Ask pupils to keep the CM for reference and revise the relevant phrases when pupils are about to do pair/group work.

4
Provide a time limit to focus minds.
To help pupils doing the ♦ activity, tell them how many adjectives each of their two sentences should

have. Remind them to use feminine endings.
♦ Alert pupils to the use of negative sentences and to the use of the masculine/feminine.

Answers
♦ **1** *Leila est sympa, drôle et bavarde.* **2** *Leila n'est pas sportive ou (très) travailleuse.*
♣ *Sébastien est sportif, mais Leila n'est pas sportive. Sébastien est travailleur, mais Leila n'est pas très travailleuse.*
Leila est bavarde, mais Sébastien n'est pas très bavard. Sébastien est très sérieux, mais Leila est très drôle.

5
Tell pupils to be careful about masculine/ feminine endings.

♦ To help pupils, either give them a choice of two adjectives for each gap (masculine/feminine), or give them the five correct adjectives to match up with the correct lines.

Encourage pupils to learn the song by heart.

Madame Aristide est timide.
Monsieur Masseur est travailleur.
Madame Vareuse est paresseuse.
Monsieur Fernand est embêtant.
Mademoiselle Rive est très sportive.
Monsieur Degas n'est pas sympa.
Ah, là, là, quel hazard,
Mes professeurs sont bien bizarres!

Answers see tapescript

6
Again, pupils need to be careful about masculine/feminine endings.

Ask pupils doing the ♦ activity to make one sentence with each adjective from the key. They can also re-use *assez* and *très* from Spread B.

Encourage pupils doing the ♣ activity to look up a few other adjectives in the dictionary. Encourage the use of link words and qualifiers – for example *mais, quelquefois* – and the use of examples: *Je suis assez sportif. Par exemple, j'aime l'athlétisme et je fais de la natation mais je n'aime pas le basket. Je suis travailleur en sciences, mais je suis assez paresseux en dessin.*

D Point Langue / Atelier

pp 8–9

Resources
CM5
Grilles 1 CM optional for *Atelier*
Cassette for *Atelier* Ex 1 & 2

Key language
Recycling of personal details and hobbies

Grammar
Present tense of *avoir* and *être*

Language learning strategies
Applying a pattern

Point Langue

1

This completes the paradigms of *avoir* and *être*, as an extension of spreads B and C. All forms except for *nous/vous* were presented in **Camarades 1**.

♦ Present the plural forms for recognition purposes only. Help pupils to learn the paradigms through chanting. Encourage pupils to improvise sentences. Use mime or simple drawings as stimuli:
Teacher: *Ils sont...*
Pupils: *Ils sont fatigués*
Answers
we have = *nous avons;* we are = *nous sommes*
you have = *vous avez;* you are = *vous êtes*

2

Only pupils doing the ♣ activity practise the plural forms (items 8–11).

Extra – Pupils read in pairs for pronunciation practice.
Answers
1 *as* 2 *a* 3 *est* 4 *il* 5 *suis* 6 *as* 7 *a* 8 *êtes*
9 *sommes* 10 *avez* 11 *avons*

Atelier

1

Preparation – Rehearse the kind of language pupils might hear under each category provided in the grid. Point out only notes are needed, for example: *bleus* and not *il a les yeux bleus.*

COUNTER

> 1 – *Martin... c'est qui, Martin?*
> – *Martin? Il a les yeux marron, et les cheveux blonds, et... assez courts.*
> – *Ah, oui, d'accord! Il est sympa?*
> – *Euh... il aime la musique, la télé, mais il n'aime pas beaucoup le sport. Il va beaucoup au cinéma. Il voudrait un club cinéma ici.*
> 2 – *Et Manuel, c'est qui?*
> – *Manuel? Regarde. Il a les yeux marron et les cheveux bruns, assez courts.*
> – *Ah, oui, d'accord.*
> – *Il est très sportif. Il fait du foot et de l'athlétisme. Il voudrait organiser des compétitions au Club des Jeunes.*

Answers
Martin (d); marron; blonds / assez courts; sympa; musique / télé; voudrait club cinéma
Manuel (c); marron; bruns / assez courts; sportif; foot / athlétisme; voudrait compétitions

2

♦ Guide pupils by pointing out the grid category each time they are about to hear key information. Not all columns need to be completed here. Alternatively, write all the key information from both interviews on the board but all mixed up, for pupils to allocate to the correct interviewee. Make the last column optional if you consider it too difficult.

COUNTER

> 1 – *Aline, tu voudrais être représentante au Club des Jeunes?*
> – *Oui, ça m'intéresse.*
> – *Pourquoi?*
> – *Ben... Je suis travailleuse, oui... je ne suis pas sportive mais j'aime beaucoup les ordinateurs... Je voudrais organiser un club d'ordinateurs ici, au Club des Jeunes...*
> – *Tu as beaucoup de copains et de copines?*
> – *Oui... je suis un peu timide, je suis assez calme... mais j'aime bien... aller au cinéma, par exemple.*
> 2 – *Mouloud, tu voudrais être représentant au Club des Jeunes. Pourquoi?*
> – *Ah? Moi, je suis drôle, j'ai beaucoup de copains... J'adore le Club des Jeunes, c'est super!*
> – *Tu es travailleur?*
> – *Euh... oui et non... Au collège, non. Mais le Club des Jeunes, ça m'intéresse! Je voudrais organiser des fêtes, faire du théâtre, organiser des activités drôles, quoi.*

Answers
Aline; travailleuse / un peu timide/calme; ordinateurs / cinéma; voudrait club d'ordinateurs
Mouloud; drôle / un peu travailleur; Club des Jeunes; voudrait fêtes / théâtre / activités drôles

3

Point out that not all columns need to be completed and that it is not necessary to understand every word (e.g. *comme*). Ask pupils to work without glossary/dictionary in order to focus on reading skills such as using context as an aid to understanding.
Answers
Virginie
  sympa / drôle / honnête / bien organisée / calme / un peu paresseuse
  activités calmes / lecture / sport / copains
  voudrait soirées-disco / soirées-jeux /sorties-piscine

4

Suggest how to carry out the group discussion by writing a few questions and key phrases on the board. For example:
Tu préfères qui? Pourquoi?
Oui, mais...
J'aime bien/je n'aime pas... parce que...
On vote?

E Voici ma famille

Objective
Introducing your family

Resources
CM6–7
Card (optional) for CM 6
Cassette for BD and Ex 2
A4 paper for Ex 6

Key language
Parle-moi de ta famille.
Tu as un frère / un demi-frère /une sœur / une demi-sœur /
un(e) cousin(e)?

Je n'ai pas de frère.
Ton père / beau-père s'appelle comment? Il s'appelle...
Ta mère / belle-mère a quel âge? Elle a... ans.
Ton grand-père / Ta grand-mère habite où?
Il / Elle habite à + town
Recycling of numbers

Grammar
Recycling of *avoir*
Language learning strategies
Learning to spell new words

Ways in
Carole now meets Ludivine's class for the first time. You can introduce the spread like this: *Carole est en classe. Ça va, c'est chouette. Elle aime bien la classe. Elle donne quelque chose à la prof de géographie. Qu'est-ce que c'est?*

Pupils read the BD while they hear the cassette. Ask them to spot the countries mentioned and guess what they are. (BD tapescript – see Pupil's Book)

1 Revise the continents by naming well-known towns or countries and asking pupils to name the continent. You can also name wild animals.
Answers
1 oui 2 oui 3 non 4 oui 5 non

2 Draw a simple family tree to revise *frère / sœur* and introduce *père / mère / grand-père / grand-mère*. Draw another to introduce *beau-père / belle-mère / demi-frère / demi-sœur*. Pupils should guess *cousin / cousine*. Use the *Famille* box to introduce the written word, and ask pupils to copy the words into two lists (masculine and feminine) or with *mon / ma*.

Préparation – ♣ revise *nord / sud / est / ouest / centre*. Not all items say where the people live. When checking the answers, ask questions (*Elle s'appelle comment?* etc.). Insist on full sentences, using *sa*, for example: *Elle s'appelle Latifa. C'est sa demi-sœur. Elle habite dans le nord.*

COUNTER

1 – *Latifa, c'est ma demi-sœur. Elle habite dans le nord, avec ma mère.*
2 – *Sandra, c'est ma sœur.*
3 – *Christophe, c'est mon frère.*
4 – *Ça, c'est Josiane, ma grand-mère Josiane. Elle habite dans le sud.*
5 – *Ma mère s'appelle Annick. Elle habite dans le nord.*
6 – *Kevin, c'est qui?*
   – *Kevin? C'est mon cousin. Il habite dans le centre.*
7 – *Tu as un grand-père?*
   – *Oui, mon grand-père s'appelle Roger. Il habite dans l'ouest de la France.*
8 – *Et Stéphanie, c'est... ta cousine?*
   – *Oui. Ma cousine Stéphanie habite dans l'est. Dans l'est de la France.*
9 – *C'est qui, ça?*
   – *Ça, c'est ma belle-mère, Elisabeth.*

Answers
1 *Latifa, g, nord*   2 *Sandra, c*   3 *Christophe, i*
4 *Josiane, b, sud*   5 *Annick, j, nord*   6 *Kevin, e, centre*
7 *Roger, d, ouest*   8 *Stéphanie, k, est*   9 *Elisabeth, l*

3 Encourage pupils carrying out the ♦ activity to do what they can without the key first.

Extra – Using the key box, ask pupils questions and demand instant replies: the idea is not to provide real information but to give any reply which answers the right question. Pupils can then practise in pairs.
Answers
1 *père*   2 *demi-sœur*   3 *grand-mère*   4 *demi-frères*
5 *belle-mère*   6 *grand-père*   7 *mère*

4 *Préparation* – Revise numbers 1–69.

Insist on pupils writing notes and not full sentences prior to the pair speaking. ♦ When speaking, you can ask pupils to provide one-word answers rather than complete sentences.

After pupils have asked their questions, they can check that the information they jotted down is right, either by reading their notes alongside their neighbour's or through speaking, for example:

A *Tu as un frère, Michael. Il a six ans.*   *Oui, correct.* B

5 Encourage pupils to work without the key initially.
Answers
Grand-père: Séraphin, 66 ans; Grand-mère: Louise, 63 ans; Père: André, 35 ans; Mère: Marie-Laure, 35 ans; Frère: Guillaume, 7 ans; Demi-frère: Karl, 15 ans; Demi-sœur: Gabrielle, 13 ans

6 Give pupils ideas and stimulate their curiosity by improvising an oral description of your family. To focus their attention on everything you say, you can instead ask them to guess whether each statement is true or false.

Pupils' posters can be used for a display or as part of a class folder for reference purposes or to be displayed on special occasions. They can also be used for writing to penfriends and link classes.

F Tu es né où?
pp 12–13

Objective
Saying in which country relatives live or were born

Resources
CM2
OHT (see **Ways in** section)
Grilles 1 CM optional for Ex 2
Cassette for BD and Ex 2 and 4

Key language
Tu habites où? / Tu es né(e) où?
J'habite... / Je suis né(e)... en Allemagne / Angleterre / Belgique /
Ecosse / Espagne / France / Grande Bretagne / Grèce / Irlande /
Italie / Suisse
... au Pays de Galles

Language learning strategies
Learning to spell new words

Ways in
Carole is in class, struggling with the geography of
Europe. You can introduce the spread like this:
*Carole aime bien le collège, mais elle a des problèmes en
géographie.*

Pupils read the BD while they hear the cassette. Revise
countries using CM2. (BD tapescript – see Pupil's Book.)

1

Extra – Do some pronunciation work using the towns.
Improvise similar questions using other towns,
including places in the UK, then ask pupils to do the
same in pairs. Remind pupils about *au Pays de Galles*
(see the key).
Answers

1 *En Belgique*	2 *En Espagne*	3 *En Italie*
4 *En Allemagne*	5 *En France*	6 *En Grèce*
7 *En Suisse*	8 *En France*	

2

Teach the difference between *J'habite* (**Camarades 1**
revision) et *Je suis né(e)* by using a few famous people
as examples: *Je m'appelle Eric Cantona. Je suis né en
France. J'habite en Grande Bretagne.*

Preparation – Revise *ville / village, maison /
appartement* and *nord / sud / est / ouest / centre.* A grid
is provided on CM to assist pupils.

♣ Point out that not all items on the cassette contain
further details.

When checking answers, ask pupils to provide
complete sentences, pretending they are the people on
cassette in order to practise the *je* structures.

> 1 – *Moi, je suis née en France et j'habite en*
> *Belgique. J'habite une ville dans le nord.*
> 2 – *Moi, je suis né en Espagne, mais j'habite en*
> *France.*
> 3 – *Tu es née où?*
> – *Je suis née en Suisse.*
> – *Et tu habites où?*
> – *J'habite en Italie. Dans un village, dans le sud.*
> 4 – *Tu es née où?*
> – *Moi? Je suis née en Grèce.*
> – *Et... tu habites où?*
> – *J'habite en Irlande.*
> 5 – *Tu es née en France?*
> – *Non, je suis née en Irlande. Mais j'habite en*
> *Angleterre, dans l'ouest de l'Angleterre. J'habite*
> *dans un appartement, dans une grande ville.*

> 6 – *Tu habites où?*
> – *Je suis née en Ecosse, mais j'habite en Belgique,*
> *avec ma mère. On habite dans une grande*
> *maison.*
> 7 – *Tu es né ici, en France?*
> – *Oui, je suis né en France, mais j'habite en*
> *Allemagne, dans un village, à la montagne.*

Answers
1 *France, Belgique, ville, nord*
2 *Espagne, France*
3 *Suisse, Italie, village, sud*
4 *Grèce, Irlande*
5 *Irlande, Angleterre, ouest, appartement, grande ville*
6 *Ecosse, Belgique, grande maison, avec mère*
7 *France, Allemagne, village, montagne*

3

Preparation – Revise the alphabet, using first names
met so far in this unit or easily recognisable European
towns. Pupils can then do the same in pairs.

4

You may wish to point out beforehand that there are
nine countries listed but one country has no symbol
(*Angleterre*). There are therefore only eight answers on
the cassette.

> 1 *Belgique b* 2 *Allemagne f* 3 *Italie h*
> 4 *Espagne c* 5 *Ecosse d* 6 *Grèce g* 7 *France e*
> 8 *Irlande a*

Answers: on cassette

5

Ask Pupil A to write his/her secret country down each
time to avoid accusations of cheating by Pupil B!

6

Make it clear to pupils that all six statements are
incorrect. ♦ Pupils can answer in note form (for
example: 1 *1300km Jamaïque*). ♣ Pupils make complete
sentences. Warn pupils not to use *je* in their answers.
Encourage pupils to work without glossary/dictionary.

Extra – Use the letter to practise reading aloud.
Answers
1 *La Martinique est à 1300km de la Jamaïque.*
2 *Bastien parle français.*
3 *Bastien est né en Martinique.*
4 *Bastien préfère la campagne.*
5 *Ses parents sont nés en Guadeloupe.*
6 *La Martinique est au sud de la Guadeloupe.*

7

Pupils can draw or use photos to illustrate their work.
They should remember to use speech bubbles since
they are practising using *je*.

Une visite de la Martinique

G Ils ont quel âge?
pp 14–15

Objective
Saying how old people are

Resources
CM 8–9
Cassette for BD, Ex 1, 2, 4 and CM 8–9

Key language
Ton grand-père a quel âge? / Ta grand-mère a quel âge?
Il / Elle a + numbers 60–79
Recycling of numbers

Grammar
Recycling of *avoir* + age

Language learning strategies
Pronunciation: *-an / -en / -on*

Ways in
Carole is designing a card on a school computer for her grandmother's birthday. You can introduce the spread like this: *Carole est au collège. Elle travaille à la bibliothèque.*

Pupils read the introduction while they hear the cassette. (BD tapescript – see Pupil's Book.)

Revise numbers 1–69, then focus more specifically on numbers 11–19.

Introduce the new numbers (70–79) slowly and ask pupils to work out the pattern. Practise using chanting, naming the number after/before, spotting the correct figure on the board, writing the correct figure on the board.

Practise descriminating between 60–69 and 70–79.

1 **Extra** – Continue the practice with numbers of your own choice if needed.

COUNTER

| 73 | 65 | 67 | 74 | 62 | 72 | 71 | 78 | 70 | 60 |

2 **Extra** – Pupils can improvise a similar activity in pairs or in groups.

COUNTER

| 72 | 69 | 77 | 66 | 60 | 75 | 70 | 74 | 65 | 71 |

3 ◆ Make sure pupils know how to pronounce *plus*.

4 A matching exercise to give more listening practise with numbers.

COUNTER

1 – *Le chimpanzé le plus âgé est mort à 59 ans.*
2 – *Record du cheval le plus âgé: 62 ans!*
3 – *L'oiseau le plus rapide est l'autruche, qui fait 72 km à l'heure.*
4 – *Fred Davis est devenu champion du monde de billard à 67 ans.*
5 – *L'escalator le plus long, à Londres, fait 60 mètres.*
6 – *L'arbre de Noël le plus grand a mesuré 67 mètres.*
7 – *Il pleut? Non, pas toujours. Record sans pluie en Grande Bretagne: 73 jours.*

Answers
1 59–c **2** 62–a **3** 72–b **4** 67–g **5** 60–e
6 67–d **7** 73–f

5 **Preparation** – After going through the grammar box with pupils, revise the paradigm of *avoir*, referring pupils back to page 8 if necessary.
Answers
avons, a, a, ont, grand-père, a, ont

6 Pupils may prefer to use a photo instead of a drawing.

Pupils can describe their real or imaginary family (e.g. *la famille Adams*).

♣ Pupils can add details in addition to ages.

H Point Langue / Atelier

pp 16–17

Resources	Key language
CM 10, 11 and 12	Numbers 50–79
Grilles 2 CM optional for Atelier Ex 1	Recycling of alphabet and family
Cassette for Atelier Ex 1	
Dictionaries for Atelier Ex 2	**Language learning strategies**
Card and scissors for CM 12	Learning through games

Point Langue provides further practice of numbers, especially of 60–79.

1

♦ Pupils will find this easier if they write each of the numbers given in figures.

Answers

1 *soixante-trois*   2 *soixante-dix*   3 *soixante-quatorze*
4 *soixante-dix-sept*   5 *soixante-neuf*

2

Pupils can spell towns, countries or any other category of words they wish instead.

3

In their own time, pupils can look up other celebrities for others to guess their age in 2020.

Atelier

1

A grid on CM is provided for this task. The listening and the reading can be done in any order. Interrupt the cassette to enable pupils to make notes. Pupils should not need the glossary for the reading. Completing the family tree can be made optional.

♣ Ask pupils to jot down additional information.

COUNTER

> *Mon petit frère a huit ans. Il aime beaucoup faire du vélo. Mon père a un prénom espagnol. Il s'appelle Antonio. Ça s'écrit A-N-T-O-N-I-O. Ma grand-mère s'appelle Mercedes, M-E-R-C-E-D-E-S. Elle a 67 ans. Mon grand-père a 73 ans. Il s'appelle Juan, J-U-A-N. Ah! Et j'ai une sœur! Mais elle habite toute seule. Elle a 21 ans.*

Answers

Personne	Age	Prénom
Moi	13	*Augusto*
Frère	16	*Carlos*
Frère	8	*Luis*
Père	48	*Antonio*
Grand-mère	67	*Mercedes*
Grand-père	73	*Juan*
Sœur	21	*(name not given)*

Extra – Pupils make up similar items with the help of dictionaries.

2

Answers

1 *Etats-Unis*   2 *Islande*   3 *Russie*   4 *Chine*
5 *Australie*   6 *Pérou*

Une visite de la Martinique

1 Ma ville? Pas mal!

Objective
Describing your town

Resources
Camarades 1 Flashcards 69–76.
Flashcards 9–14
CM 13, 14 and 15
Cassette for introduction, Ex 1 and CM 13
Dictionaries for Ex 3 and 6
A4 paper or larger for Ex 6

Key language
C'est comment, ta ville / ton village?

*Ma ville / Mon village, est / n'est pas... calme / moderne / joli(e) /
bruyant(e) / ancien(ne) / industriel(le)*
J'aimerais bien habiter à...
Pourquoi? Parce que...
Recycling of alphabet

Grammar
... plus... que... / ... moins... que...

Language learning strategies
Recognising irregular adjectives in the dictionary

Ways in
Carole compares her town with Chartres.

Revise places in town (**Camarades 1** Flashcards
69–76). Teach the adjectives using *Ma ville est...*
(Flashcards 9-14).

Pupils then read the introduction while they hear it on
cassette. See if pupils can guess what *... plus... que...*
means by saying: *La Rochelle est très jolie! Lille... bof, oui
et non* and using local towns as examples.
(Introduction tapescript – see Pupil's Book)

1

Preparation – Check pupils understand the pictures.

COUNTER

To train pupils to spot key words, ask them to copy the
new adjectives, then to listen to the cassette, simply
ticking the adjectives whenever they hear them. They
can then listen again and do the task.

1 – *Ma ville, c'est... c'est une ville industrielle. Elle
est très grande. Lille, c'est dans le nord de la
France.*

2 – *Moi aussi, j'habite à Lille. C'est bruyant. C'est
une ville assez bruyante. Mais pour le shopping,
c'est génial!*

3 – *Ma ville, La Rochelle, c'est une ville très, très
jolie. C'est superbe! Et puis, il y a la mer, et
moi, j'aime beaucoup la natation.*

4 – *Moi, j'aime beaucoup les villes anciennes, parce
que j'adore l'histoire. Donc, Chartres, c'est très
bien pour moi. Toute ma famille est née à
Chartres.*

5 – *J'habite à La Rochelle, comme Marine. C'est
bien, parce que c'est une ville calme, assez calme.
Mais... il y a beaucoup de touristes, il y a trop
de touristes!*

6 – *Fort-de-France, c'est assez moderne comme ville.
Ma rue, c'est moderne. Mais mon collège, oh, là,
là, c'est vraiment ancien!*

7 – *Thierry, c'est mon frère. Il aime Chartres, mais
moi, non. Pas du tout! Dans ma rue, c'est
bruyant! Et puis... j'aimerais bien habiter en
Espagne, moi!*

8 – *J'habite à Fort-de-France, moi aussi. Carole
trouve que c'est une ville moderne? Ah, non, je
ne suis pas d'accord! Moi, j'habite dans le centre
de Fort-de-France, et c'est très ancien. J'aimerais
bien visiter Chartres, moi aussi.*

Answers
1 *f, très grande, nord*   2 *d, shopping génial*
3 *c, (il y a la) mer, (elle aime la) natation*
4 *e, adore l'histoire, famille née à Chartres*
5 *b, beaucoup de touristes*   6 *a, collège ancien*
7 *d, n'aime pas Chartres (frère aime Chartres), voudrait
habiter en Espagne*   8 *e, centre ancien, aimerait bien
visiter Chartres*

2

Preparation – Use the key to point out the difference
between the masculine and the feminine of the new
adjectives. Compare *calme / moderne* to *rouge / jaune*.
Practise pronunciation of *ancien / ancienne*.

3

Extra – To enhance dictionary practice you can also
ask pupils to list the masculine and the feminine forms
of each of the adjectives.

♣ Pupils can learn these new adjectives in addition to
the key language.

Answers
1 *touristique*   2 *historique*   3 *ennuyeuse*
4 *intéressants*   5 *fantastique*   6 *agréable*
7 *célèbres*   8 *pauvre*

Grammaire
Practise the use of *plus... que... / moins... que...* by
improvising examples using descriptions of towns or
people: *Madonna est plus grande que Tom Cruise?*

4

Extra – ♣ Ask pupils to generate a few sentences of
their own with the help of the pictures.

Answers
1 *faux, La Rochelle est moins bruyante que Lille / Lille est
plus bruyante que La Rochelle.*   2 *vrai*   3 *vrai*   4 *vrai*
5 *faux, Lille est moins jolie que Chartres / Chartres est
plus jolie que Lille.*   6 *faux, Lille est plus bruyante que
Fort-de-France / Fort-de-France est moins bruyante que
Lille.*   7 *vrai*   8 *faux, Lille est plus industrielle que
Chartres / Chartres est moins industrielle que Lille.*

5 Pupils can use other towns as well as those in
Ex 4.

6 Pupils may prefer to work in pairs or groups. They can
use the introduction on page 18 as a model and
should use the new key language as much as possible.
Pupils can use photos from local tourist office
brochures and write a factual sentence below each
picture. ♣ In addition, pupils can write a paragraph
stating and justifying their personal opinions.
♣ Encourage pupils to re-use adjectives from Ex 3.

Unité 1

Une visite de la Martinique

J C'est comment, ton collège?

pp 20–21

Objective
Talking about your school

Resources
CM3 and 16
OHT (see **Ways in** section)
Cassette for BD and Ex 2, 3 and 4

Key language
Est-ce que vous faites des voyages / vous travaillez le samedi?
Qu'est-ce que vous portez au collège / vous faites à midi / vous faites comme sports?
Nous portons / faisons / jouons / allons / mangeons...
Recycling of clothes and days of the week

Grammar
Present tense with *nous* and *vous* (regular *-er* verbs)

Language learning strategies
Looking up French verbs in the dictionary

Ways in
Carole has prepared a dossier of general information on her school. You can introduce the spread like this: *Carole travaille beaucoup en géographie. Elle a préparé un dossier sur son collège en Martinique.*

Ask pupils to tell you as much as they can about their school, for example: *Il y a une bibliothèque, J'aime le dessin*, etc.

Refer to CM3 notes for suggestions about introducing question forms.

1 ***Preparation*** – Check that pupils remember what *nous* means.
Answers
1 e 2 f 3 d 4 b 5 a 6 c

2 ♣ Pupils can jot down extra information.

COUNTER

1 – *Nous portons un jean ou une jupe. Moi, je préfère les jeans.*
2 – *Je mange à la cantine, parce que c'est bon!*
3 – *Ma copine et moi, nous jouons au basket. Dans l'équipe juniors.*
4 – *Quelquefois, nous faisons des voyages. En Guadeloupe, par exemple.*
5 – *Vous portez un uniforme dans ton collège?*
6 – *A midi, mon copain Bastien va à la maison.*
7 – *Et vous travaillez le samedi?*
 – *Le samedi matin. Ici aussi?*
 – *Ah oui, oui.*
8 – *Vous travaillez cinq jours par semaine?*
 – *Cinq jours et demi.*

Answers
1a 2e 3d 4c 5a 6f 7b 8b

Grammaire
After showing the *nous / vous* pattern to pupils, use the key to generate as many answers as possible using *nous*. Point out the oddity in *mangeons*: can pupils work out the reason?

3 ***Extra*** – For extension work using a more extensive listening passage, replay the Ex 2 recording and ask different groups of pupils to raise their hands when they hear verbs with *nous* or verbs with *vous*.

COUNTER

Section A
Nous mangeons. Nous jouons. Vous mangez. Nous faisons. Nous portons.
Vous jouez. Vous allez. Nous regardons. Vous portez. Vous écoutez.

Section B
Vous allez au cinéma jeudi? Nous faisons du sport le mardi. Nous jouons au tennis le week-end. Vous mangez à la cantine? Nous allons en ville samedi? Vous jouez au foot? Nous mangeons à sept heures. Vous faites des voyages? Vous regardez souvent la télévision! Nous écoutons la radio.

4 ***Preparation*** – Pupils can listen to the model provided on cassette (not reproduced in the Pupil's Book) for ideas. Encourage pupils to avoid mere yes/no answers.

Emphasise the importance of clear, convincing speech when carrying out interviews. The interviewers can comment on the replies instead of merely asking questions. If you ask pupils to act out their dialogues, encourage them not to stay glued to their script.

– *Vous travaillez le mercredi?*
– *Non, nous ne travaillons pas.*
– *Vous faites du sport?*
– *Oui. Nous faisons de l'athlétisme, par exemple.*
– *Vous mangez à la cantine?*
– *Nous mangeons à la cantine ou à la maison.*
– *Vous faites des voyages?*
– *Oui. Nous faisons des voyages avec le prof d'histoire et le prof d'anglais.*
– *C'est chouette!*
– *Oui, j'adore les voyages.*
– *Vous portez un uniforme?*
– *Ah, non! Nous portons un jean ou un pantalon. Ma copine préfère les jupes.*
– *Vous écoutez la radio en classe?*
– *Non, mais nous regardons la télé.*

5 ♣ Emphasise the need for notes as opposed to a full script.

Extra – ♦ After writing and reading, pupils can stretch themselves further by copying their sentences with words missing and trying to reproduce them by speaking from memory.

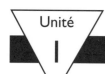

K Ta sœur travaille où? pp 22–23

Objective
Saying where your relatives work

Resources
Flashcards 15-24
OHT (optional) for Ex 5: see notes
CM 17-18
Cassette for BD and Ex 1
Dictionaries for Ex 3 and 6
A4 paper optional for CM 17 Ex 3 and CM 18 Ex 2

Key language
Ton père / Ta sœur / Tes parents travaille(nt)?
Il / Elle / Mon frère / Mes parents travaille(nt)... à la maison;
... dans un bureau / hôtel / magasin / hôpital / grand magasin;
... dans une usine / banque / ferme
Il(s) / Elle(s) ne travaille(nt) pas
Recycling of names for family members

Grammar
Recycling of the present tense with *ils* and *elles* (regular *-er* verbs)
Recycling of *ne... pas*

Language learning strategies
Checking gender in the dictionary

Ways in
Carole and Ludivine are off to see Ludivine's sister, who works at a cinema. You can introduce the spread like this: *Carole est avec Ludivine, à la maison. Elle parle avec son père au téléphone. Ah! La Martinique, c'est loin* (explain *loin* through action).

Pupils read the BD while they listen to the cassette. Then use Flashcards 15–24 to teach the new place names. Point out the masculine and the feminine places. Put particular emphasis on accurate pronunciation (*hôtel / hôpital / ferme/ banque / bureau*). (BD tapescript – see Pupil's Book.)

1

Preparation – Point out that pupils will hear either two or three places of work under each item. Also point out that ♣ only applies to 1, 6, 7 & 8.

Extra – Write some of the jobs on the board to reinforce pronunciation: *docteur / porteur / directeur*.

Use the key to remind pupils of the *-ent* verb ending (**Camarades 1**) and *mon / ma / mes*.

COUNTER

> **1** – *Je travaille dans un hôpital. Je suis docteur. (...) Moi, je travaille dans un magasin, un magasin de vêtements...*
> **2** – *un bureau (...) une ferme (...) une usine*
> **3** – *un magasin (...) un hôpital (...) une banque*
> **4** – *un hôtel (...) un grand magasin (...) un hôpital*
> **5** – *Je travaille dans une usine (...) Je travaille à la maison (...) Je travaille dans une ferme.*
> **6** – *Je travaille dans un hôtel, je suis réceptionniste (...) Alors, moi, je travaille dans un hôtel. Je suis porteur.*
> **7** – *Je ne travaille pas. J'ai un petit bébé (...) Moi, je travaille dans une banque. Je suis directrice.*
> **8** – *Moi, je travaille dans une usine; je prépare des pizzas (...) Eh bien, moi, je ne travaille pas. Je cherche du travail. Normalement, je suis électricien...*

Answers
1 c (doctor), i (clothes shop) **2** a, g, e **3** b, c, f
4 d, i, c **5** e, h, g **6** d (receptionist), d (porter)
7 j (baby), f (manager – accept director)
8 e (pizzas), j (electrician)

2

Emphasise peer checking of pronunciation: pupil **A** should refuse to answer if pupil **B** appears to be careless with pronunciation.

3

Preparation – Set a time limit to encourage fast dictionary work. Ask pupils to make a guess at translation before looking up the words. ♣ Pupils need to be careful about the use of *un / une*.

Some pupils may wish to learn these place names in addition to the key language. Some of them are, in fact, taught later on in **Camarades 2**.
Answers
gare (f) = station   *aéroport* (m) = airport
boucherie (f) = butcher's   *mairie* (f) = town hall
marché (m) = market   *commissariat* (m) = police station   *station-service* (f) = petrol station
pharmacie (f) = chemist's

4

Do an example as a whole class before pupils start working in groups. ♦ To help pupils, write a sample sentence on the board instead, underlining the words that can be changed each time: *Mon père travaille dans un hôtel à Coventry avec ma sœur et il aime ça parce que c'est moderne.*

5

Encourage pupils to read full sentences to complete the task more easily. They should also learn to adopt good test/exam techniques by doing the items they find easiest first, then coming back to the remaining ones if there is time. When doing the corrections, analyse carefully with pupils the clues provided by the text: parts of speech, context, common sense, grammatical clues, etc.

Extra – Reproduce the letter in full on an OHP transparency, then blank out more and more words and ask one pupil at a time to reproduce a sentence orally from memory.
Answers
1 *ne* **2** *il* **3** *soir* **4** *hôpital* **5** *pas* **6** *travaillent*
7 *ont* **8** *sœur* **9** *fatigant* **10** *restaurant* **11** *un*

6

♦ Pupils should use the key as much as possible.

Encourage pupils to use language they have learnt rather than making excessive use of dictionaries. Encourage them to ask each other questions about words they may have forgotten rather than asking you. Ask pupils to check each other's work in pairs before producing their final draft. Explain what they should check, for example, gender (use of articles, *mon / ma / mes*), agreement of verbs and adjectives, punctuation, spelling of difficult words, etc.

L Point Langue / Atelier   pp 24–25

Resources
CM 19
OHT (see notes on *Atelier*)

Grammar
Present tense of regular *-er* verbs
on / nous

Key language
Recycling of school routine and personal details

Language learning strategies
Bringing variety into productive work

Point Langue

This page reinforces the work done on *nous / vous* (Spread J), provides explanations on *tu / vous* and *on / nous* and presents the full present tense paradigm of *travailler*.

1 ♦ Write an example of a verb with *nous* and an example of a verb with *vous* on the board to help pupils.

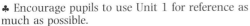

♣ Encourage pupils to use Unit 1 for reference as much as possible.

Answers
♦ **1** *portez* **2** *portons* **3** *regardez* **4** *regardons*
  5 *mangez* **6** *mangeons* **7** *Vous* **8** *nous*

Atelier

♦ To assist pupils with *personnage 1*, complete a form similar to that on page 25 and show it on an OHP. Provide an example for *personnage 2*.

Personnage 3 is being interviewed and providing information about himself/herself. Rehearse possible questions with pupils before they prepare the interview.

CAMARADES 2		OVERVIEW – UNITE 2 – ON FAIT DU SHOPPING				NATIONAL CURRICULUM	
	Topics/Objectives	Key language	Grammar	Strategies		PoS coverage	AoE
A	**Encore des numéros!** Learning new numbers	Numbers 80–1000 Recycling of numbers 1–79		Learning through games		1 a, c, d 2 a, b, f	B
B	**Je cherche...** Shopping for clothes	*Vous désirez? Je cherche (une veste bleu foncé). De quelle couleur? Vous avez un pull en rose? Je n'aime pas le violet / l'orange / le bleu clair. Ça fait combien? Ça fait ... francs. C'est cher / Ça va / Ce n'est pas cher.* Recycling of clothes, numbers and colours	Adjectives (colours): agreement or not?	Adapting a model conversation Checking gender in the dictionary		1 a, d, f, g, h, i 2 a, c, d, e, f, h, n 3 a, b, c	C
C	**Ça va?** Discussing problems when buying clothes	*Je peux essayer? Bien sûr, pas de problème, là-bas. Ça ne va pas. C'est un peu / très / trop... grand / petit / long / court / large / juste. Ça va. C'est joli / parfait.* Recycling of numbers and colours	C'est + invariable adjectives	Selecting the correct translation when looking up English words in a dictionary		1 a, c, d, f, g, h 2 a, d, e, g, h 3 c, d	C
D	**Point Langue Atelier**	Numbers 1–1000 Recycling of shopping for clothes		Applying a pattern Using spider webs to learn or revise		1 c, j 2 a, f, n 3 b	C
E	**Bonjour! Je voudrais...** Buying food	*Je voudrais... un demi-litre de lait / un kilo de tomates / 500 grammes de viande hachée / fromage / une bouteille de limonade / une boîte de tomates / une tranche de jambon / un paquet de beurre / un pot de yaourt / un tube de dentifrice / une tarte aux fraises / une baguette.*		Alphabet practice as an aid to learning new words		1 a, h, i, j 2 a, d, e, g, k, n 3 b, d	C
F	**Pardon, où est... ?** Finding your way round the supermarket	*Où est ... le poisson / la boucherie / la boulangerie / la laiterie / la pâtisserie / l'alimentation générale? Où sont ... les boissons / les surgelés / les fruits et légumes? Allée numéro trois. Au fond. / à gauche / à droite.*	*Où est ...? Où sont ...?*	Pronunciation: *-i-, -o-, -oi-*		1 a, c, g, h, i 2 a, b, d, e, f 3 4 a	C

| CAMARADES 2 | OVERVIEW – UNITE 2 – ON FAIT DU SHOPPING | | Cont. | | NATIONAL CURRICULUM | |
	Topics/Objectives	Key language	Grammar	Strategies	PoS coverage	AoE
G	C'est devant ou derrière? Saying where products are at the supermarket	C'est avant / après / derrière le poisson. C'est entre les fruits et les légumes. C'est en face / à côté du poisson. C'est près / loin de la charcuterie. C'est à gauche / droite des surgelés / de l'alimentation générale. Recycling of supermarket sections	Prepositions	Adapting a model dialogue	1 a, c, d, g, h, i 2 a, b, c, d, e, g, k 3 a, c, f	C
H	Point Langue Atelier	Recycling of supermarket vocabulary	Prepositions with du / de la / de l' / des	Applying a pattern	1 a, c, d, k 2 a 3 f, g	C
I	Pour Noël, j'aimerais... Saying what you would like for Christmas	J'aimerais... / Je vais acheter... un CD / une cravate / une cassette vidéo / un jeu pour ordinateur / un porte-feuille / du papier à lettres / des articles de toilette / des boucles d'oreille / des chaussettes / un jouet / un poster. Recycling of personal possessions and opinions	Recycling of je vais / tu vas + infinitive	Using the dictionary as an aid to working independently	1 a, f, g, i 2 a, d, e, h, i, j 3 d 4 a	BC
J	On fête Noël chez toi? Talking about what you do at Christmas time	Chez moi, / en France, / en Angleterre, / en Écosse,... on fête le jour de Noël avec des amis / la famille. Je fais / On fait un grand repas / un sapin / des décorations. On met des chaussures / chaussettes pour le père Noël. On offre des cadeaux. On va à l'église.	Present tense of faire Use of on	Using link words in writing	1 a, c, f, g, i, j 2 a, d, e, j, k, l 3 d, f 4 c	BC
K	Point Langue Atelier	Recycling of Christmas and presents	Present tense of faire	Applying a pattern Using the textbook for reference	1 d, i 2 k 3 d, f	B
L	On révise	Recycling of Units 1–2			1 a, c, i 2 a, d, h, j 4 a	

IT Opportunities

CORE ACTIVITIES

Text manipulation

Spreads A–I
Produce a model text in the first person in which a young person writes about:
(a) what he/she would like for Christmas
(b) what he/she is buying for others
(c) how Christmas is celebrated at home

Word processing – guided writing

Spreads B–D
Create and save the text of a conversation in which somebody is buying clothes in a shop. Highlight or under-line a number of words that could be substituted, e.g. items of clothing, colours, sizes, prices. Pupils replace the highlighted words with others that would be appropriate.

Presentation

Spreads E and F
Using a word processor offering different fonts, borders and possibly clipart, pupils produce a leaflet advertising up to ten special offers in a supermarket.

If a multi-media package is available, a similar presen-tation could be made using text, sound and images scanned from magazines or taken with an ion (disk) camera.

Provide pupils with helpful phrases, such as *prix choc, offre spéciale, bonne affaire* to describe the offers.

Pupils should ensure that prices are realistic. They could look up articles in dictionaries as well as using ones that are found in the book.

ADDITIONAL ACTIVITIES

Word processing – extended writing

Spread B
Exercise 2
Pupils use the three sets of rhyming words to write a poem. The advantages of doing this task on a word processor include:

• opportunities to revise and improve an original draft
• opportunities for collaborative work
• opportunities to present a poem in an imaginative way – with different fonts, font sizes and possibly colours

The Internet

Information on the Web can be found by using search engines. These are systems which collect and index vast numbers of pages. Among the most popular search engines are:

Alta Vista: http://www.altavista.digital.com/
Lycos: http://www.lycos.com/
Infoseek: http://www.infoseek.com/
Yahoo! http://www.yahoo.com/

Search engines work by asking you to type in a word, or a series of words. A list of related links is then produced for you to browse through.

Unfortunately searches do not always take you straight to the information you want. For example, if you were looking for information on tourism in France and typed the word 'Paris' into a search engine you would probably be presented with several thousand links, most of which would be irrelevant to your needs.

A successful search can never be 100% guaranteed, since the contents of the Internet are constantly changing, but all the suggested entries in **Camarades 2** have been tested in terms of their relevance to the unit of the book, as well as their ability to produce a manageable number of links to browse through.
• Type *hypermarché* into a search engine. Try to find pictures and information in French about some of the leading French hypermarket chains.
• Type *Auchan* into a search engine. The *Auchan* hypermarket chain opened its own website in 1996.
• Type *fromage* into a search engine. You should be able to access information about cheeses from different regions of France
• Type *boulangerie* into a search engine. You might find information about bread, as well as pictures of shops.

Copymasters

The *présentation* and the *grilles* copymasters should be used as indicated.
The other copymasters (worksheets and vocabulary sheets) should be used with or after the spread indicated.

Pupil's Book Spread	Corresponding Copymaster
A	19–20 *Glossaire*
B	–
C	1 *Présentation*; 4–5 *On écoute*; *Grilles 2*
D	6 *Grammaire*; 7-8 *On parle*
E	–
F	2 *Présentation*; 9–10 *On lit*; *Grilles 2*
G	3 *Présentation*; 11 *On s'amuse*
H	12 *Grammaire*; 13 *Que sais-tu?*
I	14 *Plaisir de lire*
J	15–16 *On écrit*
K	17 *Grammaire*; 18 *Que sais-tu?*
L	–

Notes to accompany Copymasters (CMs)

Feuille 1
Presentation sheet to revise clothes and to present the adjectives. Use pupils of different sizes in the class for further practice: *Le pull de Jérémy pour Fiona, ça va?*

Feuille 2
Presentation sheet to introduce the different sections in the supermarket as well as the key direction words. Integrate revision of food and drink by saying a section (recognition) and asking pupils to name as many items as they can that could be found in that section. Then repeat the activity the other way round for pupils to manipulate the new language.

Feuille 3
Presentation sheet to teach the new prepositions.

Feuilles 4–5 On écoute
These practise numbers, prices and shopping for clothes.

Feuille 4 ♦
Ex 1 – Repeat the numbers after the cassette if necessary. Allow plenty of time for pupils to check through all three cards.

93 ... je répète ... 93	82 ... je répète ... 82
97 ... je répète ... 97	95 ... je répète ... 95
86 ... je répète ... 86	81 ... je répète ... 81
89 ... je répète ... 89	88 ... je répète ... 88
87 ... je répète ... 87	80 ... je répète ... 80

Answers *carte C (bottom line)*

Ex 2 – Write the prices on the board for multiple choice instead.

1 – *Je cherche un pull.*
– *Regarde le pull bleu. Ça coûte 85f.*

2 – *Je cherche une jupe.*
– *Regarde la jupe rouge. Elle coûte 95f.*

3 – *Je cherche une veste.*
– *Regarde la veste noire. Elle coûte 160f.*

4 – *Je cherche un T-shirt.*
– *Regarde le T-shirt rose. Ça coûte 80f.*

5 – *Je cherche un pantalon.*
– *Regarde le pantalon gris.*
– *Ça fait combien?*
– *Ça fait 350f.*

6 – *Je cherche une chemise.*
– *Regarde la chemise verte.*
– *Ça fait combien?*
– *Ça fait 90f.*

Answers
1 C, bleu, 85f   **2** D, rouge, 95f   **3** F, noire, 160f
4 A, rose, 80f   **5** E, gris, 350f   **6** B, verte, 90f

Feuille 5 ♣
Ex 1 *Preparation* – Recap on colours and on reasons for buying/not buying clothes.

1 – *Regarde la veste à 195f. Ça t'intéresse?*
– *La veste, là? A 195f? Bon, oui, ce n'est pas cher, mais regarde la couleur! Moi avec une veste jaune? Ah, non alors!*

2 – *Oh, les baskets! C'est cher?*
– *Ben, regarde, là.*
– *345f...*
– *345f, ça va, mais... non! C'est trop petit. Ça, c'est du 39. Moi, je prends du 41.*

3 – *Ah, moi aussi, je cherche une jupe.*
– *Regarde. Ça va?*
– *Oui, elle est bien!*
– *Et ce n'est pas trop cher, non?*
– *189f? Oui, c'est vrai. Mais... elle est un peu courte, non?*
– *Un peu courte? Non, non, je ne suis pas d'accord. J'aime bien les jupes courtes, moi. Pas de problème! Ça va!*

4 – *Bon, alors, ça va, la chemise, oui ou non?*
– *Ben, je ne sais pas... 145f... Et la couleur? Tu trouves ça bien, la couleur?*
– *Ben, écoute, c'est joli, le bleu foncé.*
– *Tu trouves?*
– *Oui, ça va avec ton pantalon.*
– *Ah, euh... non, personnellement, j'aimerais bien bleu clair. Oui, bleu clair.*

5 – *Excusez-moi. C'est combien, le pantalon?*
– *Il y a une réduction. Il est à 180f.*
– *Je peux essayer?*
– *Oui, bien sûr, c'est là-bas.*
– *C'est un peu juste, non?*
– *Un peu juste? Non, non, c'est votre pull! Regardez.*
– *Ah oui, en effet. C'est parfait!*

6 – *Qu'est-ce que tu cherches?*
– *Regarde la casquette. Tu aimes ça?*
– *Bof, ouais...*
– *Tu préfères la casquette en orange ou en vert?*
– *Euh... Oh là! Regarde le prix!*
– *Quoi? Ça fait combien?*
– *249f!*
– *249f?? Ah, là, il y a un problème! J'ai seulement 100f.*

Answers
1 veste   195f   non   couleur (jaune)
2 basket   345f   non   trop petit (c'est du 39; voudrait 41)
3 jupe   189f   oui   aime les jupes courtes
4 chemise   145f   non   préfère bleu clair
5 pantalon   180f   oui   parfait
6 casquette   249f   non   trop cher (a seulement 100f)

Ex 2 – Make sure pupils understand A–D before playing the cassette. Point out that what matters here is not detailed information but the overall theme of each exchange. When doing the corrections, play the cassette again and discuss with pupils which words were crucial to the selection of the correct answer.

> **1** – *Qu'est-ce qu'il y a? Il y a un problème?*
> – *Ben oui. C'est les jeans. A la radio, on dit: «offre spéciale, jeans à 85f,90», mais regardez: sur le jean, il y a écrit 115f.*
>
> **2** – *Vous avez un problème?*
> – *Oui, euh... je voudrais changer ce T-shirt, s'il vous plaît. C'est possible?*
> – *Pourquoi?*
> – *Ben... c'est un T-shirt vert clair mais ma copine n'aime pas beaucoup ça. Elle aimerait bien un T-shirt vert foncé.*
>
> **3** – *Je peux vous aider?*
> – *Oui, euh... c'est la jupe, là... J'ai acheté la jupe ce matin, mais elle est sale. Regardez.*
> – *C'est sale? Mais non, mais non, c'est normal, ça. Ce n'est pas sale, ou pas beaucoup.*
> – *Ah, écoutez, pour moi, c'est sale. Je peux changer la jupe, oui ou non?*
>
> **4** – *Bonjour, je voudrais changer ce pull, s'il vous plaît.*
> – *Qu'est-ce qui ne va pas?*
> – *Ben, c'est... c'est tout. Ça... ça ne va pas.*
> – *Qu'est-ce que c'est? La couleur?*
> – *La couleur, ça va, mais c'est un peu juste.*
> – *Un peu juste? Mais, c'est bien. C'est très populaire en ce moment.*
> – *Ah non, non, pas pour moi.*
>
> **5** – *Je voudrais changer ce sweat-shirt, s'il vous plaît.*
> – *Ça ne va pas?*
> – *Il est joli, mais c'est moins cher au magasin «Bon Marché».*
> – *Moins cher au «Bon Marché»? Ah, mais la qualité, c'est différent!*
> – *Non, non. Ce sweat-shirt, taille 40, vert foncé. Ici, c'est 239f. Au «Bon Marché», c'est 195f. Une différence de 44f. C'est beaucoup pour un sweat-shirt!*

Answers
(part 1) **1** A **2** C **3** D **4** B **5** A
(part 2) **1** F **2** G **3** I **4** H **5** E

Feuille 6 Grammaire
This CM practises adjectival agreements.

Ex 1 *Extra* – Pupils make up extra examples of their own.
Answers
1 *noires* **2** *blanc* **3** *vert / rose*
4 *rouge / orange* **5** *vert foncé* **6** *bleu clair*

Ex 2: *Extra* – Pupils draw and colour in items 1–7.
Answers
ms = masculine singular *fs* = feminine singular
mpl = masculine plural *fpl* = feminine plural
1 *bleue* **2** *verts* **3** *jaunes* **4** *noire* **5** *grises* **6** *orange*
7 *vert foncé*

Feuilles 7–8 On parle
Role-play practice on buying clothes.

Feuille 7 ♦
Explain to pupils that role-play 2 is identical to role-play 1 but provides less support.

Extra – Pupils improvise slightly different dialogues, changing the item, the problem and the price.

Feuille 8 ♣
Preparation – Brainstorm using the strategy box.

Feuilles 9–10 On lit
These two CMs provide additional reading practice on supermarket shopping.

Feuille 9 ♦
Ex 1 **Answers**
1 R **2** R **3** P **4** P **5** R **6** P **7** P **8** R **9** P **10** P

Ex 2 *Extra* – After drawing the supermarket, ask pupils to rewrite the shopping list in a time-saving order, in line with the supermarket plan.
Answers
1 D **2** A **3** G **4** F **5** B **6** C **7** E

Feuille 10 ♣
Pupils should work without dictionaries in order to build up reading skills, such as making sense of the unknown from what you do understand; awareness of cognates; awareness of context; awareness of parts of speech.
Answers
Ex 1: **1** *vrai* **2** *vrai* **3** *faux* **4** *faux* **5** *faux* **6** *faux*
Ex 2: **1** *chou-fleur* **2** *gratuit(e)* **3** icing sugar
4 *jusqu'à* **5** *frais* **6** *prix* **7** low calorie
8 *ananas* **9** *brosses à dents* **10** glass
11 *pressing* **12** extra points

Feuille 11 On s'amuse
Ex 1 – The aim is to reach the end box first. Pupils miss a turn when falling on a *fermé* box and move as indicated when they fall on an instruction box.

Ex 2 – Elicit any comprehension problems there might be through mime and facial expression only.

Play the cassette again, one or two lines at a time. Devise a gestual routine for the song. Pupils can then sing along with gestures. (Tapescript – see CM.)

Feuille 12 Grammaire
This CM provides further practice of prepositions with *du / de la / de l' / des*.

Ex 1 ♦ Encourage pupils to do peer checking.
Answers
baguette fromage gâteaux yaourts
bananes (biscuits) (poisson) lait
tarte jambon (poulet) dentifrice

Ex 2 ♣ Ask pupils to be extra careful about the use of *du /de la / de l' / des* as they speak.

Feuille 13 Que sais-tu?

This copymaster revises topics 1 and 2.

Ex 1 – Emphasise that all the items contain a mistake (product or price).

Answers

1 *Le fromage, ça fait quatre-vingts francs.* **2** *La viande, ça fait quatre-vingt-deux francs.* **3** *La tarte, ça fait cent quinze francs.* **4** *Les yaourts, ça fait dix francs quatre-vingt-dix.* **5** *La baguette, ça fait trois francs quatre-vingt-cinq.* **6** *Le dentifrice, ça fait vingt-sept francs quinze.*

Ex 2 – Suggest pupils reply within five seconds.

Ex 3 – Pupils should carry out the dialogue without writing it out first.

Feuille 14 Plaisir de lire

Extra – In small groups, pupils write a story on the pictures in the third person. They can invent details.

C'est le 19 décembre. Barnabé travaille dans un grand magasin ...

Answers

Le costume,... Bonjour,... Donne-moi... Moi, je veux... Et moi, je veux... Reste avec... Il est moche!... Fatigué?...

Feuilles 15–16 On écrit

These two CMs are about Christmas.

Feuille 15 ♦

Answers

Ex 1: *bonbons nounours sapin père Noël jouet cravate portefeuille chaussettes chocolats décembre papier à lettres décorations cadeaux boucles d'oreilles église repas → Bon Noël, Camarades!*

Feuille 16 ♣

Ex 1 – Pupils add collage or drawings.

Ex 2 – More able pupils should work without the suggested phrases. They could first brainstorm in small groups on each question..

Feuille 17 Grammaire

This CM offers additional practice of *faire* in the present tense.

Feuille 18 Que sais-tu?

This CM offers some revision of topic 3.

Ex 1 **Answers**

1 *articles de toilette* **2** *boucles d'oreilles* **3** *chaussettes* **4** *chocolats* **5** *cravate* **6** *jouet* **7** *poster* **8** *jeu pour ordinateur* **9** *papier à lettres* **10** *portefeuille* **11** *CD*

Ex 2 Pupils should speak without notes.

A Encore des numéros!

pp 26–27

Objective
Learning new numbers

Resources
Cassette for BD and Ex 1, 2, 4 and 5
CM 19–20 for reference throughout Unit 2

Key language
Numbers 80–1000
Recycling of numbers 1–79

Language learning strategies
Learning through games

Ways in
Shopping can be a delight or a nightmare. In topic 1, Thierry's shopping for clothes. In topic 2, he goes to the supermarket. Topic 3 finds him planning Christmas. In this spread, he meets his mum to go shopping with her.

Revise numbers 1–79. Then start teaching 80–100 through sound only. Encourage pupils to try and work out the pattern for themselves as they listen to you, then play the number games pupils already know for intensive practice. For more recognition work, say some numbers and ask different groups of pupils to repeat odd/even numbers or numbers below/above 90.

Pupils can then read the short BD while they hear it on cassette. (BD tapescript – see Pupil's Book.)

1
Pupils listen, follow the song and then sing along.

Extra – Improvise aural discrimination tasks with numbers that can easily be confused, for example 67, 77, 87 and 97.

quatre-vingts	quatre-vingt-onze
quatre-vingt-un	quatre-vingt-douze
quatre-vingt-deux	quatre-vingt-treize
quatre-vingt-trois	quatre-vingt-quatorze
quatre-vingt-quatre	quatre-vingt-quinze
quatre-vingt-cinq	*(Oh, zut! Je déteste*
(Oh là là! Je déteste	*travailler!)*
travailler!)	quatre-vingt-seize
quatre-vingt-six	quatre-vingt-dix-sept
quatre-vingt-sept	quatre-vingt-dix-huit
quatre-vingt-huit	quatre-vingt-dix-neuf
quatre-vingt-neuf	cent
quatre-vingt-dix	*(Oh, excellent! C'est le*
(Oh super! c'est le	*rayon des vêtements!)*
libre-service)	

2
Preparation – Do some aural discrimination practice (along the lines suggested above) between sounds like *deux / douze, cinq / quinze*, etc.

a	quatre-vingt-trois	**d**	cent
b	quatre-vingt-douze	**e**	quatre-vingt-seize
c	quatre-vingt-six	**f**	quatre-vingt-cinq

Answers
a F b F c F d V e F f F

3
First demonstrate ♦ and ♣ to the whole class.

♦ Set a time limit of 5 seconds for **B** to gain a point.
♣ Ask pupils to record the number of guesses.

4
Preparation – 200, 300, etc., with emphasis on 500 (silent -q-), 600 (silent -x-) and 800 (silent -t-). Then practise numbers such as 201, 202, etc.

deux cents	trois cents
trois cents	neuf cents
quatre cents	quatre cents
cinq cents	mille
six cents	six cents
sept cents	huit cents
huit cents	deux cents
neuf cents	sept cents
mille	

5
As a step between ♦ and ♣, write or draw the items (*baskets*, etc.) on the board for pupils to select.

1 – *Les baskets? Six cents francs.*
– *Six cents?*
– *Oui.*

2 – *Le pantalon, c'est combien?*
– *Trois cents.*
– *Trois cents? C'est cher...*

3 – *C'est combien, le chien?*
– *Cinq cents francs!*
– *Cinq cents?*

4 – *Oh, regarde les T-shirts!*
– *Deux cents francs!*
– *Deux cents? Pas possible!*

5 – *La veste? Quatre cents francs.*
– *Quatre cents? Mmm...*

6 – *Le baladeur, c'est combien?*
– *Sept cent quatre-vingts.*
– *Sept cent quatre-vingts? Oh, c'est trop...*

7 – *La télévision? Neuf cents quatre-vingt quinze.*
– *Neuf cent quatre-vingt quinze... Mmm...*

Answers
1 600f, les baskets **2** 300f, le pantalon
3 500f, le chien **4** 200f, les T-shirts **5** 400f la veste
6 780f, le baladeur **7** 995f, la télévision

6
♦ Pupils may find it easier to work in pairs. Suggest they look out for *cent* and *mille* as pointers.
Answers
♦ **f** = 80 **i** = 85 **c** = 93 **d** = 101 **h** = 271
e = 422 **b** = 589 **a** = 600 **g** = 1057
♣ **a** quatre-vingt-deux **b** 19 **c** sept cent trois
d 83, 38 **e** 518, 815, huit cent quinze
f 916, 619, six cent dix-neuf

7
Pool ideas as a whole class to assist less imaginative pupils. Insist that pupils suggest activities which can be carried out entirely in French.

B Je cherche...   pp 28–29

Objective
Saying what someone looks like

Resources
Flashcards 25–28
Cassette for BD and Ex 1, 3 and 4
Dictionaries for Ex 3 and 5

Key language
Vous désirez?
Je cherche (une veste bleu foncé).
De quelle couleur?

Vous avez un pull en rose?
Je n'aime pas le violet / l'orange / le bleu clair.
Ça fait combien? Ça fait ... francs.
C'est cher / Ça va / Ce n'est pas cher.
Recycling of clothes, numbers and colours

Grammar
Adjectives (colour): agreement or not?

Language learning strategies
Adapting a model conversation
Checking gender in the dictionary

Ways in
Thierry is having difficulty choosing a new jacket.

Revise clothes with the help of Flashcards 25–28.
Build in revision of numbers and prices:
– *La veste, ça fait combien?* (write a price on the board)
– *La veste, ça fait 375f.*
Pupils then read the BD as they hear it on cassette.
Ask questions: *Thierry cherche un pantalon?*

1

♦ Pupils could first try without any support.
Answers
♦ **1** *Vous désirez?* **2** *Je cherche une veste.*
3 *Je n'aime pas le bleu.* **4** *Ça fait combien?*
5 *C'est cher.* **6** *Ce n'est pas cher.* **7** *Ça va.*
♣ **1** *Thierry* **2** *Maman* **3** *Thierry* **4** *Thierry* **5** *Maman*

2

♣ Introduce a challenge after a few minutes. If pupils answer without hesitation they gain one point.

3

Pupils should use the dictionary only when necessary.

Extra – Pupils create their own rhythm, learn the rap by heart or make up their own. (Tapescript – see Pupil's Book.)

4

Preparation – Use item 1 (example) for aural recognition of individual words. ♦ Pupils write down the words *T-shirt, couleur, rouge, combien, vingt-cinq, pas cher*, and tick them as they hear them. ♣ Give the words to pupils jumbled and ask them to number them in the order in which they hear them.

COUNTER

```
1 –  Bonjour, vous désirez?
   –  Je cherche un T-shirt.
   –  De quelle couleur?
   –  Rouge.
   –  Voilà... un joli T-shirt rouge...
   –  Ça fait combien?
   –  Vingt-cinq francs.
   –  C'est bien. Ce n'est pas cher!

2 –  Bonjour!
   –  Bonjour, vous désirez?
   –  Je cherche un pull.
   –  Et de quelle couleur?
   –  Noir. C'est pour l'école.
   –  Bon, voilà – un pull noir.
   –  Ça fait combien?
   –  Quatre-vingt-cinq francs.
   –  Quatre-vingt-cinq? Bon, ça va.
```

```
3 –  Bonjour!
   –  Vous désirez?
   –  Je cherche une casquette.
   –  De quelle couleur?
   –  Vous avez une casquette verte?
   –  Verte? Oui – voilà.
   –  Et ça fait combien?
   –  Seize francs.
   –  Seize francs? Oh, ce n'est pas cher!
   –  D'accord.

4 –  Vous désirez?
   –  Je cherche une veste. Ça fait combien, la veste grise?
   –  La veste grise? Ça fait... mille quatre cents.
   –  Mille quatre cents? Oh là là là! C'est cher!

5 –  Vous désirez?
   –  Je cherche un pantalon bleu.
   –  Un moment... un pantalon bleu... Ah, voilà!
   –  Ça fait combien?
   –  Cent soixante-cinq francs.
   –  Cent soixante-cinq... Oh, c'est cher.

6 –  Vous désirez?
   –  Je cherche un short. Ça fait combien, les shorts?
   –  Cinquante-neuf francs.
   –  Cinquante-neuf? Ça va.
   –  Et de quelle couleur?
   –  Blanc et bleu.
   –  Un moment... blanc et bleu... Oui, voilà!
   –  Oh, super!
```

Answers
1 *T-shirt, rouge, 25f, pas cher* **2** *pull noir, 85f, ça va*
3 *casquette, verte, 16f, n'est pas cher* **4** *veste, grise, 1400f, cher* **5** *pantalon, bleu, 165f, cher*
6 *short, blanc et bleu, 59f, ça va*

5

Extra – Pupils use the English-French part of their dictionaries to make up a poster of their own.
Answers (reading across)
un, une, une, un, une, un, une, un, un, un

6

Pupils can use the realia from Ex 5. The conversations can then be acted out and recorded on video or cassette, with pupils performing from a script or from memory. Scripts can be word processed and displayed with photos of the performance.

On fait du shopping

C Ça va?

Objective
Discussing problems when buying clothes

Resources
CM 1, 4 & 5
OHT (see **Ways in** section)
Grilles 2 CM for Ex 4
Cassette for BD, Ex 1, 2, 5 and CM 4–5
Dictionaries for Ex 4

Key language
Je peux essayer? Bien sûr, pas de problème, là-bas.
Ça ne va pas. C'est un peu / très / trop... grand / petit / long /
court / large / juste.
Ça va. C'est joli / parfait.
Recycling of numbers and colours

Grammar
C'est + invariable adjectives

Language learning strategies
Selecting the correct translation when looking up English
words in a dictionary

Ways in
Thierry bumps into classmates who are also shopping
for clothes... and he is not helping much!

Use CM1, which can be put onto OHT, to revise clothes
and to present the adjectives. Use pupils of different
sizes in the class for further practice: *Le pull de Jérémy –
pour Fiona, ça va?*

Pupils then read the BD as they hear the cassette. Do
some practice on intonation in questions and
exclamations. (BD tapescript – see Pupil's Book.)

1

You may prefer to do this purely as a listening activity
at first, using the reading as reinforcement afterwards.

1 *Ça va.*	**4** *C'est large.*
2 *Ça ne va pas.*	**5** *C'est joli.*
3 *C'est long.*	

Answers
1 e **2** d **3** c **4** a **5** b

2

Encourage pupils to reuse the interjections in their
own work.

1 – *Vous l'aimez? Ça va?*
– *C'est très joli.*
– *Ah, bon?*
– *Oui, c'est parfait!*

2 – *Alors, ça va?*
– *Ça ne va pas!*
– *Oh, là là! C'est trop court!*
– *Oui, c'est court...*

3 – *Ça va?*
– *Ça ne va pas du tout!*
– *Non?*
– *Non, c'est un désastre! C'est trop grand!*
– *Grand?*
– *Oui, c'est énorme!*

4 – *Madame?*
– *Oui, ça va?*
– *Je regrette, mais c'est... euh... trop juste.*
– *Ah, bon? C'est juste? Attendez – je vais voir s'il
y en a un autre...*

5 – *Ça ne va pas?*
– *Non! C'est petit!*
– *Oh, là là! C'est vrai! C'est petit ...*

Answers
1 *Laureline; Ah, bon?* **2** *Erik; Oh, là là* **3** *Magali; Non?*
4 *Marc; ça va?* **5** *Virna; Oh, là là*

3
♦ Reiterate the importance of intonation.
♣ Pupils should use Spread B language.

4
Give a time limit to limit dictionary use.

Extra – Pupils make up a similar task, either by using
adjectives previously learnt or by looking up new
adjectives of their choice.
Answers
1 *vraiment* **2** *laid* **3** *démodé* **4** *affreux* **5** *minuscule*
Mot mystère: idéal

5
Extra – Pupils practise the role-play several times,
looking at the speech bubbles less and less, until they can
carry out the role-play with the picture support only.

– *Vous désirez?*
– *Je cherche une veste noire.*
– *Voilà une veste...*
– *Je peux essayer?*
– *Pas de problème.*
– *Oh, c'est trop long.*
– *Ah, bon? Et ça, ça va?*
– *Non, c'est trop juste.*
– *Oh là, là! Et ça alors.*
– *C'est parfait. Ça fait combien?*
– *200 francs.*
– *Oh, ça va! Merci, au revoir!*
– *Merci, au revoir!*

Answers
1 *noire* **2** *Pas de problème* **3** *long* **4** *juste* **5** *parfait*
6 *200 francs* **7** *ça va*

6
Pupils can work in groups of three instead: shopper,
friend and shop assistant, as in the BD. Encourage
them to memorise their conversation. Pupils can then
act out in front of a jury (other teachers/sixth
formers/French assistants).

D Point Langue / Atelier   pp 32–33

Resources
CM 6, 7 and 8
Cassette for **Point Langue** Ex 1 and 2
Magazines or old catalogues for **Atelier** Ex 1
A4 paper and dictionaries for **Atelier** Ex 3

Key language
Numbers 1–1000
Recycling of shopping for clothes

Language learning strategies
Applying a pattern
Using spider webs to learn or revise

Point Langue

These three activities offer more number practice.

1

Prononcer ou pas?
- *Les chaussettes, ça fait cinq francs.*
- *Combien?*
- *Cinq.*
- *Pour le T-shirt, ça fait six francs.*
- *Six?*
- *Oui, six.*
- *Pour le short, ça fait huit francs.*
- *Combien?*
- *Huit.*
- *Pour la casquette, ça fait dix francs.*
- *Dix?*
- *Oui, dix.*

Cinq francs – cinq,
Six francs – six,
Huit francs – huit,
Dix francs – dix,
Attention à la prononciation!

a – *Il y a combien de casquettes?*
  – *Casquettes? Il y en a dix.*
  – *Dix.*
b – *Et des chemises?*
  – *Attendez un moment... Il y a six chemises.*
  – *Six chemises.*
c – *Il y a combien de pantalons, là?*
  – *Il y a cinq pantalons.*
  – *Cinq pantalons.*
d – *Combien de pulls est-ce qu'il y a?*
  – *Au total, il y a quatre-vingt-huit pulls.*
  – *Quatre-vingt-huit pulls? Oh là là!*
e – *Et les paires de baskets?*
  – *Baskets... Trente-six paires.*
  – *Trente-six paires de baskets. D'accord.*
f – *Il y a combien de shorts?*
  – *Des shorts? Il y a... soixante-dix shorts.*
  – *Soixante-dix? Pas possible! Vérifie encore.*

Answers
a 10 **b** 6 **c** 5 **d** 88 **e** 36 **f** 70

2

un, une	*onze*
deux	*douze*
trois	*treize*
quatre	*quatorze*
cinq	*quinze*
six	*seize*

a *quatorze*
b *seize*
c *deux*
d *quinze*
e *trois*
f *onze*

Answers
a 14 **b** 16 **c** 2 **d** 15 **e** 3 **f** 11

3

Extra – Pupils improvise a similar activity for their partners.
Answers
87 = *quatre-vingt-sept* 103 = *cent trois* 300 = *trois cents* 710 = *sept cent dix* 180 = *cent quatre-vingts* 2590 = *deux mille cinq cent quatre-vingt-dix*

Atelier

1
This can be done in groups for a display.

2
Pupils may wish to use words other than those provided for writing their own poems. ♦ Pupils should be encouraged to adhere to the format of the poem provided.
Answers
désirez cherche va long aime bleu avez

3
This is best done on large sheets of paper. ♣ Pupils should do as much as they possibly can using their own knowledge before they start using dictionaries. Explain to pupils that ideograms are a good way of revising: can they think of any Unit 1 topics to which this method could be applied?

E Bonjour! Je voudrais... pp 34–35

Objective
Buying food

Resources
Flashcards 29–40 + Packets, tins, etc, to introduce new language
Cassette for BD and Ex 1 and 5
Dictionaries for Ex 3 and 7

Key language
Je voudrais... un demi-litre de lait / un kilo de tomates /

500 grammes de viande hachée / 100 grammes de fromage / une bouteille de limonade / une boite de tomates / une tranche de jambon / un paquet de beurre / un pot de yaourt / un tube de dentifrice / une tarte aux fraises / une baguette
Recycling of the alphabet

Language Learning Strategies
Alphabet practice as an aid to learning new words

Ways in
Thierry's mother is exhausted after their shopping trip. She asks Thierry to go to the supermarket for her and tells him what to buy. You can introduce the spread like this: *Thierry est dans un café avec sa mère. Le shopping, c'est fatigant... mais ce n'est pas fini!*

Introduce the key language using the Flashcards (see Teacher's Book introduction) and any realia you may have. Explain how to say *cinq cents* (the -*q* should not be heard).

Integrate alphabet revision into practising the new language.

Ask a pupil to say a food – with quantity/container. The next pupil repeats it and adds one, etc.

Pupils can then read the BD while they hear the cassette. Ask questions: *Thierry est tout seul? Ils sont où? Ils sont au magasin de vêtements? Ils vont acheter des vêtements? Thierry aime aller au supermarché?* (BD tapescript – see Pupil's Book.)

1

COUNTER

– *Bon, Thierry. Maintenant, tu vas au supermarché.*
– *Mais je déteste ça!*
– *Je suis fatiguée, moi! Prends des notes! Je voudrais... numéro un – un demi-litre de lait.*
– *Un demi-litre de lait...*
– *Numéro deux. Un kilo de pommes de terre.*
– *Un kilo de pommes...*
– *Pommes de terre.*
– *D'accord.*
– *Et puis, cinq cents grammes de viande hachée.*
– *Cinq cents grammes de viande hachée ...*
– *Cent grammes de fromage.*
– *Cent grammes de fromage ...*
– *Une bouteille de limonade.*
– *Bouteille de limonade. C'est tout?*
– *Non. Ecris – numéro six, une boîte de tomates.*
– *Boîte de tomates ...*
– *Une tranche de jambon...*
– *Une tranche de jambon?*
– *Oui, c'est pour ta grand-mère. Numéro huit, un paquet de biscuits.*
– *Un paquet de biscuits... C'est tout?*

– *Pas encore. Numéro neuf, un pot de yaourt.*
– *Un pot de yaourt... Grand ou petit?*
– *Grand. Et puis un tube...*
– *Attends! Un tube...*
– *De dentifrice.*
– *Un tube de dentifrice.*
– *Et une tarte aux fraises.*
– *Tarte aux fraises? Mmm, délicieux! J'adore ça.*
– *Et une baguette.*
– *C'est tout?*
– *Oui, c'est tout. Ah, non, tu as besoin d'argent...*

Answers
♦ 1 f   2 i   3 e   4 b   5 g   6 a   7 k   8 c   9 j   10 h
11 d   12 –   ♣ a *Maman*   b *Thierry*   c *Thierry*

2

♦ After a little practice, encourage pupil B to answer without looking at the key.

To enhance motivation, suggest pupils score a point for each correct answer.

3
🎲 🖐

Give a time limit to encourage fast dictionary use.

4
🎲

Give a time limit as an extra challenge.
Answers
1 *non*   2 *oui,* d   3 *non*   4 *non*   5 *non*   6 *oui,* b
7 *non*   8 *oui,* f

5
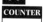
COUNTER

When checking the answers orally, encourage pupils to speak in full sentences. Note that the price of the fruit in **d** has been rounded up to 34 francs.

a – *Bonjour!*
– *Bonjour! Vous désirez?*
– *Je voudrais des bananes. Un demi-kilo.*
– *Un demi-kilo de bananes? D'accord.*
– *Et avec ça?*
– *Rien. C'est tout. Ça fait combien?*
– *3f50.*
– *Voilà. Merci.*
– *Merci, au revoir!*

b – *Bonjour!*
– *Bonjour! Vous désirez?*
– *Je voudrais du lait.*
– *Du lait? Un litre ou un demi-litre?*
– *Deux litres.*
– *Deux litres? Ça fait six francs.*
– *Six francs... Voilà.*
– *Merci.*
– *Au revoir!*

c – *Bonjour monsieur, Vous désirez?*
– *Je cherche du poisson. Vous avez du thon?*
– *Oui, on a du thon au naturel en boîte.*
– *En boîte? Mmm... d'accord. Deux boîtes, s'il vous plaît.*
– *Deux boîtes – ça fait onze francs quatre-vingt-dix.*
– *Onze francs...?*
– *...quatre-vingt-dix.*
– *Et voilà. Merci!*
– *Au revoir...*

d – *Bonjour!*
– *Bonjour – vous désirez?*
– *Vous avez des fraises?*
– *Des fraises? Bien sûr.*
– *Un demi-kilo.*
– *Un demi-kilo... Et avec ça?*
– *Du jus d'orange. Deux bouteilles.*
– *Deux bouteilles de jus d'orange. C'est tout?*
– *Oui, c'est tout.*
– *Au total, ça fait trente-quatre francs.*
– *Trente-quatre. Merci!*
– *Merci. Au revoir!*

e – *Vous désirez?*
– *Je voudrais du beurre. Vous avez du beurre «Le Villageois»?*
– *Mais oui, bien sûr.*
– *Deux, s'il vous plaît. Ça fait combien?*
– *Deux beurres... ça fait quinze francs quatre-vingt.*
– *Quinze francs quatre-vingt? Voilà.*
– *Merci – au revoir!*

f – *Bonjour! Je voudrais du fromage, s'il vous plaît.*
– *Bien sûr. Quelle sorte de fromage?*
– *Vous avez du fromage hollandais?*
– *Oui. Combien?*
– *Deux cents grammes.*
– *D'accord. Deux cent grammes... Ça fait six francs cinquante.*
– *Six francs...?*
– *...cinquante.*
– *Voilà. Merci, au revoir!*
– *Au revoir.*

Answers
a photo 4, *1 demi-kilo* (♣ *3F50*)
b photo 8, *2 litres* (♣ *6F*)
c photo 3, *2 boîtes* (♣ *11F90*)
d photo 2, *1 demi-kilo*
photo 1, *2 bouteilles* (♣ *34F*)
e photo 5, *2* (♣ *15F80*)
f photo 6, *200g* (♣ *6F50*)

6

Pupils need to be extra careful as two utterances in a row may need to be spoken by the same person.
Answers
g b h c d k a j f e i

7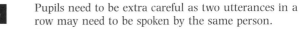

♦ Ask pupils to reuse key language and **Camarades 1** language only to reinforce practice of language already practised. They can vary the quantities if they wish. Suggest a minimum number of items.

Pupils should then practise their dialogue orally with as few prompts as possible, ideally just their shopping list.

F Pardon, où est...?

pp 36–37

Objective
Finding your way round the supermarket

Resources
CM 2, 9 and 10
OHT (see **Ways in** section)
Grilles 2 CM for *Gigi Magique*
Cassette for BD and Ex 1 and 3
A4 paper optional for CM 9, Ex 2

Key language
Où est ... le poisson / la boucherie / la boulangerie / la laiterie /
la pâtisserie / l'alimentation générale?
Où sont... les boissons / les surgelés / les fruits et légumes?
Allée numéro trois
Au fond / à gauche / à droite
Recycling of food, drink and quantities

Grammar
Où est ...? Où sont ...?

Language learning strategies
Pronunciation: *-i / -o / -oi*

Ways in
Thierry has difficulty finding his way round the
supermarket. He asks an assistant for help.

Use **CM 2** on the OHP to introduce the different
sections in the supermarket as well as the key direction
words. Integrate revision of food and drink. Say a
section (recognition) and ask pupils to name as many
items as they can in that section. Then repeat the
activity the other way round for pupils to manipulate
the new language.

After a while, introduce the rest of the key language.
You can then ask pupils to place the different
supermarket sections from memory, in teams. Teams
score one point for each correct answer.

Pupils then read the BD while they listen to the
cassette. (BD tapescript – see Pupil's Book.)

1

Extra – After the corrections, pupils compare the
answers with the CM 2 map: are the two supermarkets
very different?

COUNTER

> 1 – Pardon, je voudrais acheter du steak haché. C'est
>   où, le rayon?
>   – La boucherie? Allée numéro cinq.
>
> 2 – Monsieur? Vous pouvez m'aider? Je cherche les
>   tartes aux fraises.
>   – La pâtisserie? Au fond.
>
> 3 – Pardon, mais où sont les bouteilles de limonade,
>   s'il vous plaît?
>   – Les boissons? A gauche.
>
> 4 – Excusez-moi, s'il vous plaît! Je cherche des
>   tomates...
>   – Les fruits et légumes sont à droite.
>
> 5 – Monsieur, s'il vous plaît? Où sont les baguettes?
>   – La boulangerie? A droite.
>
> 6 – Pardon, mais... où sont les yaourts?
>   – Ça, c'est la laiterie. Allée numéro un.

Answers
♦ **1** *boucherie* **2** *Au fond* **3** *boissons* **4** *à droite*
    5 *boulangerie* **6** *la laiterie*
♣ **1** *cherche steak haché* **2** *cherche les tartes aux fraises*
    3 *cherche les bouteilles de limonade* **4** *cherche les*
    tomates **5** *cherche les baguettes* **6** *cherche les yaourts*

2

♦ As an extra challenge, pupil **B** scores a point for
each utterance: fewest overall wins.

3

Preparation – Explain that more than one clue to the
correct supermarket section may be provided each
time, for example a food/drink may be named as well
as the correct section each time.

COUNTER

> 1 – Bonjour, mesdames, messieurs. Promotion steak
>   haché aujourd'hui. Allez vite à la boucherie, allée
>   cinq. Oui c'est ça, la boucherie, allée cinq. Ne la
>   ratez pas!
>
> 2 – Attention, attention! Amateurs de fraises,
>   occasion aujourd'hui, mardi seulement! Allez au
>   rayon fruits et légumes, où il y a des fraises
>   délicieuses. Rayon fruits et légumes, à droite.
>   Oui, à droite. Allez vite!
>
> 3 – Offre spéciale au rayon boissons! Quatre
>   bouteilles d'eau minérale Perrier pour le prix de
>   trois. Rayon boissons, à gauche.
>
> 4 – Vous achetez des baguettes aujourd'hui? Eh bien,
>   vous avez de la chance! Achetez trois baguettes à
>   la boulangerie, allée quatre, et on vous offre une
>   tarte aux pommes gratuite. Allez à la
>   boulangerie, allée quatre!
>
> 5 – Attention, tous les enfants! Vous aimez les
>   yaourts, non? Bon, il y a une offre spéciale
>   aujourd'hui au rayon laiterie. Achetez six
>   yaourts Baba, et on vous donne une balle. Oui,
>   une belle balle pour jouer au tennis ... Vite!
>   dites-le à maman ou papa! C'est la laiterie, allée
>   quatre. Promotion yaourts Baba avec une Baba

Answers
1 *boucherie, allée 5*   **2** *fruits et légumes, à droite*
3 *boissons, à gauche*   **4** *boulangerie, allée 4*
5 *laiterie, alleé 4*

4

Preparation – To help develop reading skills, ask
pupils to scan page 36 and decide in no more than 2
minutes which task to do first/which task to do in class
and which task to do for homework.

Answers
Gigi Magique: boulangerie, boucherie, boissons, fruits,
pâtisserie, surgelé. Mot Magique: GENIAL
Gigi Logique: boissons, laiterie, fruits, surgelés, charcuterie,
boulangerie, pâtisserie, boucherie (suggested order – open
to discussion)

G C'est devant ou derrière?

pp 38–39

Objective
Saying where products are at the supermarket

Resources
CM 2 optional for Ex 2 and 6
CM 3 & 11
OHT (see **Ways In** section)
Cassette for BD, Ex 1, 2 and CM 11
Dice and counters (rubbers, paper clips etc.) for CM 11

Key language
C'est avant / après / devant / derrière... le poisson.

C'est entre les fruits et les légumes.
C'est en face / à côté du poisson.
C'est près / loin de la charcuterie.
C'est à gauche / droite des surgelés / de l'alimentation générale.
Recycling of supermarket sections

Grammar
Prepositions

Language learning strategies
Adapting a model dialogue

Ways in
Thierry cannot find the tomatoes. You can introduce the spread like this: *Le shopping au supermarché, c'est très, très difficile. Le fromage... ça va, les baguettes... ça va. Mais où sont les tomates?*

Pupils read the BD while they listen to the cassette. Improvise a few true/false statements on the BD. (BD tapescript – see Pupil's Book.)

Use CM 3 to teach the new prepositions.

1
Pupils can complete the song as they listen, or try to guess first. (Tapescript – see Pupil's Book.)
Answers
1 *avant* **2** *derrière* **3** *à coté* **4** *loin* **5** *droite*

2
Preparation – Give pupils time to read 1–6 first. For added motivation, ask them to do blind guessing (*vrai / faux*).

♣ When pupils give their answers, encourage them to speak in full sentences.

Extra – After the corrections, ask pupils to look at 1–6 and the key and to work out the use of *du / de la / de l' / des* after some of the prepositions. Reuse CM2 and the map from page 37 for some practice.

1 – *Pardon! Je cherche la boucherie.*
– *Ça, c'est en face du poisson.*
– *En face du poisson?*
– *Oui, c'est ça.*
– *Merci!*
2 – *Pardon, mais où sont les tartes aux pommes?*
– *Les tartes? Oh, ça c'est la pâtisserie. Il y a des tartes délicieuses, là! Alors, c'est près de la boulangerie.*
– *Près de la boulangerie? Merci.*
3 – *Je cherche des boîtes de légumes.*
– *Vous trouverez des boîtes de légumes au rayon de l'alimentation générale.*
– *C'est où, ça?*
– *Avant... la charcuterie.*
– *Avant la charcuterie. Merci beaucoup.*
– *Je vous en prie.*

4 – *Pardon, mais je cherche les glaces...*
– *Ça c'est le rayon des surgelés.*
– *Et les surgelés sont...?*
– *A côté de l'alimentation générale.*
– *A côté de l'alimentation...*
– *Là, vous voyez? Allée numéro deux.*
– *Ah, oui, merci.*
5 – *Pardon, mais vous avez des baguettes aujourd'hui?*
– *Oui. Il y a des baguettes à la boulangerie.*
– *Et la boulangerie est...?*
– *A gauche. A gauche des fruits et légumes.*
– *Ah bon, d'accord, je vois maintenant. Merci.*
6 – *Des yaourts? Oui, il y a des yaourts à prix spécial aujourd'hui...*
– *A la laiterie?*
– *Oui, bien sûr.*
– *Et c'est où, ça?*
– *C'est juste en face des boissons.*
– *En face des boissons... Ah, oui, je vois maintenant. Merci.*

Answers
1 *faux, en face* **2** *vrai* **3** *faux, avant* **4** *faux, à côté*
5 *vrai* **6** *faux, en face*

3
Answers
1 b *à gauche* **2** a *derrière* **3** c *en face* **4** f *à droite*
5 e *entre* **6** d *loin*

4
Encourage peer checking before doing class corrections.
Answers
1 *des* **2** *de l'* **3** *de la* **4** *du* **5** *de la*

5
Answer
c

6
Pupils can reuse CM 2 or the map page 37. Encourage pupils to use interjections and conversational words as taught in Spread C, for example.

H Point Langue / Atelier

pp 40–41

Resources
CM 12 & 13
Cassette for **Atelier** Ex 1
OHP optional for **Atelier** Ex 1 and CM 12
A4 paper/card and colour pens (optional) for **Atelier** Ex 3
Scissors for CM 12

Key language
Recycling of supermarket vocabulary

Grammar
Prepositions with *du / de la / de l' / des*

Language learning strategies
Applying a pattern

Point Langue
This page provide extra practice of *du / de la / de l' / des.*

1

Answers
de   du   de l'   des   de la

2

Encourage pupils to work in pairs and to refer to the explanations at the top of the page for each item.

♦ Warn pupils that some items may have more than one correct answer.

♣ Pupils should discuss the answers in French, as suggested in the notes on Ex 4, page 39.

Answers
♦ **1** b   **2** e   **3** d/f/h   **4** b/g   **5** d   **6** a   **7** f/h   **8** c
♣ **1** *de*   **2** *de la*   **3** *des*   **4** *de l'*   **5** *de*   **6** *de la*   **7** *de l'*   **8** *du*

Atelier

1

Preparation – To train pupils to jot down what is essential only, remind them to look carefully at the rubric first. Then show pupils the first dialogue in full on the board or the OHP and underline only the words that are needed to perform the task. The example provided on page 41 could even be shortened further to: *demi litre lait – cher.*

> **COUNTER**
>
> **1** – *Bonjour, vous désirez?*
> – *Vous avez un demi-litre de lait?*
> – *Oui, bien sûr.*
> – *Ça fait combien?*
> – *Quatre francs vingt.*
> – *Oh, là là! C'est cher, le lait ici!*
>
> **2** – *Bonjour!*
> – *Bonjour – je peux vous aider?*
> – *Oui. Vous avez des tomates?*
> – *Oui. A huit francs le kilo.*
> – *Mais ... ces tomates sont jaunes!*
> – *Oui, madame. C'est une nouvelle variété. Mais les tomates jaunes sont délicieuses, je vous assure.*
> – *Non, merci. Je n'aime pas la couleur. Des tomates jaunes? Ce n'est pas normal!*

> **3** – *Bonjour. Vous désirez?*
> – *Vous avez des fraises?*
> – *Oui. Voici des fraises délicieuses...*
> – *Mais, les fraises sont très grosses! Elles sont énormes! Je préfère les petites fraises, pour faire une tarte.*
> – *Je regrette mais je n'ai plus de petites fraises.*
> – *Bon, je vais au marché! Là, il y a toujours un grand choix...*
>
> **4** – *Bonjour, monsieur. Vous désirez?*
> – *Bonjour. Vous avez des pommes de terre?*
> – *Oui. Vous en voulez combien?*
> – *Deux kilos. Je peux voir?*
> – *Oui, voilà.*
> – *Mais elles sont trop petites, ces pommes de terre!*
> – *Petites?*
> – *Oui! Petites! Minuscules! Je veux de grosses pommes de terre pour faire des frites!*
> – *Bien, je regrette mais, c'est tout ce qu'on a.*
> – *Bof! Je vais au supermarché, moi. Je déteste les petits magasins!*

2

Ask pupils to write several mini-sketches (not long dialogues) and to select their favourite. Have a jury (older pupils/French assistants/PGCE students). Instead, you can ask pupils to record themselves, or you can video them and use the video as part of a special event.

3

Encourage pupils to think up other ideas for games, so long as no English is required to play the games. Pupils may prefer to work collaboratively, and should have a go at playing games devised by other pupils. Some of the games could also be made into a booklet for future use or for future generations of pupils.

On fait du shopping

1 Pour Noël, j'aimerais...

pp 42–43

Objective
Saying what you would like for Christmas

Resources
Realia to teach the key language
CM 14
Cassette for BD and Ex 1
Dictionaries for Ex 4 and for CM 14 (optional)

Key language
Qu'est-ce que tu aimerais pour Noël?
Qu'est-ce que tu vas acheter pour...?

*J'aimerais... / Je vais acheter... un CD / une cravate /
une cassette-vidéo / un jeu pour ordinateur / un portefeuille /
du papier à lettres / des articles de toilette / des boucles d'oreille /
des chaussettes / des chocolats / un jouet / un poster*
Recycling of personal possessions and opinions

Grammar
Recycling of *je vais / tu vas* + infinitive

Language learning strategies
Using the dictionary as an aid to working independently

Ways in
Mail order shopping might be the answer to Thierry's shopping problems. Flicking through a catalogue, Thierry plans his Christmas shopping. You can introduce the spread like this: *Thierry déteste le shopping, mais le 25 décembre, c'est... Noël! Encore du shopping! Mais avec un catalogue, c'est plus facile!*

Explain what *Noël* means (*c'est le 25 décembre*). Pupils then read the BD while they listen to the cassette. Afterwards, to encourage short-term retention and speed scanning, ask pupils to say as quickly as possible whether the words you say appear in the BD or not. For example: *veste, génial, anniversaire, Noël, père, shopping, mère, Ludivine, super, acheter, chocolats, bonbons.* (BD tapescript – see Pupil's Book.)

Use realia to teach the key language from page 42. Some of the presents are revised from **Camarades 1**. You can then use the artwork page 42 to introduce the new words in writing.

1

Preparation – Revise the language of opinions (see *Rappel* box). Say one of the phrases and ask pupils to respond through facial expression.

1	*Un CD... oh, super!*
2	*Une cassette-video? Chouette!*
3	*Une cravate? Ça, c'est nul!*
4	*Un jeu pour ordinateur... génial!*
5	*Un jouet... pas mal.*
6	*Un poster... oui, c'est bien.*
7	*Un portefeuille... bof, ça va.*
8	*Du papier à lettres? Non, c'est moche.*
9	*Des affaires de toilette... oh, ennuyeux.*
10	*Des boucles d'oreille... , c'est peut-être bien, pour une fille.*
11	*Des chaussettes? Nul! Absolument nul!*
12	*Des chocolats? Hm, ça va.*

Answers

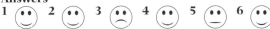
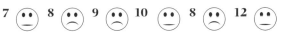

2

Preparation – Do a few examples as a whole. First, you ask the questions, then get the pupils to ask you the questions.

Encourage pupils to use previously learnt vocabulary as well as the new words. In their answers, pupils should respond with a facial expression to match their stated opinion.

3

♦ *Preparation* – This task emphasises awareness of context. Encourage pupils to read whole sentences to find the necessary clues.

♣ *Preparation* – Encourage pupils to read the rubric and look at visual clues (words in bold) to narrow down their search. Pupils should work without dictionaries.

Answers
♦ **1** *jeu pour ordinateur* **2** *livre* **3** *CD* **4** *cassette-vidéo* **5** *chocolats* **6** *chaussettes*
♣ (suggested answers)
  a *train / voiture / maquette / cassette-vidéo / livre*
  b *cassette / CD / jeu pour ordinateur / poster / article de toilette / bic / gomme / feutre* **c** *papier à lettres / porte-monnaie / savon / gel de bain / jeu de société / Monopoly / livre* **d** (see b) **e** (see b) **f** *cahier / stylo / chocolats*

4

♦ You may prefer to ask pupils to use words they know – for reinforcement – rather than looking up new words. Alternatively, set a maximum number of words to look up.

Remind all pupils to check the gender of words they look up in the dictionary.

⬛J On fête Noël chez toi?

pp 44–45

Objective

Talking about what you do at Christmas time

Resources

CM 15 and 16
Cassette for Ex 1, 2 and 5
Photos (optional) to be provided by pupils for Ex 6
Paper (A4 or larger) for CM 16
Christmas-related magazines pictures optional for CM 16

Key language

On fête Noël chez toi? Chez moi, / en France, / en Angleterre, / en Ecosse,... on fête le jour de Noël avec des amis / la famille.

... on ne fête pas Noël.
Qu'est-ce que tu fais / vous faites?
Je fais / On fait un grand repas / un sapin / des décorations.
On met des chaussures / chaussettes pour le père Noël.
On offre des cadeaux. On va à l'église.
Recycling of the date, presents and relatives

Grammar

Present tense of *faire*
Use of *on*

Language learning strategies

Using link words in writing

Ways in

Thierry's friend is going to Guadeloupe for Christmas this year. This leads to them discussing Christmas time. You can introduce the spread like this: *Thierry et ses copains parlent de Noël: Noël en famille, Noël à la maison, Noël avec les grands-parents. Et on parle des traditions de Noël.*

First revise the date. For example:
• *Dites le mois après / avant*
• *Devinez ma date de naissance.* (→ *Non, avant / après*)
You can then introduce the special days listed on the calendar. Give pupils some background information but point out there are no 'hard and fast rules' about Christmas in France.
• Schoolchildren have approximately three weeks off.
• Muslims from north Africa do not celebrate Christmas.
• People send New Year cards and only to close relatives and friends.
• Children put a pair of shoes under the Christmas tree.
• Small shops that sell food are open in the morning on Christmas day, as people are fond of fresh food and need their freshly baked baguettes! Supermarkets are closed.
• More and more people also celebrate on Christmas Eve. Christmas carols are not a tradition in France.
• People spend a lot on food on Christmas day (turkey, oysters, venison and seafood...) A typical dessert is *La Bûche de Noël.*
• Boxing day doesn't exist.
• New Year's Day is also a very big day in France. Some people give presents for the New Year. Shops and other businesses also tend to give their most loyal customers small presents such as keyrings, calendars, etc.

1

COUNTER

1 – *Bonjours, chers auditeurs! Aujourd'hui, voici les réponses à notre question «On fête Noël chez toi, et comment?» Et pour notre première réponse, on va directement au Canada, et chez Catherine. Bonjour, Catherine!*

– *Bonjour!*

– *Dis-moi, Catherine. On fête Noël chez toi, au Canada?*

– *Oui, bien sûr.*

– *Et le jour le plus important pour toi, c'est...?*

– *Le vingt-quatre décembre, la veille de Noël.*

– *Et qu'est-ce que tu fais chez toi, à Noël?*

2 – *On va parler maintenant à notre numéro deux, Jacqui. Jacqui, tu habites où?*

– *J'habite en Belgique.*

– *Et chez toi, on fête Noël?*

– *Oui, on fête Noël, mais ce n'est pas très important pour nous.*

– *Non?*

– *Non, nous ne sommes pas très réligieux. On fête plus la Saint-Sylvestre.*

– *La Saint-Sylvestre? Et qu'est-ce tu fais ce jour-là?*

3 – *Pour interview numéro trois, on va maintenant à l'île de la Réunion. Salut, Michel. C'est où, exactement, l'île de la Réunion?*

– *C'est près de l'Afrique. A l'est.*

– *Et dis-moi, on fête Noël chez vous?*

– *Oui, on fête Noël. C'est une fête très importante ici.*

– *Et, chez toi, quel jour est le plus important?*

– *Chez moi, on fête le vingt-cinq décembre, le jour de Noël.*

– *Pourqoui ça? Qu'est-ce vous faites exactement?*

4 – *Et maintenant, numéro quatre. On va parler à Christian. Christian, tu viens d'où?*

– *J'habite à Lille, dans le nord de la France.*

– *Et chez toi, en fête Noël?*

– *Non. On ne fête pas Noël.*

– *Non? Pourquoi pas?*

– *Je suis Témoin de Jéhovah. On ne fête pas Noël chez nous.*

– *Ah oui? Chez vous on fête le Jour de l'An?*

– *Oui, le Jour de l'An est plus important.*

5 – *Ensuite, numéro cinq. On parle à Laurent. Tu es d'où Laurent?*

– *J'habite en Corse.*

– *Ah! La Corse, au sud de la France – très jolie. Dis-moi, on fête Noël chez toi?*

– *Oui, bien sûr. La Vielle de Noël, le vingt-quatre, est un jour très important chez nous.*

– *Est-ce qu'il y a des traditions particulières en Corse?*

Answers

1 ✔, *Canada, la veille de Noël*
2 ✗, *Belgique, la Saint-Sylvestre*
3 ✔, *l'île de la Réunion, le 25 décembre*
4 ✗, *France, Lille, le 1 janvier*
5 ✔, *France, la Corse, la veille de Noël*

2

Preparation – Pupils read all the items before they listen to the cassette to ensure comprehension. Discuss the use of *on* in the questions. Pupils then read each item individually before they listen to the relevant passage.

COUNTER

– Marc! Dis, c'est vrai que tu vas en Guadeloupe à Noël cette année encore?

– Oui! On va à l'Hotel Désirade, à Gosier, comme l'année dernière.

– Oh, tu as de la chance! Mais – on fête Noël en Guadeloupe?

– Bien sûr.

– On fait un sapin?

– Oui, dans le séjour. C'est un sapin vraiment énorme!

– On fait des décorations?

– Oui, pour la table. On met des décorations sur toutes les tables pour le réveillon. C'est très joli.

– On mets quelque chose pour le père Noël? Il vient aussi en Guadeloupe?

– Oui, on met les chaussures comme en France. Il y a aussi une visite du père Noël pour les enfants pendant le Réveillon. Les petits enfants adorent ça.

– On va à l'église?

– Oui, à minuit. Il y a une grande cathédrale qui n'est pas loin.

– On fait un grand repas?

– Oui, avec la famillle. Et puis il y a aussi tous les clients de l'hôtel. C'est vraiment super.

– On offre des cadeaux?

– Oui, le jour de Noël, on offre des cadeaux à la famille. Et l'hôtel aussi offre de petits cadeaux aux clients – des chocolats, des bonbons, du champagne...

Answers
1 b   2 a   3 b   4 a   5 a   6 a

3

Extra – Ask pupils if they can think of a few more questions to ask, or ask a few more questions yourself, for example: *On ouvre les cadeaux à quelle heure? Qui prépare le repas de Noël? On mange à quelle heure chez toi le jour de Noël?*

4

Preparation – Give a time limit to encourage the use of effective reading skills. Discuss with pupils the best way to proceed:
♦ Pupils should scan for key words with the help of the pictures;
♣ Pupils should use context and awareness of cognates, synonyms and parts of speech.

After the corrections, discuss with pupils in what way the words in italics can help in written or in oral work (link words; avoiding short sentences).
Answers
♦ a, f, c, d, b, e
♣ 1 *on fait les préparatifs*   2 *Qu'est-ce que vous faites (à Noël)?*   3 *on se donne des cadeaux.*   4 *nous faisons un grand repas*   5 *mes grands-parents font le sapin*
et = and   *mais* = but   *ou* = or   *après* = after   *Ensuite* = Afterwards/Next   *D'abord* = First   *puis* = then

5

COUNTER

– Rémy, qu'est-ce que tu fais à Noël cette année?

– Je vais chez mes grands-parents en Angleterre.

– On fête Noël en Angleterre?

– Bien sûr! C'est une fête importante.

– On fête la Saint-Sylvestre chez tes grands-parents?

– Non, le jour de Noël c'est plus important. Ce que j'aime le plus, c'est qu'on fait deux sapins.

– Deux sapins?

– Oui. Il y a un sapin dans le salon, et puis j'ai un sapin dans ma chambre.

– Oh, tu en as de la chance!

– Mais oui! Cette année comme cadeau, j'aimerais avoir beaucoup de CD.

– Des CD?

– Oui, en Angleterre, les CD ne sont pas chers.

– Et toi, Thierry, qu'est-ce que tu aimerais pour Noël?

– Un jeu pour ordinateur. Maman a un ordinateur, et elle me laisse faire des jeux.

– Tu fêtes Noël chez ton père?

– Non, chez ma mère et mon beau-père. Et puis, je vais fêter la Saint-Sylvestre chez mon père.

– Tu aimes ça?

– Oui, la Saint-Sylvestre est très importante chez mon père. J'aime surtout le repas du soir – on invite les cousins, on fait des jeux, on chante – c'est super.

– Et toi, Hayoon? On ne fête pas Noël chez toi, je crois.

– Non, on ne fête pas Noël. Mais le jour de l'an, c'est important chez nous.

– Qu'est-ce que tu fais le jour de l'an?

– On sort, on fait un grand repas...

– Et qu'est-ce que tu aimes le plus?

– Les cadeaux! On offre des cadeaux, parce que c'est mon anniversaire le vingt-six décembre.

– Qu'est-ce que tu aimerais comme cadeau?

– Oh, je sais pas... Une cassette vidéo, ou des posters. Hup, allons-y mes amis! Tu viens Thierry? On a informatique, je crois...

Answers
♦ 1 Hayoon   2 Rémy   3 Thierry
♣ 1 Hayoon: *fête jour de l'an, grand repas, anniversaire le 26 décembre, aimerait cassette-vidéo ou poster*
2 Rémy: *Noël chez grands-parents (Angleterre), un sapin dans le salon et un sapin dans sa chambre, aimerait des CD*
3 Thierry: *Noël chez sa mère, Saint-Sylvestre chez son père. Invite cousins, chante, fait des jeux*

Preparation – Build up pupils' ability to use reference materials by asking them to reuse/adapt any materials from this spread.

6

♦ Pupils may prefer to write short sentences – using bullet points, for example. ♣ Pupils should produce more continuous writing. Although pupils must write about themselves, they should help each other in pairs or in small groups. To ensure maximum recycling, limit the number of words to look up in the dictionary and the number of questions pupils can ask you.

K Point Langue / Atelier   pp 46–47

Resources
CM 17 & 18
Dictionaries for **Atelier** Ex 3
Dice, counters and scissors for CM 17
Card and scissors for CM 18 (*Bilan / Conseil*)

Key language
Recycling of Christmas and presents

Grammar
Present tense of *faire*

Language learning strategies
Applying a pattern
Using a textbook for reference

Point Langue

1

This page presents and practises the whole paradigm of *faire* in the present tense. ♦ The task focuses on the singular form only.

Answers
1 *je* **2** *Tu* **3** *on*

2

Answers
♦ *fais fais fait fait fais*
♣ *fais fait fait faisons font fait faites*

Atelier

1

Answers
cassette cravate vidéo jouet chocolats poster papier → *TROUSSE*

2

Pupils can use Ex 2, page 46 for reference.

3

Preparation – Discuss with pupils how best to proceed. It is a good idea to look up the words at the bottom in the French-English half of a dictionary rather than starting from the pictures and using the English-French section.
Answers
gâteau farine œufs sucre beurre chocolat houx verre champagne.

L On révise pp 48–49

Resources
Cassette for Ex 1

Key language
Revision of Units 1-2

1

These tasks provide some revision of Units 1 and 2 in preparation for *Epreuve 1*.

Preparation – Revise foods and prices. Pupils carrying out the ♣ activity should note down the quantity that the customer actually buys.

COUNTER

1 – Bonjour, vous désirez?
– Bonjour. Je voudrais du fromage. C'est combien, le kilo?
– Le fromage hollandais? C'est à dix-sept francs quatre-vingt quinze.
– C'est bien. Alors, cinq cents grammes.
– Merci.

2 – Bonjour! Je voudrais des chips. Ça fait combien, un paquet?
– Des chips? Quatre francs quatre-vingts.
– Alors, deux paquets. Un moment, je vais voir si j'ai de la monnaie...

3 – Bonjour?
– Vous avez de la mayonnaise?
– Bien sûr. Vous en voulez combien?
– C'est combien, le pot?
– Il y a une offre spéciale: trois pots pour vingt francs soixante-dix.
– Mmm... non, merci. Je veux seulement un pot.
– D'accord.

4 – Vous désirez, mademoiselle?
– Les tomates sont à combien?
– A neuf francs quatre-vingt-quinze le kilo.
– Bon, euh, je voudrais deux cent cinquante grammes, alors.
– Pas de problème.

5 – Je peux vous aider, monsieur?
– Oui, je cherche du jus d'orange.
– C'est là.
– Ah, oui. C'est combien?
– Quatre francs soixante-quinze.
– D'accord.
– Mais il y a une offre spéciale.
– Ah, oui?
– Si vous en achetez trois bricks, on vous donne le quatrième gratuit.
– Excellent. Je prends les quatre, alors.

6 – Bonjour!
– Bonjour, madame. Vous désirez?
– Je voudrais des raviolis. Vous en avez en boîte?
– En boîte? Oui.
– C'est combien?
– Six francs quatre-vingt-quinze.
– Une boîte, s'il vous plaît.

7 – Oui, monsieur?
– Vous avez un bon vin mousseux?
– On a du vin Laurent Bertin...
– C'est combien?
– Un moment ... C'est à trente-deux francs quatre-vingt-quinze.

– C'est pas mal.
– Et avec l'offre spéciale, vous payez une bouteille et on vous donne la deuxième.
– Alors, c'est une bouteille gratuite?
– Oui, c'est ça.
– En ce cas, donnez-en-moi quatre!
– Quatre au total?
– Oui. Deux payées, et deux gratuites.

8 – Vous avez de la pizza?
– Fraîche ou congelée?
– Congelée. Ça fait combien?
– Vingt-cinq francs soixante.
– Oh, là là, c'est cher, ça!
– Oui, mais c'est délicieux – jambon, fromage, olives...
– Bon, je la prends. Une pizza alors.

9 – Je peux vous aider?
– Vous avez du jambon?
– Oui, on a du jambon de Bayonne ...
– Oui, celui-là. C'est combien le kilo?
– Cinquante-deux, quatre-vingt dix.
– Six tranches, alors.
– Six tranches? D'accord.

Answers
1 a *17f95 500 grammes* **2** i *4f80 2 paquets*
3 c *20f70 (pour 3) 1 pot* **4** h *9f95 250 grammes*
5 g *4f75 4 bricks* **6** b *6f95 1 boîte* **7** e *32f95 4 bouteilles* **8** d *25f60 1* **9** f *5290f 6 tranches*

2

Preparation – Revise foods and the supermarket.
Answers
a = *laiterie* b = *alimentation générale* c (see b)
d (see b) e = *boissons* f = *charcuterie* g = *boissons*
h = *fruits et légumes*

3

Preparation – Revise personal details (Unit 1).

4

Preparation – Revise presents.

5

Preparation – Revise shopping for clothes.
Answers
1 d 2 f 3 a 4 e 5 b 6 c

6

This task follows on from Ex 5.

7

This is a realia-based task about a Christmas holiday in a Guadeloupe hotel, re-capping reading skills so far.
Answers
♦ a ✔ b ✔ c ✗ d ✔ e ✔ f ✔ g ✗ h ✔
♣ 1 *Oui* 2 *On fait un repas traditionnel.* 3 *Oui, il y a un déjeuner tropical de 12h à 15h et un dîner avec des spécialités guadeloupéennes à 20h.* 4 *Oui, on danse, on écoute de la musique et il y a un barbecue.* 5 *Ça fait 1 000f par personne par jour.*

A – Epreuve d'écoute

Exercice 1

Pupils are tested on their ability to understand short statements, spoken clearly with good quality recording and no background noise. This is an example of performance at Level 1 on AT 1.

COUNTER

Exemple

- *Salut! Je m'appelle Catherine et j'ai douze ans.*

1 – *Bonjour! Je m'appelle Marc. J'ai treize ans.*
2 – *Et moi, je m'appelle Annie. Moi, j'ai onze ans.*
3 – *Bonjour tout le monde! Je m'appelle Ahmed et j'ai quinze ans.*
4 – *Salut! Je m'appelle Nabila. J'ai quatorze ans.*
5 – *Moi, je m'appelle Luc. J'ai douze ans.*

Exemple

- *Salut! Je m'appelle Catherine et j'ai douze ans. La date de mon anniversaire est le 21 janvier.*

1 – *Bonjour! Je m'appelle Marc. J'ai treize ans et mon anniversaire est le 13 mars.*
2 – *Et moi, je m'appelle Annie. J'ai onze ans et mon anniversaire, c'est le 18 avril.*
3 – *Bonjour tout le monde! Je m'appelle Ahmed et j'ai quinze ans. La date de mon anniversaire est le premier août.*
4 – *Salut! Je m'appelle Nabila. J'ai quatorze ans et je suis née le 24 juin.*
5 – *Moi, je m'appelle Luc. J'ai douze ans et mon anniversaire est le 17 octobre.*

A 1 mark for each correct answer. Total 5.
Pupils scoring at least 4 correct answers are showing some characteristics of performance at Level l.

1 13 **2** 11 **3** 15 **4** 14 **5** 12

B 1 mark for each correct answer. Total 5.
Pupils scoring at least 3 correct answers are showing some characteristics of performance at Level l.

1 H **2** G **3** D **4** A **5** I

Exercice 2

This tests pupils' understanding of familiar vocabulary (clothes) and numbers in the form of prices. It tests performance at Level 2, but success on both parts of the exercise (8 or more out of 10) represents performance approaching Level 3 standard.

COUNTER

Exemple

- *Bonjour mademoiselle. Vous désirez?*
- *Je voudrais ce T-shirt. C'est combien?*
- *C'est 55 francs, mademoiselle.*

1 – *Bonjour monsieur. Je peux vous aider?*
- *Oui. Je veux acheter cette paire de baskets. Elles coûtent combien?*
- *Les baskets? Cette paire coûte 160 francs.*

2 – *Mademoiselle? Vous désirez?*
- *J'aime bien ce pull rouge.*
- *Très bien mademoiselle. Ce pull coûte 220 francs.*
- *Oh là, là! C'est trop cher!*

3 – *Bonjour monsieur. Qu'est-ce que vous désirez?*
- *Je voudrais une chemise. Elle coûte combien, cette chemise?*
- *Celle-là? Elle coûte 75 francs, monsieur.*

4 – *Oui madame? Je peux vous aider?*
- *J'aime bien cette veste. C'est combien?*
- *Elle est belle, n'est-ce pas? Ça coûte 280 francs, madame.*
- *Bon. Je la prends.*

5 – *Monsieur? Qu'y a-t-il pour votre service?*
- *Bonjour. Je cherche un pantalon. Vous en avez?*
- *Oui bien sûr. Ce pantalon-ci, par exemple?*
- *Il coûte combien?*
- *Il coûte 195 francs, monsieur.*
- *Ça va. Merci.*

1 mark for correct letter + 1 mark for correct price. Total 10.

1 H 160 **2** B 220 **3** A 75 **4** C 280 **5** D 195

Exercice 3

The material is now a little more dense, in the form of a short passage. Success in noting the main points from the text represents work at Level 3 standard.

> **Exemple**
>
> – *Excusez-moi. Je veux acheter du lait.*
> – *Alors, allez tout droit. Il y a un magasin à droite, dans la rue de la République.*
>
> **1** – *Je voudrais acheter du pain.*
> – *Alors si tu veux du pain, prends la première à gauche. C'est la rue Monceau. Il y a une boulangerie dans cette rue.*
>
> **2** – *Où est-ce que je peux acheter de bonnes pâtisseries?*
> – *Alors il faut descendre la rue de la République. Continuez tout droit, tout droit et vous trouverez une pâtisserie à gauche.*
>
> **3** – *Excusez-moi! J'ai soif! Je veux quelque chose à boire. Où est-ce que je peux aller?*
> – *Mais regardez! Il y a un café là-bas, tout près dans cette rue, à gauche.*
>
> **4** – *Où est-ce que je peux acheter du jambon, du saucisson et du paté?*
> – *Dans la rue Monceau. Allez tout droit, prenez la première à droite et vous avez le magasin à droite.*
>
> **5** – *Je veux acheter du bœuf. Il y a une boucherie dans la ville?*
> – *Oui bien sur! Descendez la rue de la République et prenez la deuxieme à gauche. C'est la rue Paul Bert.*

$^1/_2$ mark for correct shop + $^1/_2$ mark for correct location. Total 5. Pupils scoring at least 3 marks are showing some characteristics of performance at level 3.

1 (5) B **2** (4) D **3** (1) A **4** (3) G **5** (2) C

B – Epreuve orale

Exercice I

Pupils work in pairs and choose three articles. They have to name the article of clothing (1 mark for each article) and their partner has to give the correct price. The roles are then reversed. Each pupil is therefore assessed on three articles of clothing and three prices. The clothes vocabulary is revision from **Camarades 1** and the numbers are those encountered in the first unit of **Camarades 2**.

Pupils scoring 4 or more (2 in each category) are showing characteristics of performance at Level 1. Total = 6 marks.

Pupils naming the items of clothing correctly are showing characteristics of performance at Level 1. ('Pupils respond briefly, with single words... to what they see...') Pupils who can correctly name at least two items of clothing and give the correct prices are showing some characteristics of performance at Level 2 ('short simple responses to what they see and hear – naming and describing people, places, objects').

Exercice 2

This exercise recycles food items from **Camarades 1** and they are combined with the quantities from Unit 2 in **Camarades 2**. The areas assessed are the item of food and the quantity. Pupils can choose their own items or alternatively the teacher could choose three.

Total = 6 marks. The pupil's performance may show characterisics of both Level 1 and Level 2. At Level 1 pupils should be able to name two or three items of food (brief response – single words – approximate pronunciation). Pupils who can add the extra detail by giving the correct quantity on at least two items show some characteristics of performance at Level 2 (short simple responses, clear meaning, naming and describing of objects).

Exercice 3

The differentiation in this exercise is related to the outcome. The Copymaster is intended to cue utterances which will enable pupils to display characteristics of performance at both Levels 3 and 4.

Level 3 characteristics of performance include the ability to initiate and respond, using memorised language and using short simple responses. Pupils who can successfully communicate at least three of the six details about themselves using short responses such as *Je suis né(e) à Paris, J'ai les cheveux blonds* are showing characteristics of performance at Level 3. If they can communicate two or three details about a brother or sister such as *Il a 14 ans, Il a les cheveux noirs* this also shows characteristics of performance at Level 3. Level 4 characteristics of performance include the ability to produce more utterances (at least three or four) with generally accurate pronunciation and intonation. Pupils who can communicate at least four or five details about themselves and at least three about their brother or sister are showing characteristics of performance at Level 4.

The details are as follows:
1 mark for communication of birthplace, 1 for age, 1 mark per detail about hair (ie: long/short, black/blonde) 1 mark for colour of eyes, 1 mark for an adjective of character (= 6 marks). There are then 4 marks available as follows: 1 for brother/sister, 1 for their age, 1 for their name, 1 for a detail about his / her hair (length or colour).

Teachers may wish to add bonus marks as below. These enable the amount of help/support needed from the teacher to be taken into account. Some pupils may be able to treat the exercise as a presentation and proceed unaided, whereas others may need extra support from the teacher in the form of questions. These marks also give the teacher the opportunity to reward the degree of accuracy shown by pupils.
1 mark – pupil manages to communicate the basic messages – language is often inaccurate but the meaning of most of the messages is there. Substantial help is needed from the teacher.
2 marks – communicates nearly all the messages despite inaccuracies in short simple responses. Some help from the teacher.
3 marks – communicates messages well. Language often very accurate. Little help needed.

C – Epreuve de lecture

Exercice 1

This test requires only the understanding of single words in the shopping context (Unit 2) which identify different departments in a supermarket. Pupils have to match pictures of different food to the appropriate French sign. This is a test of performance at Level 1. Total = 7 marks. Pupils scoring 5 or more marks are showing some characteristics of performance at Level 1.

1 C **2** H **3** G **4** F **5** A **6** D **7** E

Exercice 2

Teachers may find it helpful to revise the location of countries prior to the test. The exercise is designed to test language skills but pupils do need to be able to find the right country on a composite style map showing several countries. Some countries have capitals and/or symbols (as in the Pupil's book in Unit 1) to give extra visual support. The clues in the descriptions also give extra support which should help pupils to find the country given that the position of France is located in the example. The questions are graded in difficulty. Pupils have to match the description to the correct country.

This is a test of performance at Level 2. Total = 6 marks. Pupils scoring 4 or more marks are showing some characteristics of performance at Level 2 (understanding of short phrases presented in a familiar context).

1 H **2** C **3** D **4** A **5** E **6** F

Exercice 3

This exercise tests personal descriptions and requires pupils to read a longer text featuring familiar language. The stimulus text is in the form of continuous prose but there is little reading required in the questions. Some of the lexical items (e.g. *jouer au tennis*) are recycled from **Camarades 1**. Pupils are required to identify main points. The exercise tests performance at Level 3. Total = 5 marks. Pupils gaining 4 marks show characteristics of performance at Level 3.

1 C **2** A **3** B **4** D **5** B

Exercice 4

This exercise concentrates on language acquired on the subject of Christmas. Pupils are expected to be able to identify main points, likes and feelings (Level 3) and some specific detail (Level 4). The text has characteristics of both Levels 3 and 4. The task (*vrai / faux*) is a relatively easy type and it is suggested therefore that pupils scoring 5 or more marks show characteristics of performance at Level 3. Total = 7 marks. Should teachers want this exercise to differentiate further, they could ask pupils to correct the four false statements, e.g. 2 = *Faux – avec sa famille / en famille*. As the task is now more difficult, pupils who successfully correct three of the four false statements (by locating and noting specific detail) show some characteristics of performance at Level 4.

1 *faux* **2** *vrai* **3** *faux* **4** *faux* **5** *vrai* **6** *faux*
7 *vrai*

D – Epreuve écrite

Exercice 1

An exercise in copying familiar words. Although pupils are deciphering anagrams, the correctly-ordered words are provided for reference. This is a Level 1 test on AT 4.

1 mark for each correctly spelt word. Total 5. Pupils scoring at least 4 marks are showing some characteristics of performance at Level 1.

1 *mai* **2** *mars* **3** *juin* **4** *octobre* **5** *janvier*

Exercice 2

In this exercise, pupils are required to write familiar words from memory. It is therefore a test of performance at Level 2.

1 mark for each if recognisable as correct word (spelling may be approximate). Ignore gender errors, if included. No marks for words written in English. Total 6. Pupils scoring at least 4 marks are showing some characteristics of performance at Level 2.

Any six of: *fromage; beurre; jambon; poisson; pain; fraises; tomates* ('tomatoes' = 0); *lait; limonade* ('lemonade' = 0).

Exercice 3

In this exercise, pupils' ability to copy familiar short phrases correctly is tested. It is therefore another test of performance at Level 2.

1 mark for each fully correctly copied phrase. $1/2$ mark if words in correct order but with copying error/s. Total 3. Pupils scoring at least 2 marks are showing some characteristics of performance at Level 1.

1 *Elle est grande.*

2 *Elle a les cheveux longs.*

3 *Il porte des lunettes.*

Exercice 4

A further test, on a different topic, of writing familiar words from memory.

1 mark for each word if recognisable as correct French word. Ignore accent and gender errors. No marks for English. Total 6. Pupils scoring at least 4 marks are showing some characteristics of performance at Level 2. If, however, all three marks on *cadeaux* are gained (and none on *pour qui*), this would of course show satisfactory learning of the 'presents' vocabulary.

Cadeau: any three from: *jouet; jeu d'ordinateur; cravate; chaussettes; chocolats; stylo; boucles d'oreille.*

Pour qui: any recognisable relative. Do not award names. Accept *mon ami/e*. Each must be different.

| CAMARADES 2 | OVERVIEW – UNITE 3 – UNE INVITÉE IDÉALE? | | | NATIONAL CURRICULUM | |
Topics/Objectives	Key language	Grammar	Strategies	PoS coverage	AoE
A **Tu as ta brosse à dents?** Packing your suitcase	*Tu as... un/ton porte-monnaie? / une (ta) brosse à dents? / une (ta) télécarte? / du (ton) dentifrice? / de l' (ton) argent? Oui, j'ai...; Non, je n'ai pas mon / de / d'...* Recycling of other personal possessions	Recycling of *j'ai du... / je n'ai pas de...*	Listening: using rubrics and visuals to make predictions	1 a, c, d, f, g, h, i, j, k 2 a, d, h, j, k 3 c, d, f	AB
B **Qu'est-ce que tu veux faire?** Making suggestions for going out	*Qu'est-ce que tu veux faire? Quand? Ce matin / Ce soir / Cet après-midi / Demain / Demain soir... J'aimerais bien / On peut / On pourrait ... rester à la maison / sortir / aller à la patinoire / aller au bowling ...ou aller à la discothèque. Moi aussi. / Moi, non.*		Listening to dialogue: listening out for key words in questions (*où? / quand?*) as an aid to understanding replies	1 a, c, d, f, g, h, j 2 a, d, e, g, h, i, l 3 d, e	B
C **Je peux prendre une douche?** Staying with a family: asking permission	*(Est-ce que) je (tu) peux...? / Tu veux...? / Marc peut (veut)...? (Est-ce qu') il / elle / on peut (veut...? prendre un bain (une douche)? / téléphoner à mes (tes) parents? / écouter un CD? / manger (boire) quelque chose?* Recycling of other home activities	Present tense of *pouvoir* and *vouloir*	Practising new language through multi-sensory activities Using context as an aid to understanding	1 a, c, d, h 2 a, d, e, g, i, k, l 3 c, b, f, g	AB
D **Point Langue Atelier**		*pouvoir* *vouloir*	Applying a pattern Learning through song and play	1 c, d, g, i 2 f, k 3 a, f	B
E **Il est quelle heure?** Saying the time (12-hour clock; minutes past the hour)	*Il est quelle heure? Il est une heure. Il est sept heures cinq / dix / et quart / et vingt / vingt-cinq / et demie. Il est midi / minuit et demi. Il faut rentrer à quelle heure? A ... heures.* Recycling of time phrases / places of entertainment	Recycling of *pouvoir* in invitations	Word order when giving the time in French	1 a, c, g, h, i, j 2 a, i, n 3 b, d, f	B
F **Qu'est-ce que tu veux regarder?** Discussing opinions on TV programmes	*Qu'est-ce qu'il y a à la télé? Il y a.../ On peut regarder... un film / du sport / un jeu-télé / les informations / un feuilleton / des variétés / des dessins animés. C'est à quelle heure? C'est à... huit heures moins vingt-cinq, etc.*		Pronunciation: *-é / -er / -ez* Learning to spell new words	1 a, c, d, f, g, h, i, j 2 a, d, e, h, j 3 b, c, e, f	B

CAMARADES 2	OVERVIEW – UNITE 3 – UNE INVITÉE IDÉALE?	Cont.		NATIONAL CURRICULUM	
Topics/Objectives	Key language	Grammar	Strategies	PoS coverage	AoE
G Tu aimes la science-fiction? Discussing opinions on TV programmes	*Tu aimes... les publicités / les informations / les feuilletons / les variétés / les dessins animés / les jeux-télé / les films policiers / le sport? / les films de violence? Pourquoi? Parce que... ça m'intéresse / m'amuse / m'ennuie / m'énerve / me fait peur.*	Verbs of opinion + *le / la/ l' / les*	Matching up two reading sources	1 a, c, d, f, g, h, i, j 2 a, d, e, h, j 3 b, c, e, f 4 a	B
H Point Langue Atelier		Verbs of opinion + *le / la/ l' / les*	Applying a pattern Developing awareness of cognates and near cognates	1 c, f, g 2 h, j 3 c, e, f, g 4 a, c, d	B
I Tu aides à la maison? Saying what you do to help at home	*(Est-ce que) Tu aides à la maison? Tu fais...? / Je fais... / Je ne fais pas... / Je ne fais jamais... la vaisselle / la cuisine / le ménage / les courses / ma (ta) chambre... tous les jours / tous les soirs / le week-end / de temps en temps. Je ne fais rien. Recycling days of the week.*	Negatives *ne ... pas* and *ne ... rien* / Recyling of *faire*	Working against the clock Matching two reading sources	1 c, d, f, g, i, j 2 a, d, e, g, h, j, k 3 b, c, f, g	A
J Je peux sortir le soir? Discussing freedom to go out	*Tu peux / Il peut / Elle peut sortir souvent? Je (ne) peux (pas)... sortir le week-end / quand je veux / aller où je veux. Il (Elle) peut aller / Il (elle) veut... II (Elle) doit / Tu dois / Il doit / Elle doit... rentrer à quelle heure? / rentrer à 11h / demander la permission.*	Present tense of *devoir* / Recycling of *pouvoir*	Using the correct subject when answering questions, e.g. *tu ... ? → je ...* / *ta sœur ... ? → elle ...*	1 c, d, f, g, h 2 a, d, e, g, h, j, k 3 b, c, f, g	AB
K C'est vraiment stupide! Stating opinions about freedom or lack of it	*A mon / ton avis... sortir tous les soirs / tout seul / le soir / avec n'importe qui. ... aller au lit a 9h.. rentrer tard, c'est bien / normal / chouette / génial / dangereux / stupide / nul. ... ce n'est pas juste. Recycling of opinions*		Pronunciation *eu* (*deux / heure*) Matching listening and reading sources	1 a, c, d, f, g, i, j 2 a, d, e, f, h, j, l 3 b, c	AB
L Point Langue Atelier		Present tense of *devoir*	Applying a pattern Matching two reading sources	1 c, d, f, g, i, j 2 h, j 3 c, e, f	AB

IT Opportunities

CORE ACTIVITIES

Text manipulation

Spreads F and G

Produce a model text in the first person in which a young person writes about:
(a) what types of programme s/he likes watching on television
(b) why s/he likes this type of programme
(c) the names and times of his/her favourite programmes
(d) how s/he helps around the house

Word processing – guided writing

Spread E

Create and save a simple text, similar to the one below, in which a young person is sending a written invitation to a friend. Highlight or underline a number of words that could be substituted. Pupils then create their own invitation to an imaginary French-speaking friend by replacing the highlighted words with others that would be appropriate.

Note: Ensure that pupils select times that make sense. For example, if *soir* is replaced by *après-midi*, the times should be in the afternoon.

Tu peux aller <u>au théâtre</u> avec moi <u>vendredi soir</u>? On a un billet pour toi. On va <u>au théâtre</u> à <u>six heures et demie</u>. Tu peux arriver chez moi à <u>cinq heures et quart</u>? Il y a <u>un train</u> à <u>cinq heures vingt-cinq</u>. Après, on peut aller <u>à la discothèque</u> avec <u>Pierre</u> et <u>Estelle</u>, mais il faut rentrer à <u>dix heures et demie</u>. Je vais mettre mon pantalon <u>bleu</u>, mon T-shirt <u>noir</u> et mes baskets <u>noirs</u>. C'est d'accord? Ecris-moi.

Presentation

Spread I

Pupils imagine that they must advertise themselves as home-helps in order to earn money for a charity event. To do this they produce a presentation, possibly a simple leaflet using borders and different fonts, giving name, age, telephone number, what they can do (e.g. *je fais la vaisselle, la cuisine et les courses*) and how much they charge (e.g. *25 francs par heure*). Additional information could be provided about their character (e.g. *je suis travailleuse*) and when they can work (e.g. *je peux travailler le vendredi soir / le weekend*).

ADDITIONAL ACTIVITIES

The Internet

Spreads F and G

If possible, find the search engine 'Yahoo France' (http://www.yahoo.fr).

Key *tele7jours* or *tele-top matin* into the search engine. Both these sites belong to French television magazines. Pupils could be asked to identify familiar programmes (i.e. programmes found on British television) in the published schedules. They could then be asked to give a spoken or written presentation in which they name the programmes, their days and their times. They could also state whether they like or dislike the programmes and give reasons.

Databases

The activity for this unit provides opportunities to explore gender differences in eating habits (connected to food and shopping – Spreads E–H in Unit 2), helping in the house (connected to Spread I of Unit 3) and bedtime (connected to Spreads J and K of Unit 3).

Teachers and pupils will need to be familiar with basic data-handling terminology (e.g. file, record, field, numeric, alpha-numeric) as well as graphing techniques and searching routines involving the use of 'and/or' and 'includes/is equal to'. They should also be aware of the need for precision and consistency in data entry.

Conduct a pupil survey, in the form of a simple and carefully constructed multiple choice questionnaire, that asks for the following information:
• gender – *M* or *F*
• whether the pupil is a vegetarian – *oui* or *non*
• what the pupil does, on a regular basis, to help in the house – tick any number of tasks from a prescribed list (e.g. *vaisselle lit chambre courses*)
• at what time the pupil normally has to be in bed during the school week – answers should be given in hours and minutes (e.g. 21.30 / 22.00)

The survey could be made across the whole year group rather than across one class only. In this way the information will have more credibility. The potential of the database to organise large amounts of information at a speed that could not be achieved manually will be more apparent.

Enter data consistently and accurately against the fields of:

• *sexe* (alpha-numeric)
• *veg* (alpha-numeric)
• *aide* (alpha-numeric)
• *couche* (numeric)

This should also be done as efficiently as possible, the best scenario probably being through reliable volunteers in the lunch hour or after school.

Pupils interrogate the database to find specific information (e.g. how many boys go to bed before 10 o'clock, what is the most common way of helping at home) as well as significant gender differences in the areas investigated.

Teach pupils effective ways in which to report back the information they have gathered. One way in which this could occur is through the reinforcement of *plus... que...* and *moins... que...* (e.g. *les garçons se couchent plus tôt que les filles / les filles mangent moins de viande que les garçons*) which were introduced in Unit 1.

Copymasters

The *présentation* and the *grilles* copymasters should be used as indicated.
The other copymasters (vocabulary and worksheets) should be used with or after the spread indicated.

Pupil's Book Spread	Corresponding Copymaster
A	20–21 *Glossaire*
B	*Grilles 3*
C	1 *Présentation*; 5–6 *On lit*
D	7 *Grammaire*; 8 *On s'amuse*; *Grilles 3*
E	2 *Présentation*
F	2–3 *Présentation*; 9–10 *On écoute*
G	4 *Présentation*; 11–12 *On écrit*; *Grilles 3*
H	13 *Grammaire*; 14 *Que sais-tu?*
I	15 *Plaisir de lire*; *Grilles 4*
J	–
K	16–17 *On parle*; *Grilles 4*
L	18 *Grammaire*; 19 *Que sais-tu?*

Notes to accompany Copymasters (CMs)

Feuille 1
Presentation Sheet to present the questions and answers connected with asking for permission. You can also use mime to encourage pupils to generate the correct questions.

Feuille 2
Presentation Sheet to teach the time. Only use times past the hour. If possible, also use a clock and allow for plenty of hands-on practice by pupils. Remind pupils of how to say *deux / trois / six / neuf / dix* before *heures*.

Feuille 3
Presentation Sheet to teach different kinds of TV programme.

Feuille 5–6 On lit
These two CMs provide additional reading practice about spreads A–C. They can easily be used concurrently as the rubrics are short and simple.

Feuille 5 ♦
Ex 1 – Note the negative sentence in item 6.

Ex 2 – Warn pupils that the items are not presented in the same order in the grid and on the graph. When completing the grid, pupils should check that their ticks add up to 20.

Extra – Ask pupils to state what they would rather do on a Saturday night by listing the first names in their order of preference.

Answers
Ex 1: **1** D **2** A **3** C **4** F **5** E **6** B
Ex 2: CD: ✔✔✔   bowling: ✔✔✔✔   patinoire: ✔✔✔
discothèque: ✔   maison: ✔✔   douche: ✔✔
copains: ✔✔✔   bain: ✔✔

Feuille 6 ♣
Pupils should avoid using dictionaries in order to develop more effective reading skills. You can help pupils by telling them that there are only three false items in Ex 2.

Answers
Ex 1: **1** *savon* **2** *bowling* **3** *porte-monnaie* **4** *douche*
5 *patinoire*

Ex 2: **1** *vrai* **2** *faux* **3** *faux* **4** *vrai* **5** *vrai* **6** *faux*
7 *vrai* **8** *vrai*

Feuille 7 Grammaire
This CM provides further practice of *pouvoir* and *vouloir*. Here agin, the ♦ task focuses on singular verb forms.

Ex 1 – Enhance motivation by asking pupils to keep score.

Ex 2 – **Answers**
1 *veux, peux* **2** *peut, veut* **3** *veux, peut* **4** *veut, peut*

Ex 3 – **Preparation** – Brainstorm for possible answers before playing the cassette.

After pupils have listened once or twice and made notes, give them time to turn their notes into complete sentences. Warn them about the need to change *je* to *il / elle*, etc.

1 – *Alexia, tu veux sortir ce soir?*
– *Ce soir? Non, je veux faire mes devoirs.*
2 – *Vous invitez Dominique?*
– *Non, nous avons un problème.*
– *Nous ne pouvons pas téléphoner ici.*
3 – *On va au bowling ce soir?*
– *Ben... non, je ne peux pas sortir le jeudi.*
4 – *David veut aller à la patinoire?*
– *Oui, mais... moi, je préfère écouter des CD.*
– *Ouais, moi aussi.*

5 – *Tu peux sortir tous les jours?!*
– *Ben, oui, et toi, Jérôme?*
– *Moi, non! Mes parents sont stricts: le week-end seulement.*

6 – *Sébastien, j'aimerais bien aller à la discothèque dimanche soir.*
– *Dimanche soir? Mais, Sandrine! Et le collège? Je veux bien aller à la discothèque, mais samedi soir.*

7 – *Alors, Sonia, le bowling à... 8 heures?*
– *Ben, non! J'ai des problèmes avec ma mère: je ne peux pas sortir ce soir.*
– *Et toi, Isabelle?*
– *Non! Je regrette, mais je dois rester à la maison avec mon petit frère.*

Answers
1 *Elle veut faire ses devoirs.* **2** *Ils ne peuvent pas téléphoner ici.* **3** *Il ne peut pas sortir le jeudi.* **4** *Elles préfèrent écouter des CD.* **5** *Non, il sort le week-end seulement.* **6** *Non, il veut/préfère aller à la discothèque samedi soir.* **7** *Non, elles doivent rester à la maison.*

Feuille 8 On s'amuse

Ex 1 – Pupils may prefer to work in small groups.

Encourage pupils to write for an audience, and make sure each member of the class has the opportunity to see all the poems written by classmates. For easier understanding, pupils should illustrate any words they looked up in their dictionaries which are not familiar to the rest of the class and not easily recognisable. For example, *rhinocéros* should not need illustrating, but *mouette* would. This also enhances awareness of cognates and near cognates.

Ex 2 – Make sure pupils remember *plus* and *moins*.

Feuille 9–10 On écoute

These two CMs provide additional listening practice on the time and on TV viewing and other leisure activities.

Feuille 9 ♦

Ex 1 **Preparation** – Say the programme titles once or twice slowly to familiarise pupils with the French sounds prior to listening to the cassette.

1 – *Tarzan, c'est à quelle heure?*
– *Tarzan? A... 8 heures et demie.*

2 – *Rambo, c'est à quelle heure?*
– *Rambo? A... 2 heures et quart.*

3 – *Le bowling, c'est à quelle heure?*
– *Le bowling? C'est à 4 heures 10.*

4 – *OK Musique, c'est à quelle heure?*
– *OK Musique? C'est à 10 heures 20.*

5 – *La natation, c'est à quelle heure?*
– *La natation? C'est à 2 heures moins 20.*

6 – *Tom et Jerry, c'est à quelle heure?*
– *Tom et Jerry? C'est à 4 heures moins cinq.*

7 – *Le judo, c'est à quelle heure?*
– *Le judo? C'est à midi.*

8 – *Dallas, c'est à quelle heure?*
– *Dallas? C'est à une heure moins vingt-cinq.*

Answers
*12h00: Judo   12h35: Dallas   1h40: Natation
2h15: Rambo   3h55: Tom et Jerry   4h10: Bowling
8h30: Tarzan   10h20: OK Musique*

Ex 2 **Preparation** – Go through a–g to check pupils know what types of TV programmes they are. Tell pupils that they will hear two types of TV programmes each time, but that they will not hear the letters a–g.

1 – *Tu préfères les feuilletons ou le sport?*
– *Je préfère le sport.*

2 – *Tu préfères les variétés ou les dessins animés?*
– *Je préfère les variétés.*

3 – *Tu préfères les informations ou les jeux-télé?*
– *J'aimerais bien regarder un jeu-télé.*

4 – *Tu préfères les films ou les variétés?*
– *Je préfère les films.*

5 – *Tu préfères le sport ou les dessins animés?*
– *Je préfère les dessins animés.*

6 – *Tu préfères les informations ou les films?*
– *Je préfère les informations.*

7 – *Tu préfères les jeux-télé ou les feuilletons?*
– *Je préfère les feuilletons.*

Answers
1 B *Sports Matin*   **2** D *Musique et Chansons*
3 F *Tu joues? Tu gagnes!*   **4** G *ET L'extraterrestre*
5 E *Wallace et Gromit*   **6** C *Flash Infos*   **7** A *X files*

Feuille 10 ♣

Ex 1 **Extra** – Copy one of the three tapescripts – with gaps – onto OHT and ask pupils to listen again and fill the gaps.

1 – *Tu veux sortir avec nous ce week-end?*
– *Quand?*
– *Vendredi soir.*
– *Vous allez où?*
– *On aimerait bien aller au bowling en face de la piscine.*
– *Il y a un bowling en face de la piscine?*
– *Oui, c'est chouette.*
– *Ah mais, euh... il y a des variétés super bien à la télé le vendredi soir!*
– *Oh, écoute, la télé, euh...*
– *Bon, d'accord! A quelle heure?*
– *Devant le bowling, à 8 heures moins le quart?*
– *OK, et... je peux inviter Nathalie?*
– *Oui, d'accord!*

2 – *Tu vas au cinéma mercredi?*
– *Oui, avec les copains. Il y a un film américain avec Robert de Niro. Et toi? Tu viens avec nous?*
– *Ben... ça dépend. A quelle heure?*
– *Euh, ça ... ça commence à 2h25.*
– *Oh, c'est..., non, ça ne va pas. J'ai un match de basket.*
– *Au stade?*
– *Non, non, au collège. On peut aller au cinéma à 4 heures, 4 heures et demie?*
– *A 4 heures et demie, c'est un film différent.*

– Qu'est-ce que c'est?

– Un film avec Al Pacino.

– Et... le film avec Robert de Niro, c'est seulement à 2h25?

– Ah ben non, c'est aussi à 5 heures et quart.

– Alors on y va à 5 heures et quart?

– D'accord. Je vais téléphoner aux copains.

3 – Monsieur! C'est quand, le week-end multi-média au collège?

– C'est le 23 mars. Chaque classe va préparer un projet.

– On prépare un jeu radio?

– Un jeu radio? Oh, non! La radio, c'est embêtant.

– On peut préparer un programme télé.

– Un programme télé?

– Ben ouais, un programme de variétés, par exemple.

– Ou un jeu-télé. C'est plus facile, non?

– Ouais, ouais, d'accord.

– J'ai une idée! Un jeu avec du sport, des chansons et de la musique!

– Et deux équipes: la classe et les profs!

Answers

1 bowling / bowling en face piscine; rendez-vous vendredi soir, 7h45, devant bowling, avec Nathalie

2 cinéma / 5h15, Robert de Niro; match de basket avant le cinéma

3 jeu-télé / avec sports, chansons et musique, pour le week-end multi-média au collège, deux équipes (classe et profs)

Ex 2 **Preparation** – Ask pupils to try and predict the answers before listening.

– Salut, Stéphanie!

– Ah, Catherine! On regarde la télé cet après-midi?

– La télé?

– Oui. J'aimerais bien aller en ville, mais il fait froid. Je préfère regarder la télé.

– Ben, moi, non, Stéphanie. Je veux aller au stade.

– Au stade? Pourquoi?

– Avec l'équipe, pour s'entraîner. On a un match mardi.

– Un match de quoi?

– Ben, un match de basket, bien sûr!

– Ah, oui, tu joues au basket! Tu finis à quelle heure?

– Oh, à... 4h et demie...

– Super! Je t'invite pour 5h! Et... devine! J'invite aussi mon cousin!

– Marc? Génial! Et tes parents?

– Ils travaillent ce soir!

Answers

aller en ville   regarder la télé   veut aller au stade / ne peut pas   un match de basket   5h00   son cousin   travaillent

Feuilles 11–12 On écrit

These two CMs provide additional practice with telling the time, TV programmes and other leisure activities. They can easily be used concurrently. Go through the ♦ rubrics while the other pupils read the ♣ rubrics on their own, then answer any queries there might be about the ♣ rubrics.

Feuille 11 ♦
Answers

Ex 1: **1** deux heures vingt   **2** cinq heures et demie **3** trois heures moins le quart   **4** huit heures dix   **5** onze heures et quart   **6** sept heures vingt   **7** Il est dix heures moins dix

Feuille 12 ♣

Discuss with pupils whether the interviewer should use tu or vous. Suggest peer checking for mistakes.

Feuille 13 Grammaire

This CM provide additional practice on the use of definite articles when stating opinions.

Answers

Ex 1: **1** J'adore les hamburgers.   **2** Et toi? Tu préfères les sandwichs..   **3** Je n'aime pas beaucoup le café. **4** A la télé, tu aimes le sport?.   **5** Non, je préfère les films policiers.   **6** Ta sœur aime le dessin?   **7** Non, elle préfère la musique.

Ex 2: **1** du, le   **2** un, les   **3** Les, des   **4** les, un **5** un, les   **6** un, les

Feuille 14 Que sais-tu?

This CM offers some revision of topics 1 and 2. For each task, pupils proceed from Préparation to Que sais-tu?, then onto Bilan / Conseil.

Ex 1– After doing the task from memory, pupils should check their answers using CM 20 (glossary) or – if applicable – their vocabulary books in order to build up their reference skills.

Ex 2

1 – Il est quelle heure?

– Il est huit heures vingt cinq.

– Huit heures vingt cinq? Je peux prendre une douche?

2 – Il est quelle heure?

– Sept heures moins dix.

– Sept heures moins dix? Je peux manger quelque chose?

3 – Il est quelle heure?

– Il est quatre heures et quart.

– Quatre heures et quart? Je peux téléphoner à mes parents?

4 – Il est quelle heure?

– Il est neuf heures et demie.

– Je peux écouter mes CD?

5 – Il est quelle heure?

– Il est dix heures moins cinq.

– Dix heures moins cinq? Je peux boire quelque chose?

6 – Il est quelle heure?

– Il est sept heures moins le quart.

– Je peux prendre un bain?

Answers

Ex 1– un porte-monnaie   une télécarte   du dentifrice une brosse à dents   de l'argent   du savon

Ex 2– **1** 8h25, douche   **2** 6h50, manger   **3** 4h15, téléphoner   **4** 9h30, CD   **5** 9h55, boire   **6** 6h45, bain

Ex 3 – After carrying out the task, pupils can do further oral practice instead of checking their notes against their partners' grids:

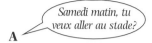
Samedi matin, tu veux aller au stade?

A

Oui. Et toi, tu veux...

B

Feuille 15 Plaisir de lire
This CM is entirely based on TV programmes. Pupils should not use dictionaries but should instead look out for cognates and near cognates, of which there are many.

Ex 1 – ♦ Pupils write two programmes per columns. ♣ Pupils categorise all the programmes.
Answers
Jeux: Le juste prix, La roue de la fortune
Enfants: Disney Club Samedi, Bonjour Babar, Club Jeunesse Vacances
Informations: Flash infos, TV5 infos, Les infos de 20h
Variétés: Pyramide de stars, Fa si la chanter, La fête en chansons
Feuilletons: Hawaï, police d'état, Le Saint, Mission Impossible
Sports: Tour de France, Téléfoot, Formule 1, Cyclisme

Ex 2 **Extra** – To reinforce awareness of cognates and near cognates, improvise translation exercise by asking pupils to scan 1–6 for phrases such as 'the French population'.
Answers
1 C 2 B 3 A 4 E 5 D 6 EastEnders

Feuille 16–17 On parle
These two CMs provide additional speaking practice based on the issues addressed in topic 3.

Feuille 16 ♦
Ex 1 – Pupils should first revise the language needed so as to carry out the interviews more smoothly.

Ex 2 – This task practises reading aloud. Emphasise the importance of speaking clearly.

Feuille 17 ♣
If using listening stations or a language lab, encourage pupils to listen to the model as many times as they wish, both for ideas and for pronunciation purposes.

Emphasise the importance of not preparing a full script, so as to practise speaking from notes.

> *Moi, je peux sortir le mardi et le week-end.... Je peux sortir avec mes copains de classe ou avec ma cousine... Je dois demander la permission à ma mère. Le mardi, je dois rentrer à huit heures et demie. Le week-end, je peux rentrer à dix heures.*
>
> *Mon copain Marc peut sortir le week-end seulement... Mais il peut sortir avec n'importe qui. C'est génial!... Il doit rentrer à neuf heures et demie.*
>
> *A mon avis, sortir seul, c'est dangereux et ce n'est pas amusant... Sortir avec n'importe qui, c'est amusant mais c'est aussi dangereux... Et sortir n'importe quand, c'est stupide parce que c'est fatigant.*

Feuille 18 Grammaire
This CM provides additional practice of modal verbs addressed so far: *pouvoir / devoir / vouloir*.

Ex 1 – Pupils need to watch out for negative sentences. They should use the context and awareness of cognates to work out the meaning of unfamilar words such as *politesse*.
Answers
Normal:
A *On peut travailler à la bibliothèque. On peut être membre d'un club.*
B *On a la permission d'aller à la bibliothèque. On peut être membre d'un club.*
Bizarre:
A *On ne doit pas travailler en silence. On ne doit pas arriver à l'heure. On doit faire de la boxe, du karaté et du parachutisme. On ne peut pas sortir à midi. On ne doit pas être poli. On peut apporter ses cahiers.*
B *On peut arriver à l'heure: ça dépend. On peut apporter ses cahiers. On doit être tres bruyant. On ne doit pas faire d'efforts. On n'a pas la permission de faire les devoirs. On n'a pas la permission de dire bonjour... On doit sortir du collège à midi.*

Ex 2
Answers
veux peux pouvez devons doit veut peut peut dois

Feuille 19 Que sais-tu?
This CM offers revision of topic 3. For each task, pupils proceed from *Préparation* to *Que sais-tu?*, then onto *Bilan / Conseil*.

Ex 1 – For genuine self-evaluation, pupils need to work without reference materials.

Ex 2 – Instead of a time limit, you may prefer to give pupils a target number of sentences to write.

Ex 3 – Pupils can refer back to the topics they used for Ex 6, page 71.

Une invitée idéale?

A Tu as ta brosse à dents?

pp 50–51

Objective
Packing your suitcase

Resources
Flashcards 41–45
Realia (optional for introducing the key language)
CM 20–21 for reference throughout Unit 3
Dictionaries for Ex 5

Key language
Tu as... un (ton) porte-monnaie / une (ta) brosse à dents /

une (ta) télécarte / du (ton) dentifrice / de l' (ton) argent?
Oui, j'ai...
Non, je n'ai pas mon / de / d'...
Recycling of other personal possessions

Grammar
Recycling of *J'ai du... / Je n'ai pas de...*

Language learning strategies
Listening: using rubrics and visuals to make predictions

Ways in
In this Unit, Anaïs spends a few days at Thierry's. Her extrovert and care-free attitude leads to small problems and discussion of how much freedom people her age have or believe they should have.

In this spread, Anaïs is packing to go and stay at Thierry's. You can introduce the spread like this:
Anaïs prépare une visite. A la maison, c'est la panique!

Note: now may also be a good time to start gathering resources for Units 4 and 5. See Spread A notes, Unit 4 for a list of useful addresses.

Introduce the key language using the Flashcards (see Teacher's Book introduction, page 9) or realia. Pupils then read the BD while they listen to the cassette. (BD tapescript – see Pupil's Book.)

Afterwards, they can play *«Le jeu de la chaîne»*:

A — *J'ai du savon...*   B — *J'ai du savon et du dentifrice...*

1

Preparation – To motivate pupils to listen, ask them to make blind guesses about the answers before they hear the cassette.

The strategy box goes with this task.

COUNTER

> **1** – *Anaïs, tu as ton savon?*
> – *Du savon? Euh... oui, oui, j'ai du savon.*
> **2** – *Tu as ta brosse à dents?*
> – *Ma brosse à dents... ma brosse à dents... Ah, oui, la voilà.*
> **3** – *Anaïs, tu as ton argent?*
> – *Mon argent? Euh... Non, il est dans le salon.*
> **4** – *Et... tu as une télécarte?*
> – *Euh... ah, non. Maman a ma télécarte.*
> **5** – *Tu as du dentifrice?*
> – *Le dentifrice... oui, il est avec ma brosse à dents.*
> **6** – *Et tu as ton porte-monnaie?*
> – *Non, il est dans le salon avec mon argent.*

Answers
1 d ✔   2 c ✔   3 a ✘   4 b ✘   5 f ✔   6 e ✘

2

Ask pupils to write down the word they are thinking of to prevent accusations of cheating.

3

Ask pupils for ideas. Those might include: only providing the consonants; only providing the vowels; providing the first and the last letters; providing jumbled up letters; providing the first or the second half of a word only.

4

Ask pupils to do as much as they can without dictionaries. If they use a dictionary, they should keep a record of how many times they used it.

Extra – ♦ When doing the corrections, ask pupils if they can explain in simple words why the words they selected are the odd ones out. ♣ When doing the corrections, go through all the clues that gave the answers away.
Answers
♦ **1** *du dentifrice*   **2** *de l'argent*   **3** *un parapluie*
   4 *du savon*   **5** *un maillot de bain*   **6** *du poulet*
♣ **1** c   **2** d

5

Preparation – Pupils may wish to look up extra items in dictionaries. To prevent problems regarding compound words, look up one or two together (e.g. hairdryer) to show that many dictionaries translate several words or phrases under the same entry.

B Qu'est-ce que tu veux faire?   pp 52–53

Objective
Making suggestions for going out

Resources
Flashcards 46–50
Grilles 3 CM (optional for Ex 4)

Key language
Qu'est-ce que tu veux faire?
Quand? Ce matin / Ce soir / Cet après-midi / Demain / Demain soir

J'aimerais bien / On peut / On pourrait... rester à la maison / sortir / aller à la patinoire / aller au bowling.
... ou aller à la discothèque
Moi aussi. / Moi, non.
Recycling of other hobbies/venues and days of the week

Language learning strategies
Listening to dialogue: listening out for key words in questions as an aid to understanding replies

---

Ways in
Anaïs is now at Thierry's. They do not appear to share the same ideas about what makes for a nice evening. You can introduce the spread like this: *Anaïs est en visite chez Thierry. C'est le soir. Anaïs et Thierry ont des projets différents.*

Brainstorm on hobbies pupils already know, in words or sentences (e.g. *le cinéma, j'aime nager*), then introduce the new hobbies with the Flashcards (see Teacher's Book introduction, page 9).

Pupils then read the BD while they listen to the cassette. Use the BD for repetition practice, breaking down difficult sentences into smaller pieces:
... ce soir?
... faire ce soir?
... tu veux faire ce soir?
... etc. (BD tapescript – see Pupil's Book.)

1 *Extra* – Once pupils have completed the task, ask them to try again and again, this time without looking at the six words provided, until they can say the short paragraph without hesitation.
Answers
1 *chez* **2** *sortir* **3** *soir* **4** *danser* **5** *maison* **6** *match*

2 *Preparation* – Warn pupils about the distractor in item 7. Encourage them to jot down additional information.

Extra – For some more detailed listening after the corrections, write down the tapescript for item 7, with gaps, on the board and ask pupils to fill the gaps with the help of the cassette. The gaps need not be key words.

COUNTER

1 – *Julien, tu vas sortir ce soir?*
    – *Ce soir? Oui. Je vais au bowling. Tu viens?*
2 – *Qu'est-ce que tu fais cet après-midi?*
    – *Cet après-midi? Oh, j'aimerais bien rester à la maison.*
3 – *Catherine, qu'est-ce que tu veux faire cet après-midi?*
    – *Mais, papa, je vais au bowling. C'est l'anniversaire de Nadia.*
4 – *Philippe, tu veux regarder la télé ce soir?*
    – *Ben non! Je vais aller à la patinoire avec les copains. A sept heures et demie.*
5 – *Salut, Valérie! Ça va?*
    – *Ouais, ça va.*
    – *Tu vas en ville?*
    – *Oui, je vais à la bibliothèque.*

6 – *Franck, qu'est-ce qu'on fait ce soir?*
    – *Tu aimes danser?*
    – *Ben oui, bien sûr!*
    – *Alors on pourrait aller à la discothèque. Ça t'intéresse?*
7 – *Tu regardes le film avec moi ce soir?*
    – *Qu'est-ce que c'est?*
    – *Un western.*
    – *Un western? Je déteste ça. Et puis... je vais sortir ce soir.*
    – *Tu vas sortir? Avec qui?*
    – *Avec mes copines!*

Answers
1 a **2** d **3** a **4** c **5** f **6** b **7** e

3 **Answers**
Ce matin (c) *A midi* (d) *Cet après-midi* (f) *Ce soir* (a)
Demain matin (g) *Demain midi* (b) *Demain après-midi* (h)
Demain soir (e)

4 A grid is provided on CM.

Pupils can use either some of the new key language or other hobbies they know in French. When comparing their choices after selecting activities individually, pupils can negotiate and complete a finalised grid together, listing their common plans for the weekend. Rehearse useful phrases for negotiating, for example:
– *Alors, on va à la piscine ce soir?*
– *Non, pas ce soir, demain matin.*
– *Bon, d'accord / Oh non, je préfère ...*

5 *Preparation* – Make sure pupils remember the difference between *ce matin / demain matin*, etc.

Extra – Pupils listen again and make notes to justify the *faux* answers.

COUNTER

1
 – Papa, je peux sortir?
 – Tu veux sortir quand?
 – Cet après-midi.
 – Qu'est-ce que tu veux faire?
 – J'aimerais bien aller à la patinoire avec Valérie.
 – Pourquoi?
 – C'est son anniversaire.
 – Bon, d'accord.

2
 – Maman, est-ce que je peux sortir?
 – Quand?
 – Demain après-midi.
 – Qu'est-ce que tu veux faire?
 – Je veux aller au bowling avec mes copains.
 – Au bowling?
 – Ben, oui. Demain, c'est samedi!
 – Ah, mais... c'est cher le bowling!
 – Oh, maman...!
 – Bon, bon, d'accord. Mais tu dois faire tes devoirs ce soir.

3
 – Papa, est-ce que je peux sortir?
 – Quand?
 – Demain soir.
 – Demain soir? Pourquoi?
 – Valérie et moi, on voudrait aller à la discothèque.
 – Avec Valérie?
 – Ben, oui... j'aime bien Valérie...
 – Ecoute, Sébastien, la piscine... la patinoire... la discothèque... C'est trop cher!
 – Oh, papa...!
 – Sébastien, c'est non! Tu dois écrire à ta grand-mère et tu dois réviser ton anglais!

Answers
a *faux (cet après-midi)*   **b** *faux (patinoire)*
c *faux (anniversaire)*   **d** *vrai*   **e** *faux (demain après-midi)*
f *faux (bowling)*   **g** *vrai*   **h** *faux*   **i** *vrai*   **j** *vrai*   **k** *vrai*
l *faux*

6

Preparation – ◆ Encourage pupils to add one question of their choice (e.g. *A quelle heure?*). ♣ Discuss with pupils what other useful structures/elements they could bring into their conversations, for example: *Il faut / Tu dois...*

Extra – Encourage pupils to learn their conversations by heart.

C Je peux prendre une douche?

Objective
Staying with a family: asking permission

Resources
CM 1, 5 and 6
OHT (see **Ways in** section)
Scissors for Ex 4

Key language
(Est-ce que) je (tu) peux...? / Tu veux...?
(Est-ce que) Marc peut / veut...?
(Est-ce qu') il (elle) peut / veut...?
(Est-ce qu') On peut...?
... prendre un bain (une douche) / ... téléphoner à mes (tes/ses)
parents /... écouter un CD /... manger (boire) quelque chose?
Recycling of other home activities

Grammar
Present tense of *pouvoir* and *vouloir*

Language learning strategies
Practising new language through multi-sensory activities
Using context as an aid to understanding

Ways in
Anaïs proves to be a very dynamic – and demanding – guest, always asking to do one thing or another. You can introduce the spread like this: *Anaïs est très active! Elle a beaucoup d'idées. Ah, là, là. C'est fatigant pour la famille de Thierry.*

Use CM 1 – which can be made into an OHT – to present the key language. You can also use mime to encourage pupils to generate the correct questions.

1
Pupils read the BD while they listen to the cassette. They then complete the task.

Extra – To encourage general language recycling, play the cassette again after the corrections – one question at a time – and ask pupils to answer no and justify their answers in any way they can think of:
– *Je peux prendre un bain?*
– *Non, Peter est dans la salle de bain.*
(BD tapescript – see Pupil's Book.)
Answers
1 d **2** b **3** c **4** e **5** a **6** f

2
Preparation – ♣ Remind pupils of the need for notes, not full sentences.

Extra – ♣ When doing the corrections, ask pupils to explain the extra details in full sentences if possible.

COUNTER

1 – *Je peux manger quelque chose?*
   – *Oui, il y a des pommes sur la table.*
2 – *Je peux prendre une douche?*
   – *Une douche? Oui, d'accord. Dans dix minutes, ça va?*
3 – *Est-ce que je peux téléphoner, s'il vous plaît?*
   – *Oui. Le téléphone est dans la cuisine.*
4 – *Thierry, je peux écouter un CD?*
   – *Oui, oui. Mes CD sont dans ma chambre.*
5 – *Est-ce que je peux boire quelque chose s'il vous plaît?*
   – *Tu veux du coca ou de la limonade?*
6 – *Je peux prendre un bain?*
   – *Un moment, s'il te plaît. Papa est dans la salle de bain.*
7 – *J'ai faim. Est-ce que je peux manger, s'il vous plaît?*
   – *Oui, bien sûr. Regarde dans la cuisine.*

Answers
1 f, *pommes sur la table*   **2** e, *dans dix minutes*
3 a, *dans la cuisine*   **4** c, *CD dans la chambre*
5 d, *coca ou limonade*   **6** b, *papa / père dans la salle de bain*   **7** f, *dans la cuisine*

3
Preparation – Remind pupils of the nature of questions beginning with *Est-ce que*. Also point out the link between nouns and personal pronouns, for example: *Lucie → Elle.*
Answers
1 e **2** f **3** d **4** a **5** b **6** c

4
Pupil B gives a positive answer if (s)he picks the same card as pupil A. If not, (s)he gives a negative answer and suggests what appears on his/her card instead.

5
♦ Before making up their own dialogue, pupils can practice the model dialogue until they know it by heart.

♣ Pupils are often good at recycling vocabulary but not so good at recycling structures across topics. Before pupils write their own dialogues, brainstorm for useful verbal structures: *il faut / je pourrais / j'aimerais bien... .*
Answers
♦ *Avec qui?   Quand?   A quelle heure?   D'accord.*

Une invitée idéale?

D Point Langue / Atelier

pp 56–57

Resources
CM 7 and 8
OHP (optional for **Atelier**, Ex 1)
Grilles 3 CM (optional for **Atelier**, Ex 2)
Dictionaries for CM 8, Ex 1

Grammar
Present tense of *pouvoir* and *vouloir*

Language learning strategies
Applying a pattern
Learning through song and play

Point Langue

This page presents and practises the full paradigms of *pouvoir* and *vouloir* in the present tense. The ♦ task focuses on the singular forms only.

1

Answers
je peux = I can   *tu peux* = you can
je veux = I want to   *tu veux* = you want to

2

Answers
♦ **1** *veux, peux*   **2** *veux, peux*   **3** *peut, veux*   **4** *veut, peux*
♣ **5** *peuvent, veulent*   **6** *voulons, pouvez*
7 *pouvons, voulez*   **8** *veulent, peuvent*

Also refer to notes for CM7 at the beginning of the unit.

Atelier

1

Preparation – To enhance listening skills, write some of the words that appear in the song on the board in chronological order. Ask pupils to listen to the song without looking at it and to tick the words as they hear them. To practise scanning a written text at speed, give pupils another list of words and give them a minute to scan the text and tick the words which appear in the song.

For more varied singing practice, you can have different pupils singing different parts of the song. Pupils can also adapt this method in pairs.

Once pupils are more familiar with the song, show it on the OHP and gradually remove words so that pupils sing from memory.

> **Vive les week-ends!**
> *Qu'est-ce que tu veux faire demain?*
> *Qu'est-ce que tu veux faire demain?*
> *Aller à la patinoire?*
> *Ou sortir très tard le soir?*
> > *Je veux travailler demain!*
> > *Je veux travailler demain!*
> > *Pour finir tous mes devoirs*
> > *Et réviser mon histoire.*
> *Tu peux travailler lundi!*
> *Tu peux travailler lundi!*
> *Le samedi, c'est pour sortir,*
> *Et le dimanche, c'est pour rire.*
> > *D'accord, je viens avec toi!*
> > *D'accord, je viens avec toi!*
> > *Le prof sera en colère*
> > *Mais vive les week-ends en plein air!*

2

A grid is provided on CM.

65

E   Il est quelle heure?

Objective
Saying the time: 12-hour clock; minutes past the hour

Resources
CM 2
OHT (see **Ways in** section)
Clock (optional)

Key language
Il est quelle heure? Il est une heure.

Il est sept heures cinq / dix / et quart / vingt / vingt-cinq / et demie
Il est midi / minuit et demi.
Il faut rentrer à quelle heure? A ... heures.
Recycling of other time phrases and of places of entertainment

Grammar
Recycling of *pouvoir* in invitations

Language learning strategies
Word order when giving the time in French

Ways in
Trouble is brewing at Thierry's as Anaïs has gone out for the evening and still isn't back.

This spread revises the hours and presents the minutes past – including quarter past and half past – using the 12-hour clock. This is preferable to trying to teach quarter past and quarter to in the same lesson – which often confuses pupils.

Use CM 2 to teach the time (see notes at the beginning of the unit).

For a change, pupils first listen to the BD tapescript without looking at the text. Play the cassette again, one section at a time, and ask as many questions as you can think of. Pupils may need to do some guessing:
Qui parle? C'est le matin? Ils sont dans le jardin? Pupils can then read the BD. (BD tapescript – see Pupil's Book.)

1

COUNTER

Preparation – Rehearse the time on each clock before pupils listen to the casette.

1 – *Il est deux heures cinq. Deux heures cinq.*
2 – *Il est quatre heures et demie. Quatre heures et demie.*
3 – *Il est six heures et quart. Six heures et quart.*
4 – *Il est trois heures dix. Trois heures dix.*
5 – *Il est quatre heures vingt-cinq. Quatre heures vingt-cinq.*
6 – *Il est quelle heure?*
   – *Il est deux heures et demie.*
   – *Deux heures et demie?*
7 – *Il est quelle heure?*
   – *Il est... huit heures et quart.*
   – *Huit heures et quart? Déjà?*
8 – *Maman, il est quelle heure?*
   – *Il est huit heures cinq.*
   – *Quelle heure?*
   – *Huit heures cinq.*
9 – *Il est quelle heure?*
   – *Il est midi et demi... euh... oui, c'est ça. Midi et demi.*
10– *Thierry, tu as l'heure?*
   – *Oui, il est dix heures vingt.*
   – *Dix heures quoi?*
   – *Dix heures vingt.*

Answers
1 f 2 h 3 g 4 e 5 i 6 a 7 b 8 k 9 l 10 c

2

Give pupils a challenging time limit.
Answers
1 g 2 c 3 j 4 e 5 i 6 a 7 k 8 l 9 d

3

Remind pupils to use TV programmes that start past the hour only at this stage.

4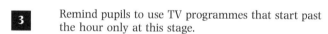

COUNTER

Items 4–7: encourage pupils to jot down other details.

1 – *Il faut rentrer à quelle heure?*
   – *A sept heures et quart.*
   – *D'accord! A sept heures et quart.*
2 – *Il faut rentrer à quelle heure?*
   – *A... huit heures et demie.*
   – *OK! A huit heures et demie.*
3 – *Il faut rentrer à quelle heure?*
   – *A... six heures vingt.*
   – *A six heures vingt? Bon, salut!*
4 – *Je dois rentrer à quelle heure?*
   – *A... trois heures dix.*
   – *A trois heures dix?*
   – *Oui. On va au supermarché.*
5 – *On peut rentrer à minuit?*
   – *Non. A dix heures et demie.*
   – *A dix heures et demie? C'est nul!*
6 – *Tu dois rentrer à quelle heure?*
   – *Oh, euh... deux heures vingt.*
   – *Pourquoi deux heures vingt?*
   – *Ben... on va chez mes grands-parents.*
7 – *Je dois rentrer à quelle heure?*
   – *Bon, disons à... six heures et quart?*
   – *Six heures et quart? Pourquoi?*
   – *La babysitter arrive à six heures et demie.*
   – *Oh, la babysitter!*

Answers
1 7h15 2 8h30 3 6h20 4 3h10 *(supermarché)*
5 10h30 *(nul!)* 6 2h20 *(va chez grands-parents)*
7 6h15 *(babysitter arrive à 6h30)*

5

♣ To develop their use of reference materials, pupils should try to adapt passages from all three messages, rather than using one message exclusively as a model.

F Qu'est-ce que tu veux regarder?

pp 60–61

Objective
Discussing what to watch on television
Full 12-hour clock

Resources
CM 2, 3, 9 and 10
OHT (see **Ways in** section)
Clock (optional)
OHT (optional for CM 10, Ex 1)

Key language
Qu'est-ce qu'il y a à la télé?
Il y a... / On peut regarder... un film / du sport / un jeu-télé /
les informations / un feuilleton / des variétés / des dessins animés
C'est à quelle heure? C'est à... huit heures moins vingt-cinq / vingt /
le quart / dix / cinq.

Language learning strategies
Pronunciation: *-é / -er / -ez*
Learning to spell new words

Ways in
Anaïs and Thierry's family are planning a TV evening, but opinions differ on the matter. You can introduce the spread like this: *Thierry est dans le salon avec sa famille et avec Anaïs. Ils vont regarder la télé, mais il y a un problème.*

This spread practises the whole 12-hour clock, so revising the minutes past the hour and introducing the minutes to the hour. Use a clock and CM 2 – which can be made into an OHT – for presentation and practice.

Pupils then read the BD while they listen to the cassette. Elicit the meaning of *variétés* and *informations* with the help of the pictures. Then see how familiar pupils are with TV schedules:

A *Les variétés?* B *Top of the Pops, vendredi soir, BBC1, 7h30.*

Teach the rest of the key language using CM3 – which can be made into an OHT. Draw on pupils' knowledge of TV programmes:

A *The Wheel of Fortune?* B *Un jeu-télé!*

(BD tapescript – see Pupil's Book.)

1

1 – *Qu'est-ce qu'il y a à la télé?*
   – *Ce soir il y a du sport.*
   – *Du sport? Chouette. A quelle heure?*
   – *A huit heures et demie.*

2 – *Qu'est-ce qu'il y a à la télé?*
   – *Il y a un jeu.*
   – *Un jeu-télé? A quelle heure?*
   – *A six heures vingt. C'est «Questions pour un Champion».*

3 – *Qu'est-ce qu'il y a ce soir à la télé?*
   – *Ben, il y a un spécial variétés à neuf heures dix.*
   – *Des variétés? J'aime bien ça.*

4 – *Et le feuilleton américain? C'est ce soir?*
   – *Non, c'est le mardi et le jeudi.*

5 – *Tu regardes les informations, papa?*
   – *Les informations? Oui, bien sûr, à huit heures du soir.*

6 – *Il y a un film ce soir?*
   – *Ouais, ouais, ils passent «Conan le Barbare» à dix heures vingt-cinq.*
   – *Mais, non, «Conan le Barbare», c'est jeudi.*
   – *Oh, zut! Oui, c'est jeudi.*

7 – *Il y a un spécial dessins animés avant le dîner.*
   – *Un quoi?*
   – *Des dessins animés. A sept heures et quart.*
   – *Oh, moi, les dessins animés...*

Answers
1 *e* ✔ *(8h30)* **2** *b* ✔ *(6h20)* **3** *g* ✔ *(9h10)*
4 *c* ✘ **5** *f* ✔ *(8h)* **6** *a* ✘ **7** *d* ✔ *(7h15)*

2
Pupils can first have a go without the key.
Answers
1 *un film* **2** *les informations* **3** *des variétés*
4 *un feuilleton* **5** *des dessins animés* **6** *du sport*
7 *un jeu-télé*

3
For a greater challenge, pupils should respond within five or ten seconds.

On prononce bien

COUNTER

Ecoute et répète:
  la télé   des variétés   des dessins animés
  une télécarte   regarder   vous pouvez   téléphoner

4
Preparation – Make sure pupils understand the connection between *sept heures moins le quart* and 6h45.

Extra – After the corrections, pupils can speak in pairs:

A *Deux heures cinq.* B *6a!*

COUNTER

1 – *Il est dix heures vingt.*
2 – *Il est 3h10.*
3 – *Il est 7h et demie.*
4 – *C'est à 7h moins 25.*
5 – *Il est quelle heure?*
   – *Il est midi moins le quart.*

6 – *Le film commence à quelle heure?*

– *A... 3h moins cinq.*

7 – *Tu vas à la piscine?*

– *Oui, demain.*

– *A quelle heure?*

– *A dix heures vingt.*

8 – *Le dentiste, c'est à quelle heure?*

– *C'est à une heure moins le quart.*

Answers
1 a **2** a **3** b **4** b **5** b **6** b **7** c **8** c

5

Pupils should work without dictionaries. When doing the answers, carefully examine the clues that led to the correct answers, including cognates and near cognates.
Answers
1 *5h45* **2** *7h45* **3** *6h05* **4** *2h15* **5** *4h50* **6** *3h55*

6

Preparation – Tell pupils there is a pause between each item. If possible, do not add to the recorded pauses. Tell pupils to write the beginning of words only if necessary and to complete their notes afterwards.

COUNTER

Ce matin, à 6h et demie, les informations complètes avec Télématin... Ensuite, notre documentaire sur le cinéma à 8h et quart... A 9h, le feuilleton. Votre feuilleton américain préféré, Amoureusement Vôtre. Après le feuilleton, des variétés, avec La Chance aux Chansons, à... 10h10... A 11h20, un autre feuilleton américain, les Aventures de Black Beauty... Ensuite, notre reportage sur l'Australie commence à midi et quart... A une heure, les informations... Après les informations, du sport: TéléSport commence à 1h25... Et à 2h05, c'est notre film de l'après-midi, Secrets Professionnels. Bonne journée!

Answers
1 *Informations* **2** *8h15* **3** *Feuilleton* **4** *10h10*
5 *Feuilleton* **6** *12h15* **7** *Informations* **8** *1h25*
9 *Film*

7

To check they have collated the correct information, each pupil should read the information gathered back to the other pupil rather than looking in the book. This provides additional reading, speaking and listening practice. Provide an example:

Il y a les informations à six heures et demie?

Oui, ça va. Il y a...?

A

B

68

G Tu aimes la science-fiction?

pp 62–63

Objective
Discussing opinions on TV programmes

Resources
CM 4, 11 and 12
OHT (optional – see **Ways in** section)
Grilles 3 CM (optional for Ex 3)
A2 paper (optional for Ex 7)

Key language
Tu aimes... les publicités / les informations / les feuilletons /
les variétés / les dessins animés / les jeux-télé / les films policiers /
le sport / les films de violence?
Pourquoi? Parce que... ça m'intéresse / m'amuse / m'ennuie /
m'énerve / me fait peur.
Recycling of verbs of opinions

Grammar
Verbs of opinion + *le / la / l' / les*

Language learning strategies
Matching up two reading sources

Ways in

Anaïs wants to watch late-night TV with Thierry You can introduce the spread like this: *Thierry est dans le salon avec sa famille et Anaïs. Il est quelle heure? Ah! On va aller au lit. Mais Anaïs n'est pas d'accord.*

Use CM 4 – which can be made into an OHT – for language presentation. First revise the TV programmes presented in Spread F. Generate pupils' opinions as much as possible using familiar language before teaching the new opinion phrases. Also encourage pupils to ask your personal opinions.

Pupils can then read the BD while they listen to the cassette. Next, 'bombard' them with *vrai / faux* statements, to which they must respond swiftly from memory. The more language recycling, the better. (BD tapescript – see Pupil's Book.)

1
Ask pupils to respond within five seconds.

2

1 – *Anaïs, tu aimes les films de violence à la télé?*
 – *Les films de violence? Oui, ça m'amuse.*

2 – *Et toi, Thierry, tu aimes les films de violence à la télé?*
 – *Les films de violence? Non, ça m'ennuie.*

3 – *Julien, tu aimes les informations à la télé?*
 – *Les informations? Ah oui, ça m'intéresse.*

4 – *Anaïs, tu aimes les films policiers à la télé?*
 – *Les films policiers? J'adore ça. Ça m'amuse.*

5 – *Et les publicités, tu aimes ça?*
 – *Les publicités? Ah, non, alors! Ça m'énerve!*

6 – *Il y a un film violent à la télé ce soir. Tu aimes les films de violence, Ludivine?*
 – *La violence? Ça me fait peur.*

7 – *Thierry, qu'est-ce que tu regardes?*
 – *Les publicités.*
 – *Les publicités?*
 – *Ben oui, ça m'intéresse!*

8 – *Papa, tu regardes le jeu-télé à sept heures et demie?*
 – *Ah oui, les jeux-télé, ça m'amuse! Ça m'amuse beaucoup!*

Answers
1 *les films de violence*, b 2 *les films de violence*, e
3 *les informations*, d 4 *les films policiers*, b

5 *les publicités*, a 6 *les films de violence*, c
7 *les publicités*, d 8 *les jeux-télé*, b

3

Preparation – Decide how many programme types pupils should interview their peers about.

4

♦ Encourage peer checking for spelling.
♣ Pupils can develop their answers further: *Les films de violence, ça m'énerve. Par exemple, je ne regarde pas...*

5

Do this in two phases. First, pupils make notes (e.g. *informations, ennuie*), then they compare their notes with their sentences from Ex 4 and put a tick where they agree and a cross where they disagree. ♦ It does not matter if some pupils only gave opinions on six programme types in Ex 4, they can still say whether or not they agree with the cassette statements.

COUNTER

 – *Ludovic, tu aimes la télé?*
 – *Ça dépend. Par exemple, je n'aime pas les informations.*
 – *Pourquoi?*
 – *Les informations, ça m'ennuie.*
 – *Tu aimes les films de violence?*
 – *Les films de violence, ça m'amuse. Par exemple, les films policiers, c'est amusant.*
 – *Il y a beaucoup de publicité à la télé.*
 – *La publicité? Oui... ça m'intéresse. C'est intéressant.*
 – *Et les feuilletons?*
 – *Ah, les feuilletons! Le matin, l'après-midi, le soir. Ça m'énerve!*
 – *Et... tu regardes les jeux-télé?*
 – *Les jeux-télé? Euh... non... pas beaucoup, parce que ça m'ennuie. Je préfère le sport. Ça m'intéresse.*

6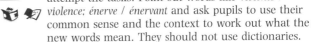

Préparation – Read the passage aloud before pupils attempt the tasks. Point out words like *violents / violence: énerve / énervant* and ask pupils to use their common sense and the context to work out what the new words mean. They should not use dictionaries.
Answers
1 *vrai* 2 *faux* 3 *vrai* 4 *vrai* 5 *faux* 6 *vrai*
7 *faux* 8 *vrai*

7
For a more authentic look, pupils may prefer to work in groups on large pieces of paper.

H Point Langue / Atelier

Resources
CM 13 and 14

Grammar
Verbs of opinion + *le / la / l' / les*

Language learning strategies
Applying a pattern
Developing awareness of cognates and near cognates

Point Langue

This page reinforces the work from Spread G by providing additional practice on the use of definite articles when stating opinions.

1
♦ Pupils can use the glossary to check on gender.
Answers

♦ **1** *le* **2** *les* **3** *les* **4** *les* **5** *le* **6** *la* **7** *les*

CM 13 provides additional practice on the use of definite articles. (See notes at beginning of unit.)

Atelier

1
Pupils should work without dictionaries.

2
Again, pupils should work without dictionaries.

1 Tu aides à la maison?

pp 66–67

Objective
Saying what you do to help at home

Resources
Flashcards 51–55
CM 15
Grilles 4 CM for Ex 1

Key language
(Est-ce que) Tu aides à la maison?
Tu fais...? / Je fais... / Je ne fais pas... / Je ne fais jamais...
la vaisselle / la cuisine / le ménage / les courses / ma (ta) chambre

... tous les jours / tous les soirs / le week-end / de temps en temps.
Je ne fais rien.
Recycling of days of the week

Grammar
Negatives: *ne ... pas* and *ne ... rien*
Recycling of *faire*

Language learning strategies
Working against the clock
Matching two reading sources

Ways in
Anaïs is surprised to find Thierry helping round the house. You can introduce the spread like this: *C'est le week-end, mais Thierry travaille beaucoup à la maison. Anaïs est très surprise!*

Use the Flashcards to present the new language and ask pupils about what they do round the house.

Next, introduce the negative phrases. You and/or pupils can then improvise some true/false statements, using negatives or not:
– *Je ne fais jamais la vaisselle.*
– *Vrai?*
– *Oui.*

Before looking at the BD, ask pupils to try and guess which three jobs Thierry does round the house. Pupils can then check their guesses against the BD, and listen to the cassette. (BD tapescript – see Pupil's Book.)

1

COUNTER

A grid is provided on CM.

> **1** – *Ludivine, tu aides à la maison?*
> – *Oui, je fais le ménage. Avec mon frère.*
>
> **2** – *Julien, tu aides à la maison?*
> – *Oui, je fais la vaisselle. Mais ça m'embête.*
>
> **3** – *Valérie, est-ce que tu aides à la maison?*
> – *Non, je ne fais rien.*
> – *Rien?*
> – *Rien!*
>
> **4** – *Grégory, est-ce que tu aides à la maison?*
> – *Oui. Je fais ma chambre.*
> – *Ta chambre? Quand?*
> – *Le samedi.*
>
> **5** – *Hayoon, tu travailles beaucoup chez toi?*
> – *Beaucoup, non, mais je fais la cuisine.*
> – *Tous les jours?*
> – *Non, le week-end.*
>
> **6** – *Karine, qu'est-ce que tu fais à la maison?*
> – *Moi, ben... je ne fais rien.*
> – *Tu ne fais rien?*
> – *Non, non, je n'aide jamais à la maison.*
>
> **7** – *Sébastien, tu aides à la maison?*
> – *Je fais le... ma chambre..., je fais la vaisselle... et je fais les courses.*
> – *Ta chambre... la vaisselle... et les courses?*
> – *Oui, mais, euh... le samedi seulement.*

Answers
1 housework, *avec frère* **2** washing up, *embête* **3** ✗
4 bedroom, *samedi* **5** cooking, *week-end* **6** ✗
7 bedroom, washing up, shopping, *samedi*

2

One correct guess = one point. Who wins?

3

COUNTER

Preparation – Pupils should first browse through 1–7, then look at each item carefully before listening to the relevant cassette passage. Warn pupils that they will hear the answers in clusters: 1; 2–4; 5–6; 7.

> – *Carole, tu aides beaucoup à la maison.*
> – *Oui. Je fais la vaisselle tous les soirs.*
> – *Tu fais la vaisselle? Tu aimes ça?*
> – *Non, ça m'énerve!*
>
> – *Tu fais la cuisine?*
> – *Oui, je fais la cuisine le matin. Je prépare le petit déjeuner.*
> – *Tu aimes ça?*
> – *Ça va, c'est amusant.*
>
> – *Et ta chambre? Tu fais ta chambre?*
> – *Oui, je fais ma chambre le samedi ou le dimanche.*
> – *Et... tu fais le ménage dans le reste de la maison?*
> – *Non, je ne fais jamais le ménage.*
>
> – *Alors... la vaisselle... la cuisine... ta chambre. Et les courses?*
> – *Ah, c'est ma mère. Elle fait les courses le vendredi. Elle va au supermarché.*

Answers
1 *faux:* ♣ *tous les soirs* **2** *faux:* ♣ *ça l'énerve / elle n'aime pas ça* **3** *vrai* **4** *vrai* **5** *vrai* **6** *faux: jamais*
7 *faux:* ♣ *sa mère*

4

Ask pupils to make negative as well as positive sentences.

Extra – Pupils, working in pairs, take it in turn to read out one of their sentences to find out whether their partners wrote identical sentences. Identical sentences are easier to spot through skimming and scanning if pupils first underline the key words in each one of their sentences (e.g. what, when and with whom).

5

Give a time challenge.
Answers
Mehdi, Dalila, Myriam, Marc, Nabila, Arnaud

6

♣ Remind pupils of the foolproof method: *Quoi? Quand? Avec qui?...*

Unité 3

Une invitée idéale?

J Tu peux sortir le soir?

pp 68–69

Objective
Discussing freedom to go out

Resources
Cassette for BD and Ex 1 and 5
Rubbers for Ex 2
Dictionaries optional for Ex 7

Key language
Tu peux / Il peut / Elle peut sortir souvent?
Je (ne) peux (pas)... sortir le week-end / quand je veux / aller où je veux.

Il / Elle peut aller ou il / elle veut.
Je dois / Tu dois / Il doit / Elle doit... rentrer à quelle heure? / rentrer à 11h / demander la permission.
Recycling of 12-hour clock and places of entertainment

Grammar
Present tense of *devoir*
Recycling of *pouvoir*

Language learning strategies
Using the correct subject when answering questions,
e.g. *Tu... → Je...*

Ways in
Anaïs is packing to go home and is already planning an evening out. Can she really go out as she pleases at home? You can introduce the spread like this: *La visite chez Thierry est finie. Anaïs est avec Thierry et ses copains. Le père d'Anaïs va arriver.*

The aim here should be for pupils to elicit the meaning of the new language by themselves.

Pupils read the BD while they listen to the cassette. Having learnt *sortir* earlier, see if pupils can work out what *Tu sors / Je sors* mean, then check if they remember *souvent* and the difference between *Je peux* and *Je veux*. They should then try to guess from the context what *rentrer* means.

Next, write *je peux* and *je dois* on the board and try to elicit the meaning of *je dois* though example, gesture and intonation: *Tu peux rentrer à minuit? Moi, je dois rentrer à neuf heures!*

Finally, see if pupils can work out what the rest of the language listed in the key means, especially *Je dois demander la permission* and *Je peux sortir quand / où je veux.* (BD tapescript – see Pupil's Book.)

1

Preparation – Check that pupils remember *soir / week-end / trois fois par semaine*. Warn them that one of the sentences they are going to hear is negative. Also emphasise that they are to listen for frequency, not specific days of the week.

COUNTER

1 – *Ludivine, tu peux sortir souvent?*

 – *Je peux sortir une fois par semaine.*

 – *Une fois par semaine?*

 – *Et je dois rentrer à 8h.*

2 – *Valérie, tu peux sortir souvent le soir?*

 – *Je peux sortir trois fois par semaine.*

 – *Trois fois par semaine?*

 – *Et je dois rentrer à 8h et quart.*

3 – *Mohamed, tu peux sortir souvent le soir?*

 – *Je peux sortir quand je veux.*

 – *N'importe quand? Et tu dois rentrer à quelle heure?*

 – *Je dois rentrer à 10h et demie.*

4 – *Julien, tu peux sortir souvent?*

 – *Je peux sortir le week-end, deux fois le week-end.*

 – *Tu dois rentrer à quelle heure?*

 – *Je dois rentrer à 9h et demie.*

5 – *Marsha, tu peux sortir souvent le soir?*

 – *Je ne peux pas sortir.*

 – *Tu ne peux pas sortir?*

 – *Le soir, jamais.*

6 – *Grégory, tu peux sortir souvent?*

 – *Je peux sortir quatre fois par semaine.*

 – *Tu dois rentrer à quelle heure?*

 – *Je dois rentrer à 10 h moins le quart.*

Answers
1 e, *8h*   2 b, *8h15*   3 a, *10h30*   4 f, *9h30*
5 c   6 d, *9h45*

2

As an alternative, pupils can copy the sentences, cut each of them in half, and compete with their partners to reconstruct the dialogue against the clock.

3

Extra – Ask a few pupils to read their answers aloud. Afterwards, ask each of those pupils one or two questions about themselves:

> *Et toi, tu peux sortir le samedi soir? Tu dois rentrer à quelle heure?*

4

Preparation – Look at the key with pupils for verb forms with *il / elle*. Pupils may find it useful to copy the singular verb forms of *pouvoir / vouloir / devoir* in a grid format. Point out that all three verbs end in *-t* with *il / elle*. When doing Ex 4, ask pupils to watch out for the link between *tu* in questions and *je* in answers. Suggest pupils first do their answers in rough as they might change their minds in the light of the items that follow. All of a–g should be used once.
Answers
♦ f, d, g, a, c, b, e

5

Preparation – Go through the pictures with pupils and ask them to predict the kind of excuses they are likely to hear, using *je dois*.

Extra – Pupils listen to each item again and provide further details, in speaking or writing, using *Il / Elle veut*, for example: *Il veut sortir ce soir.*

COUNTER

1 – *Ludivine, tu peux sortir ce soir?*

– *Désolée, je dois aller au supermarché.*

2 – *Julien, tu peux sortir ce matin?*

– *Désolé, je dois faire ma chambre.*

3 – *Valérie, tu peux sortir cet après-midi?*

– *Désolée, je dois aller à la bibliothèque.*

4 – *Mohamed, tu peux sortir ce soir?*

– *Désolé, Valérie, je dois rester à la maison.*

5 – *Myriam, tu peux sortir à 7h?*

– *Ah, non, je ne peux pas, je dois faire la vaisselle.*

6 – *Frédéric, tu viens en ville avec nous?*

– *Quand?*

– *Maintenant, tout de suite. Vite, vite!*

– *Impossible! Je dois téléphoner à mon grand-père. C'est son anniversaire.*

7 – *Tu viens au cinéma?*

– *A quelle heure?*

– *Le film commence à sept heures moins vingt.*

– *Sept heures moins vingt? Ben... non, je ne peux pas. Je dois prendre un bain. Le travail dans le jardin, c'est sale!*

Answers
1 h **2** e **3** f **4** g **5** a **6** c **7** d

6

Preparation – Brainstorm for excuses. Encourage as much language recycling as possible. Tell pupils that washing your hair is not a very French excuse at all!

COUNTER

– *Tu veux sortir ce soir? On va chez Nadja?*

– *A quelle heure?*

– *A sept heures, ça va?*

– *Tu dois rentrer à quelle heure?*

– *A huit heures et demie.*

– *Zut, je ne peux pas! Je dois faire ma chambre.*

7

Because pupils need to learn to exploit familiar language in every way they can, it is best not to use dictionaries here, or to allow each pupil to look up a maximum of three words only. Point out that pupils should only use dictionaries for looking up words, not whole structures.

♦ Pupils should write about themselves only.

♣ Pupils could mention friends or brothers/sisters to vary verb forms.

Encourage peer checking. Tell pupils what you want them to watch out for when doing checking, for example: punctuation, capitals, spelling difficult words, verb endings, etc.

K C'est vraiment stupide!

pp 70–71

Objective
Stating opinions about freedom or lack of it

Resources
CM 16 and 17
Grilles 4 CM optional for Ex 5

Key language
A mon / ton avis,... sortir tous les soirs / tout seul le soir / avec

n'importe qui, / ... aller au lit à 9h / ... rentrer tard
... c'est bien / normal / chouette / génial / dangereux / stupide / nul.
... ce n'est pas juste.
Recycling of opinions

Language learning strategies
Pronunciation: *-eu (deux / heure)*
Matching listening and reading sources

Ways in
Anaïs and friends are waiting for her father and discussing freedom for people their age. You can introduce the spread like this: *Les copains de Thierry n'aiment pas beaucoup l'attitude d'Anaïs. Mais le père arrive, et... surprise.*

There is little new language in this spread. Pupils read the BD while they listen to the cassette. Then ask pupils to look at the key and improvise some statements using *A mon avis.* Ask pupils to respond using *d'accord / pas d'accord.* (BD tapescript – see Pupil's Book.)

1

COUNTER

1	*C'est bien.*	7	*C'est chouette.*
2	*C'est dangereux!*	8	*C'est génial.*
3	*C'est nul!*	9	*C'est nul!*
4	*C'est génial.*	10	*C'est dangereux!*
5	*C'est normal.*	11	*C'est bien.*
6	*C'est stupide!*	12	*C'est génial.*

2
Ask pupils to be careful about 5 and 6.
Answers
1 e **2** a **3** f **4** c **5** d **6** b

3

COUNTER

1 – *A ton avis, sortir avec n'importe qui, c'est bien?*
   – *Sortir avec qui je veux? C'est génial!*

2 – *A ton avis, sortir tous les soirs, c'est bien?*
   – *Sortir tous les soirs? C'est stupide.*

3 – *A ton avis, rentrer tard, c'est bien?*
   – *Rentrer tard le soir? C'est chouette, oui.*

4 – *Aller à la discothèque à 12 ans, à ton avis, c'est normal?*
   – *Ben oui! A mon avis... à 12 ans, c'est normal!*

5 – *Sortir tout seul le soir, à ton avis, c'est bien?*
   – *Ben, tu sais, euh... non. A mon avis, c'est dangereux, hein?*

6 – *Aller au lit à neuf heures, à ton avis, c'est bien?*
   – *La semaine, à mon avis, c'est normal. Oui, aller au lit à neuf heures, c'est normal à 12 ans.*

Answers
1 f, *c'est génial* **2** b, *c'est stupide* **3** e, *c'est chouette*
4 a, *c'est normal* **5** d, *c'est dangereux*
6 c, *c'est normal*

4

♦ ♣ The tapescript and answers are the same. While the cassette is running, pupils should never attempt to listen and read at the same time. They should read the relevant statement before they listen to the cassette. They can then listen, making notes if it helps before reading again. Allow plenty of time between each item.

COUNTER

1 – *Moi, à mon avis, aller à la discothèque à 12 ans, c'est normal.*

2 – *A mon avis, euh... Rentrer après minuit le samedi ou le dimanche... c'est chouette.*

3 – *A mon avis, sortir avec n'importe qui? Non, ce n'est pas dangereux! C'est amusant!*

4 – *Aller au lit à 9h le soir? Tous les soirs? Pourquoi? Quelquefois, à 9h, je veux dormir, et quelquefois, je préfère lire. C'est différent tous les jours.*

5 – *A mon avis, sortir tout seul le soir, c'est bien pour les garçons, mais c'est dangereux pour les filles.*

6 – *Rentrer après minuit? A mon âge? C'est dangereux! Quelquefois, il y a de la violence dans la rue. Je préfère rentrer à neuf heures, neuf heures et demie.*

7 – *Sortir tous les soirs, moi, à mon avis, c'est embêtant. Quelquefois, j'aime bien rester à la maison avec ma famille... ou avec mon chien! C'est sympa, non?*

Answers
♦ and ♣ **1** *vrai* **2** *vrai* **3** *faux* **4** *vrai* **5** *vrai*
6 *vrai* **7** *faux*

5

A grid is provided on CM.

On prononce bien
COUNTER

Répète:

   travailleur, ordinateur, seul, heure, beurre

   deux, dangereux, il peut, elle veut, délicieux, paresseux

6

Preparation – Brainstorm for suitable topics.

L Point Langue / Atelier   pp 72–73

Resources
CM 18 and 19

Grammar
Present tense of *devoir*

Language learning strategies
Applying a pattern
Matching two reading sources

Point Langue

This page supplements Spread J by presenting and practising the whole paradigm of *devoir* in the present tense. The ♣ task focuses on singular verb forms.

1

 Answers
♦ **1** *doit* **2** *doit* **3** *dois* **4** *dois* **5** *doit* **6** *doit*
♣ **1** *dois* **2** *dois* **3** *devons* **4** *devez* **5** *devons* **6** *doit*
  7 *doivent* **8** *doit* **9** *dois*

Atelier

1

As well as adding humour to the this task, the animal pictures are meant to help reinforce the message that many language items can be used in a variety of contexts.
Answers
1 c **2** a **3** b **4** e **5** d

2

When doing the corrections, examine carefully with pupils the clues that led to the correct answers.
Answers
1 c **2** e **3** a **4** d **5** b

3

Pupils can work in pairs if they wish.

CAMARADES 2 — OVERVIEW – UNITE 4 – ON VA À PARIS?

NATIONAL CURRICULUM

	Topics/Objectives	Key language	Grammar	Strategies	PoS coverage	AoE
A	**Qu'est-ce qu'on peut faire?** Discussing what to do on a day out	*Qu'est-ce qu'on peut (pourrait) faire? On peut (pourrait) / Vous pouvez / J'aimerais bien... visiter un musée / visiter la tour Eiffel / faire du shopping / faire du bateau / aller au zoo / aller au parc / aller à Disneyland* Recycling of leisure activities and time phrases	*Aller + au / à la / à l' / aux'* Recycling of verb + infinitive	Avoiding repetition in written work	1 a, c, d, f, g, h, i, j, k 2 a, d, h, i, j, m 3 f, g	B
B	**En car ou en train?** Discussing how to travel	*Je vais aller à Paris. On va voyager comment? On va / On peut / On pourrait voyager en... avion / train / bus / car / vélo / voiture. C'est plus / moins... confortable / pratique / rapide. C'est trop cher.*	Recycling of verb + infinitive	Pronunciation: *r* Using context as an aid to understanding	1 a, c, d, f, g, h, i 2 a, d, e, f, g, h, i, j 3 d, e	CE
C	**Qu'est-ce qu'on va faire?** Finalising detailed plans for a day out	*Qu'est-ce qu'on va faire? / A quelle heure? / Et ensuite? D'abord / Ensuite / Finalement / A deux heures, on va (pourrait)... D'accord? / Ça t'intéresse? Oui, d'accord. / Oh, non, pas vraiment.* Recycling of the 12-hour clock and leisure activities	Recycling of verb + infinitive	Using the textbook for reference	1 a, c, f, g, h, i 2 a, d, g, h, i, k, l 3 e, g	BCE
D	**Point Langue Atelier**	Recycling of making plans for the weekend	*Aller + au / à la / à l' / aux'*	Applying a pattern Using context and key words as an aid to understanding	1 c, d, g, i, j 2 j, n 3 e, f 4 a	BCE
E	**Ça ouvre à quelle heure?** Enquiring about opening hours	*Le musée, ça ouvre / ferme à quelle heure le matin / l'après-midi / le soir? Ça ouvre / ferme à + 24-hour clock. La cathédrale, c'est ouvert le lundi? C'est ouvert/fermé de... à.... sauf le....* Recycling of the time and days of the week		Awareness of negatives as a clue to understanding Giving a short presentation	1 a, c, d, g, h, i, k 2 a, d, e, j, l, n 3 g 4 a	BCE
F	**Vous avez de la monnaie?** Asking for change	*Tu as / Vous avez de la monnaie / une pièce de...? J'ai seulement un billet de... / Je voudrais... en pièces (billets) de ... / Je voudrais... en pièces (billets) de... Désolé(e). / Voilà, monsieur / madame / mademoiselle.*	Recycling of *avoir*	Pronunciation: silent letters at end of words	1 a, c, d, g, h 2 a, d, e, f, h, l	C

CAMARADES 2	OVERVIEW – UNITE 4 – ON VA À PARIS?	Cont.		NATIONAL CURRICULUM	
	Topics/Objectives	Key language	Grammar	Strategies	PoS coverage	AoE
G	**Au musée** Enquiring about facilities at a tourist venue	*Je voudrais... billets pour adultes / enfants. Vous avez un tarif groupes / des dépliants? C'est une visite guidée? Où est la cafétéria? Où sont les vestiaires / toilettes? Où est-ce qu'on peut manger / acheter des souvenirs?* Recycling of directions (*près de / à gauche*, etc.)	*Est-ce que...? Où est-ce que...? Qu'est-ce que...?*	Using new language creatively	1 a, c, d, g, h, i, j, k 2 a, d, e, g, j, l 3 f 4 a	BCE
H	**Point Langue Atelier**	Recycling of plans for a day out	*Est-ce que...? Où est-ce que...? Qu'est-ce que...?*	Applying a pattern Learning through song and games	1 c, d, g, h, i 2 d, e, f 3 a, f	B
I	**Qu'est-ce que tu vas acheter?** Buying souvenirs	*Qu'est-ce que tu vas acheter? Je cherche... / Vous avez... un badge / un porte-clés / un livre sur l'Afrique / des autocollants / des cartes postales? C'est combien? Il n'y a pas de badges / d'autocollants.* Recycling of personal possessions and prices	*Il n'y a pas + de / d'*	Selecting the correct translation when looking up English words	1 a, c, d, g, h, i 2 a, d, e, g, k, n 3 c, d, f, g	C
J	**A Paris en métro** Travelling on the underground	*C'est quelle station / direction pour...? C'est... C'est direct? Il faut changer? Il faut changer à... Un ticket / carnet, s'il vous plaît.*	Impersonal verbs (*il faut / on doit*) + infinitive	Answering listening comprehension questions	1 a, c, d, g, h 2 a, b, d, e, g, l 3 f 4 a	C
K	**Point Langue Atelier**	Recycling of visits to a museum and classroom routine	Verb + infinitive	Applying a pattern Preparing yourself for listening tasks Using context as an aid to understanding	1 g, i 2 a, j, k, l 3 d, e, f 4 a	ABCE
L	**On révise**	Revision of Units 3–4			1 a, c, d, f 2 a, d, e, g, h, i, k 3 g	

IT Opportunities

CORE ACTIVITIES

Text manipulation

Spreads A–D

Produce a model letter in which a young person is inviting a friend to go out. The text could resemble the one set out below:

Cher Paul,
Qu'est-ce qu'on va faire ce weekend?
Samedi on va à Paris?
On pourrait visiter la tour Eiffel le matin et aller au zoo l'après-midi. J'aimerais aussi faire du shopping, aller au musée du Sport et manger au restaurant.
On va à Paris en train ou en car? Le train, c'est plus confortable et plus rapide; mais le car, c'est moins cher. Je préfère le car.
Et dimanche matin, on va au bowling ou à la patinoire? Tu peux choisir. Ensuite on pourrait déjeuner dans le parc, et le soir, à sept heures et demie, on pourrait aller au cinéma ou au café avec tes sœurs et ton frère.

Encourage pupils to identify points of language which add to the quality of the text (e.g. use of expressions of time, such as *le matin, l'après-midi, dimanche matin, le soir, samedi, ensuite*). This should help them to emulate the model text by producing a similar letter of their own.

Word processing – guided writing (i)

Spread I

Create and save a shopping list in which inappropriate presents are chosen for different people, e.g. *pour mon frère – un torchon à vaisselle; pour ma grand-mère – une cravate*. The list could include new items that pupils look up in a dictionary, as well as the presents and souvenirs from pages 90 and 91.

Presentation

Spread B

Pupils choose a favourite form of transport. They then make a presentation (leaflet, brochure, poster, audio or video advertisement, multi-media display) expressing their preference and giving reasons (e.g. *Je préfère voyager en train. C'est rapide et pratique.*).

ADDITIONAL ACTIVITIES

Word processing – extended writing (i)

Spreads A–D

Create and save a simple text, in the form of an invitation, such as the one below:

On va en ville? On va voyager en train.
On pourrait aller aux magasins de sport.
Je vais acheter des baskets.
On pourrait aller au centre de loisirs.
On pourrait manger au café.

Pupils develop the text by inserting words and phrases found in the notes and texts in pages 74–80, for example:

On va en ville samedi avec Sylvie?
On va voyager en train parce que c'est rapide et pratique. D'abord on pourrait aller à la bibliothèque et aux magasins de sport.
Je vais acheter des baskets pour l'anniversaire de mon frère.

Word processing – extended writing (ii)

Spread E

Pupils expand on the notes *Paris Touristes* to describe the opening times of the different attractions in continuous prose, e.g.

Le musée du Sport, c'est ouvert de neuf heures et demie à midi et demi, et de quatorze heures à dix-sept heures, sauf le mercredi et le dimanche.

The Internet

Major French tourist attractions

Type 'Disneyland Paris' and 'Futuroscope' into a search engine. Your search will give you access to unofficial as well as the official sites (currently listed as *www.disneylandparis.com/disney/smain.html* and *www.actufax.com/futuroscope.html*).

Copymasters

The *présentation* and the *grilles* copymasters should be used as indicated.
The other copymasters (worksheets and vocabulary lists) should be used with or after the spread indicated.

Pupil's Book Spread	Corresponding Copymaster
A	18–19 *Glossaire; Grilles 5*
B	*Grilles 5; Grilles 6*
C	3–4 *On lit*
D	5 *Grammaire*
E	6–7 *On écrit*
F	1 *Présentation*
G	2 *Présentation; 8–9 On écoute*
H	10 *Grammaire; 11 Que sais-tu?; 12 On s'amuse;*
I	13 *Plaisir de lire; Grilles 5*
J	14–15 *On parle*
K	16 *Grammaire; 17 Que sais-tu?*
L	–

Notes to accompany Copymasters (CMs)

Feuille 1–2
Presentation Sheets to teach vocabulary connected with French money, tickets and museum visits.

Feuille 3–4 On lit
These two copymasters provide additional reading practice on transport, museum visits and outdoor activities on a day out.

Feuille 3 ♦
Make sure pupils understand that there are no right or wrong answers.

Feuille 4 ♣
Answers
Ex 1: **1** Sylvain **2** Gilles **3** Marianne **4** Ismaël
   5 Justine **6** Marianne **7** Sylvain
Ex 2: **a** Justine **b** Sylvain **c** Gilles **d** Ismaël
   e Marianne **f** Justine

Feuille 5 Grammaire
This CM offers additional practice of *au / à la / à l'/ aux* and encourages pupils to write longer sentences.

Extra – For practice on speaking and on matching listening and reading sources, ask pupils to read out some of their sentences. The other pupils should scan their sentences to see if they wrote identical ones.

Feuilles 6–7 On écrit
These two copymasters provide additional writing practice on Spread E. They can easily be used concurrently. ♣ Ask pupils to go through the CM 7 rubrics on their own while you go through the CM 6 rubrics with the other pupils. You can then check the CM 7 rubrics are clear to pupils.

Feuille 6 ♦
For both tasks, refer pupils back to the key on page 83 if necessary.
Answers
Ex 1: *Le centre sportif: jours / ouvre / lundi matin*
Le club des jeunes: ouvert, sauf / samedi, dimanche / fermé
La salle multi-loisirs (sample answer): *C'est ouvert tous les jours sauf le lundi* (or: *C'est fermé le lundi*). / *En semaine, c'est fermé le matin. / Le soir, ça ferme à 21h30.*

Feuille 7 ♣
Set a minimum or a maximum number of words. Allow dictionary use, but within limits: explain you will be looking essentially for maximum reuse of familiar language, and tell pupils why (good for memory, saves time, flexible use of 'old' language in new contexts).

Feuilles 8–9 On écoute
These two CMs provide additional listening practice on topic 2.

Feuille 8 ♦
Ex 1 – Pupils only need the cassette for sections A and B.

Section A
1 *Je voudrais changer un billet de 200f, s'il vous plaît.*
2 *Je voudrais changer un billet de 50f, s'il vous plaît.*
3 *Je voudrais changer une pièce de 20f, s'il vous plaît.*
4 *Je voudrais changer une pièce de 5f, s'il vous plaît.*
5 *Je voudrais changer une pièce de 50 centimes, s'il vous plaît.*

Section B
1 *Je voudrais changer un billet de 200f en billets de 100f, s'il vous plaît.*
2 *Je voudrais changer un billet de 50f en pièces de 10f, s'il vous plaît.*
3 *Je voudrais changer une pièce de 20f en pièces de 5f, s'il vous plaît.*
4 *Je voudrais changer une pièce de 5f en pièces de 1f, s'il vous plaît.*
5 *Je voudrais changer une pièce de 50 centimes en pièces de 10 centimes, s'il vous plaît.*

Answers
Section A: **1** b **2** e **3** d **4** f **5** c
Section B: **1** c **2** b **3** f **4** a **5** e
Section C: **1** *billet de 200f → deux billets de 100f*
2 *billet de 50f → cinq pièces de 10f* **3** *pièce de 20f → quatre pièces de 5f* **4** *pièce de cinq francs → cinq pièces de 1f* **5** *pièces de 50c → cinq pièces de dix centimes*
Argent de Danielle Désordre: c

Ex 2

– *Ici, le musée du Jouet. Allô!*
– *Allô! Bonjour madame. Le musée ouvre à quelle heure le matin?*
– *Le matin, ça ouvre à 9h30 (neuf heures trente)*
– *9h30*
– *Et l'après-midi?*
– *Ça ouvre à 14 h et ça ferme à 17h.*
– *17h?*
– *Oui, 17h.*
– *C'est ouvert tous les jours?*
– *Non, c'est fermé le lundi.*
– *On peut manger?*
– *Il y a une cafétéria.*
– *Vous avez un tarif groupes?*
– *Pour les groupes? Oui, c'est moins cher.*
– *Et vous avez un tarif enfants?*
– *Ah... euh... les adultes et les enfants, c'est 25f.*

Answers
9h30   17h   lundi   OUI   OUI   NON

Feuille 9 ♣
Ex 1 – Ask pupils to write in note form.

1 – *Tu as 10f en pièces de 1f?*
– *10f en pièces de 2f? C'est pour quoi?*
– *C'est pour les vestiaires.*
– *Attends... oui, mais j'ai seulement quatre pièces.*
2 – *Tu as 20f en pièces de 5f?*
– *20f en pièces de 5f?*
– *Oui, c'est pour la machine à boissons.*
– *Ah... j'ai seulement des pièces de 10f.*

3 – Dis, j'ai 100f. Tu as de la monnaie?
 – C'est pour quoi?
 – C'est pour la caisse. L'employé n'a pas de monnaie à la caisse.
 – Qu'est-ce que tu veux?
 – Deux billets de 50f.
 – Non, mais demande à la prof de géographie.

4 – Pardon, vous avez de la monnaie, s'il vous plaît?
 – Ça dépend. Qu'est-ce que c'est?
 – J'ai un billet de 20f et je voudrais des pièces de 2f. C'est pour le téléphone. J'ai oublié ma télécarte.
 – 5 pièces de 20f et une pièce de 10f, ça va?
 – Oui, ça va. Merci!

5 – Pardon monsieur, vous pouvez me changer des pièces?
 – Qu'est-ce que vous avez?
 – J'ai cinq pièces de 20f.
 – Et qu'est-ce que vous voulez?
 – Je voudrais un billet de 100f. Mon porte-monnaie est trop petit!
 – Ah, oui, d'accord. Moi, je préfère la monnaie pour la caisse.

6 – Tu as de la monnaie? J'ai seulement une pièce de 5f.
 – Une pièce de 5f? Et qu'est-ce que tu veux?
 – Des pièces de 1f ou des pièces de 2f.
 – C'est pour quoi faire?
 – C'est pour Julien. Chaque personne va donner 2f, et Julien va acheter une maxi boîte de chocolats pour la classe au magasin du musée.
 – Ah, ben d'accord. Moi aussi!

Answers
1 *10f Pièces de 2f Vestiaires*
 Non: a seulement 4 pièces
2 *20f Pièces de 5f Machine à boissons*
 Non: a seulement des pièces de 10f
3 *100f Deux billets de 50f Caisse*
 Demande à la prof de géo
4 *20f Pièces de 2f Téléphone Oublié sa télécarte*
5 *Cinq pièces de 20f Un billet de 100f Porte-monnaie trop petit Oui: préfère monnaie*
6 *Une pièce de 5f Pièces de 5f ou 2f Pour Julien (chocolats pour la classe) Oui*

Ex 2 – To integrate speaking practice into the task, pupils can work in pairs. They listen to the cassette once individually and compare their notes. They then listen again to check and complete their information, before comparing again and preparing a poster together.

 – Ici le musée du Jouet. Allô!
 – Allô, oui, bonjour madame, euh... je voudrais des renseignements...
 – Oui, monsieur. Je vous écoute.
 – Le... le musée est ouvert tous les jours?
 – Eh bien c'est ouvert, euh... tous les jours sauf le lundi et le jour de Noël.
 – Vous êtes fermé le lundi.
 – Oui, c'est ça. Et à Noël.
 – Et... les autres jours, euh... vous êtes ouverts toute la journée?

 – Alors, c'est ouvert de 9h30 à midi, puis... euh... de 14h... à 17h!
 – 9h30 à midi... C'est fermé pour le déjeuner?
 – Oui, de midi à 14h. Et le soir ça ferme à 17h.
 – D'accord... Et... euh... vous avez des tarifs spéciaux?
 – Des tarifs spéciaux?
 – Oui, euh... pour les groupes... ou pour les enfants.
 – Ah, pour les groupes c'est moins cher, mais pour les adultes et les enfants, c'est 25f.
 – Il n'y a pas de tarif spécial pour les enfants?
 – Non, monsieur!
 – Et... il y a... on peut manger au musée?
 – Il y a une petite cafétéria.
 – Bon, eh bien, euh... c'est tout. Merci madame!
 – De rien, monsieur.

Answers
Key information: *Ouvert tous les jours sauf lundi et Noël 9h30–12h; 14h–17h Tarif groupes Tarif adultes et enfants: 25f Cafétéria*

Feuille 10 Grammaire
This CM provides additional practice on the *Point Langue* question forms.

Ex 1
Answers
1 *Est-ce que tu manges beaucoup le matin?* 2 *Où est-ce que tu manges le matin?* 3 *Qu'est-ce que tu manges?* 4 *Est-ce que tu vas au collège en bus?* 5 *Où est-ce que tu mets ton vélo?* 6 *Qu'est-ce que tu préfères: le vélo ou le bus?* 7 *Est-ce que tu sors le mercredi?* 8 *Qu'est-ce que tu fais le jeudi soir?* 9 *Où est-ce que tu vas exactement?*

Ex 2 – ♣ You can add a competitive edge for group or whole-class practice. For each question, ask pupils in turn to generate as many different answers as possible with only five seconds' thinking time. Pupils who exceed the time limit or give an answer already used are out of the game.

Feuille 11 Que sais-tu?
This CM offers some revision of topics 1 and 2.

Ex 1

1 – On va où?
 – D'abord, on va au musée des trains. A neuf heures et demie. Ça t'intéresse?
 – Ah, oui, d'accord! Et ensuite?
 – Ensuite, on va déjeuner dans le parc.
 – Et l'après-midi, on pourrait rester au parc?
 – D'accord. Mais ensuite, à 3h, je dois faire du shopping.
 – Et finalement?
 – Eh bien, le train est à six heures et quart.

2 – Qu'est-ce qu'on va faire le matin?
  – D'abord, on va faire du bateau.
  – A quelle heure?
  – Vers dix heures. Ensuite, on pourrait faire du shopping.
  – Et ensuite, on va déjeuner où?
  – On va déjeuner dans un café vers une heure et demie.
  – Une heure et demie!
  – Et oui! Mais l'après-midi, on va aller au zoo.
  – Tout l'après-midi?
  – Ah, oui. Et finalement, on va rentrer à la maison... à... sept heures et demie?
3 – Véronique, c'est ton anniversaire, tu choisis!
  – Bon, alors, le matin... d'abord, on peut aller au zoo, non?
  – Oui, bonne idée.
  – Oh, moi, je voudrais faire du shopping!
  – Il y a un magasin au zoo. Donc, ensuite, on pourrait aller au magasin?
  – Bon, et pour déjeuner?
  – Alors, pour déjeuner, je voudrais bien aller dans une cafétéria. On pourrait déjeuner à une heure?
  – Et l'après-midi?
  – D'abord, on pourrait visiter le musée des jouets, et le soir, à huit heures on va tous au centre sportif!

Answers
A train (6h15) **B** bateau (10h00) **C** café (1h30)
D zoo **E** zoo / ✗ **F** zoo **G** cafétéria (1h00)
H centre sportif (8h00)

Ex 2 – After a while, pupil **A** can say a time and pupil **B** name the programme from memory.

Ex 3 – Reuse CM1 to remind pupils about the notes and coins that exist.

Feuille 12 On s'amuse
This Jeu de familles is played like Happy Families, in groups of three to five players. Photocopy the CM onto cards which can be laminated for regular use. The cards can be enlarged for easier handling. Each pupil needs a copy of the wordlist to be able to ask for the correct cards in French. For example:

Au musée du Cinéma, je voudrais la lanterne magique.

Preparation – All the words are either familiar words or cognates/near cognates. Do some pronunciation practice to reinforce all the work done until now on pronunciation patterns and to highlight the fact that words may look the same in French and in English but rarely sound the same.

Feuille 13 Plaisir de lire
This CM provides advice for making attractive wrapping paper for special occasions.

Extra – Ask pupils to use one of the suggestions at home and show you the result. Ask them to devise a suggestion of their own, using dictionaries and recycling some of the words and phrases used on the CM.
Answers
1 C a **2** A d **3** E c **4** D b **5** B e

Feuille 14–15 On parle
These two CMs provide additional speaking practice about going on a school trip, buying souvenirs and travelling on the underground.

Feuille 14 ♦
Ex 1 – Set a context: Imaginez: on fait un voyage scolaire. On visite un musée et on va dans un magasin de souvenirs.

Ex 2 – Pupils should practise until they can do Dialogue B without referring back to Dialogue A at all.

Feuille 15 ♣
The aim here is to practise semi-improvisation from notes. It is therefore important for pupils to follow the instructions to the letter. Allow for sufficient preparation time.

Feuille 16 Grammaire
This CM complements the work of **Point Langue** on verbs.

Ex 1 ♦ – Encourage pupils to work collaboratively.

Ex 2 ♦ / ♣ **Extra** – Pupils can turn this paragraph into a rap, with actions to reinforce meaning.
Answers
articuler (to articulate) avaler (to swallow) choisir (to choose) réviser (to revise) attendre (to wait) courir (to run) s'entraîner (to train)

Ex 3
Rap text provided in Teacher's Resource File, page 87.
Answers
ouvrir (to open) accueillir (to welcome) essayer (to try) souhaiter (to wish, hope) recevoir (to receive) répondre (to answer, reply) nettoyer (to clean) casser (to break) découvrir (to discover)

Feuille 17 Que sais-tu?
This CM offers some revision of topic 3 on buying souvenirs and travelling by métro.

Ex 1
Answer
picture 3

Ex 2
Answers
1 Trocadéro **2** Clichy **3** Roosevelt **4** Stalingrad
5 Sèvres

A Qu'est-ce qu'on peut faire?

pp 74–75

Objective
Discussing what to do on a day out

Resources
Cassette for BD and Ex 1 and 4
Flashcards 56–61
Grilles 5 CM (optional for Ex 4)
CM 18–19 for reference throughout Unit 4

Key language
Qu'est-ce qu'on peut / pourrait faire?
On peut / On pourrait / Vous pouvez /

J'aimerais bien... visiter un musée / visiter la tour Eiffel / faire du shopping / faire du bateau / aller au zoo / aller au parc / aller à Disneyland.
Recycling of leisure activities and time phrases (*matin*, etc.)

Grammar
Aller + au / à la / à l' / aux
Recycling of verb + infinitive

Language learning strategies
Avoiding repetition in written work

Ways in
The class are making plans for a science trip to Paris. Grégory is the main character. This is how you could introduce the unit: *La classe de Thierry, Ludivine et Julien va visiter Paris pour un projet en sciences. Ils ont beaucoup d'idées pour la visite. Grégory a des idées... différentes.*

Useful addresses:

Office de Tourisme de Paris
127 Avenue des Champs-Elysées
75008 PARIS
tél. 010 33 1 47 23 61 72

Musée de l'Homme
Place du Trocadéro
75016 PARIS
tél. 010 33 1 45 92 46 83

CIDJ (Centre d'Info. et de Documentation de la Jeunesse)
101 Quai Branly
75015 PARIS
tél. 010 33 1 45 66 40 20

Information Villette
Maison de la Villette
30 avenue Corentin-Cariou
75019 PARIS
tél. 010 33 1 40 03 75 03

Pupils read the BD while they listen to the cassette. (BD tapescript – see Pupil's Book.)

Use the Flashcards (see Teacher's Book introduction page 9) to teach the new activities, using *on peut*.

1

Preparation – Warn pupils that they will not necessarily hear *oui / non*. They should make deductions from the opinions or the intonation.

COUNTER

> 1 – *On peut aller dans un parc?*
>   – *Dans un parc? Pour déjeuner, oui, d'accord.*
>
> 2 – *On peut faire du shopping?*
>   – *Du shopping? Et les sciences? Et ton projet?*
>
> 3 – *On pourrait aller au zoo.*
>   – *Le zoo? Les animaux, la biologie... Oui... peut-être. Bonne idée!*
>
> 4 – *On peut visiter un musée?*
>   – *Un musée de sciences, oui, d'accord. C'est intéressant.*
>
> 5 – *Moi, j'aimerais bien aller à Disneyland.*
>   – *Disneyland?*
>   – *Ben... oui, c'est amusant, non?*
>   – *Amusant, oui, mais pour le projet, non!*
>
> 6 – *On va voir la Tour Eiffel?*
>   – *La Tour Eiffel? Pour les sciences? La physique? Oui, peut-être. C'est une bonne idée!*
>
> 7 – *Moi, j'aimerais bien faire du bateau.*
>   – *Faire du bateau? Mais enfin!*
>   – *Ben quoi?*
>   – *On va à Paris pour travailler!*

Answers
1 e, *oui* 2 a, *non* 3 d, *oui* 4 c, *oui* 5 b, *non*
6 f, *oui* 7 g, *non*

2

To increase motivation, ask pupils to keep track of how many times they guess right in one go only: *Tu es télépathe?* ♣ Pupils can use *On peut / On pourrait / J'aimerais bien* as they prefer.

3

Pupils should work without dictionaries, focusing on familiar language and cognates.

Answers

♦ 1 *aller au parc* 2 *visiter la tour Eiffel* 3 *faire du bateau* 4 *aller au zoo* 5 *faire du shopping* 6 *aller à Disneyland* 7 *visiter un musée*

♣ 1 *Non, avec Nadège.* 2 *Non, chez le dentiste.* 3 *Non, il voudrait déjeuner.* 4 *A midi.* 5 *Non, avec Nadège.* 6 *Nadège.* 7 *Non, chez Marc, dans une semaine.*

4

A grid is provided on CM.

Preparation – Revise the days of the week if necessary. Warn pupils that some of the activities are recycled from previous units. Also tell them that they will sometimes hear *Quand?* before the activity. Improvise a few sentences using the structures from the tapescript to make sure pupils understand the difference between *Définitif*, *Suggestion* and *Question*.

COUNTER

> 1 – *Allô? C'est Guillaume. On va au parc samedi matin?*
>
> 2 – *Dimanche après-midi? Ah... je vais visiter un musée avec ma sœur.*
>
> 3 – *On pourrait faire du shopping, jeudi, par exemple.*
>
> 4 – *Alors, jeudi soir... zut! Je dois faire mes devoirs.*
>
> 5 – *Dimanche matin? Moi, je vais faire du bateau avec mes parents.*
>
> 6 – *Tu vas au zoo avec moi mercredi?*
>
> 7 – *J'aimerais bien regarder le film policier ce soir.*
>
> 8 – *Tu vas acheter les cadeaux lundi? Je peux aller en ville avec toi?*

Answers
1 *parc, samedi matin, question* 2 *musée, dimanche après-midi, définitif* 3 *shopping, jeudi, suggestion* 4 *devoirs, jeudi, définitif* 5 *bateau, dimanche matin, définitif* 6 *zoo, mercredi, question* 7 *film policier, ce soir, suggestion* 8 *acheter cadeaux, lundi, question*

5

Brainstorm for ideas, recycling as much familiar language as possible: *faire de la natation, jouer au tennis,* etc. Weaker pupils can produce one-word activities instead of phrases with verbs.

B En car ou en train? pp 76–77

Objective
Discussing how to travel

Resources
Cassette for BD and Ex 1 and 3
Flashcards 62–66
Grilles 5 CM (optional for Ex 2)
Grilles 6 CM (optional for Ex 3)
Dictionaries for Ex 5
OHT optional for Ex 6

Key language
Je vais aller à Paris. On va voyager comment?
On va / On peut / On pourrait voyager en... avion / train / bus / car / vélo / voiture.
C'est plus / moins... confortable / pratique / rapide. C'est trop cher.

Grammar
Recycling of verb + infinitive

Language learning strategies
Pronunciation: *r*
Using context as an aid to understanding

Ways in
Some members of the class are busy discussing how to travel to Paris. Grégory is not being very realistic. This is how you could introduce the spread, using gestures to facilitate communication:
La classe de Grégory va aller à Paris... en vélo? en train? en avion?... Je ne sais pas... .

Introduce the means of transport with the Flashcards (see Teacher's Book introduction page 9). Then present the three new adjectives and recycle *cher / trop cher.*

Pupils then read the BD while they listen to the cassette. For practice in speed reading, say some words and ask pupils to say as quickly as possible whether they are in the text. For example: *train, confortable, vélo, avion, Julien, fatigant, car, Grégory, rapide,* etc.
(BD tapescript – see Pupil's Book.)

1

Items 5–9 are longer. ♦ To help pupils, you can put your hand up when they are about to hear the means of transport. Items 6 and 7 contain distractors.

1	*Je préfère voyager en train.*
2	*J'adore voyager en avion!*
3	*Moi, j'aime bien voyager en voiture.*
4	*Voyager en car, c'est bien, c'est sympa.*
5	*J'aime beaucoup le vélo. Je fais du cyclisme le week-end.*
6	*Pour voyager, euh... En général, je voyage en bus, quand je vais en ville ou chez ma grand-mère.*
7	*Le train? Ah, non! Je préfère l'avion. L'avion, c'est plus amusant!*
8	*J'aime bien le train, mais je préfère la voiture. On peut regarder la campagne.*
9	*Oh, euh... le vélo, c'est super! Et c'est bien pour la protection de l'environnement.*
10	*Moi, mon père a une voiture turbo. Je vais au collège en voiture. J'adore ça.*

Answers
1 c   **2** b   3 e   **4** d   **5** f   6 a   **7** b   8 e   9 f   **10** e

2

A grid is provided on CM.

If you do not want all pupils to walk around the class, this can be done in groups instead. You can then collate the results for the whole class.

3

A grid is provided on CM.

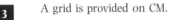

Preparation – Warn pupils that the items are increasingly long and difficult. There are a few distractors. Before pupils listen to item 7, brainstorm for predictions.

1	– *On va en ville en bus? C'est moins cher.*
2	– *On va à Paris en train? C'est plus rapide.*
3	– *J'aimerais bien aller en Italie en avion. C'est plus pratique.*
4	– *On peut aller à la mer en train.*
	– *En train ou en car.*
	– *Oui, c'est vrai.*
	– *On y va en car! C'est plus confortable.*
	– *D'accord!*
5	– *Bon, on peut voyager en train ou en avion.*
	– *L'avion? C'est trop cher!*
	– *Oui, mais c'est plus rapide.*
	– *D'accord, on voyage en avion!*
6	– *Bon, alors, tu veux aller à Boulogne?*
	– *Ouais, ouais, à Boulogne. J'aimerais bien visiter.*
	– *Alors, on va voyager comment?*
	– *Ben, je ne sais pas, euh...*
	– *Tu as une idée?*
	– *On pourrait aller à Boulogne en car?*
	– *Oui, euh... mais... c'est confortable, le car?*
	– *Non, pas vraiment.*
	– *Et voyager en car, c'est long. Trois ou quatre heures.*
	– *Alors on y va en train?*
	– *Oh, oui! C'est plus confortable.*
7	– *Bon, alors, on va voyager comment pour aller au concert? Tu as une idée, Catherine?*
	– *Ben... je ne sais pas, Nicolas... euh... en bus?*
	– *Mais non, c'est impossible. Il n'y a pas de bus! Le concert, c'est à 15 kilomètres de la ville!*
	– *Ben... alors... euh... il y a des cars?*
	– *Oui, mais... le soir, c'est impossible.*
	– *Alors, on pourrait prendre un taxi?*
	– *Un taxi? Mais enfin! C'est trop cher!*
	– *Alors, écoute, je vais demander à mes parents.*
	– *Pourquoi?*
	– *Ben, ils ont une voiture.*

Answers

1 *bus, moins cher*   **2** *train, plus rapide*   **3** *avion, plus pratique*   **4** *car, plus confortable*   **5** *avion, plus rapide*
6 *train, plus confortable*
♣ **7** a *bus,* b *15,* c *car,* d *soir,* e *trop cher,* f *voiture*

On prononce bien

> *Ecoute:*
>
> en car   en train
>
> *Répète:*
>
> en train   en voiture
>
> c'est cher   c'est super   c'est pratique   c'est rapide

4

Extra – For more reading practice and to enhance the idea of writing for an audience, pupils can read the sentences of more than one other person.

5

♦ **Preparation** – Ask pupils to do as much as they can through awareness of cognates before they start using dictionaries.
♣ Pupils must first attempt the task without help. They should only use dictionaries for checking afterwards. Point out that the words are listed in the order in which they appear in the letter.

Answers

♦ *fusée* (rocket)   *hélicoptère* (helicopter)   *parachute* (parachute)   *taxi* (taxi)   *aéroglisseur* (hovercraft)   *camion* (lorry)   *tandem* (tandem)
♣ **1** *un pays*   **2** *la gare*   **3** *à pied*   **4** *avant*   **5** *beaucoup de monde*   **6** *une usine de vêtements*   **7** *employés*

6

Preparation – Put the model dialogue on OHT for some practice in pronunciation, intonation and memorising.

C Qu'est-ce qu'on va faire?

pp 78–79

Objective
Finalising detailed plans for a day out

Resources
Cassette for BD and Ex 2, 4 and 6
Clock and/or Unit 3 CM 2 for Ex 2
CM 3 and 4

Key language
Qu'est-ce qu'on va faire? / A quelle heure? / Et ensuite?

D'abord / Ensuite / Finalement / A deux heures, on va (pourrait)...
D'accord? / Ça t'intéresse? Oui, d'accord. ? Oh, non, pas vraiment.
Recycling of the 12-hour clock, time phrases and leisure
activities

Grammar
Recycling of verb + infinitive

Language learning strategies
Using the textbook for reference

Ways in
The science teacher briefs the class about the trip to
Paris. This is how you could introduce the spread:
*Le prof de science donne l'information nécessaire sur le
voyage à Paris.*

1 Pupils read the BD while they listen to the cassette.
Ask if they can work out the meaning of *d'abord /
ensuite / finalement*. If necessary, give examples:
D'abord, on entre dans la classe. Ensuite, ...

Point out the similarity between *sept heures quarante*
and *huit heures moins vingt;* and between *huit heures
trente-cinq* and *neuf heures moins vingt-cinq.*
Answers
1 *faux* **2** *vrai* **3** *faux* **4** *vrai*

2 **Preparation** – Revise the time, using a clock or Unit 3
CM 2. Practise using *quarante* for *moins vingt*, etc. but
still using the hours 1–12 only.

COUNTER

1 – *On doit arriver au collège à quelle heure le
matin?*
– *Vous devez arriver à 7h40.*
2 – *Le bus pour la gare, le matin, c'est à quelle
heure?*
– *Le bus? C'est à 7h50.*
3 – *Le train, c'est à quelle heure le matin?*
– *Le train, c'est à 8h44.*
4 – *On arrive à Paris à quelle heure?*
– *On arrive à Paris à 9h33.*
5 – *La visite au musée de l'Homme, c'est à quelle
heure?*
– *La visite au musée? C'est à 10h15.*
6 – *On va déjeuner à quelle heure?*
– *On va déjeuner vers... 12h30.*
7 – *Le train, le soir, c'est à quelle heure?*
– *Le soir, c'est à 7h55.*
8 – *On va arriver à Chartres à quelle heure le soir?*
– *On va arriver le soir à 8h48.*

Answers
1 g, *7h40* **2** e, *7h50* **3** h, *8h44* **4** a, *9h33*
5 c, *10h15* **6** f, *12h30* **7** d, *7h55* **8** b, *8h48*

3 **Extra** – For extra speaking practice, pupils check their
notes are correct by reporting back to their partners,
using *On va aller... / On va faire...*

4 Pupils must do the reading task and write down the
names of the four museums before listening to the
cassette.

COUNTER

– *Je vais au musée du Sport cet après-midi. Ça
t'intéresse?*
– *On va au musée de la Préhistoire dimanche. Ça
t'intéresse?*
– *Nous allons visiter le musée Picasso ce week-
end. Ça t'intéresse?*
– *On pourrait visiter le musée de l'Homme samedi
matin. Ça t'intéresse?*
– *Bon, c'est décidé, on va au musée de Radio-
France ce matin. Ça t'intéresse?*
– *Il y a une exposition spéciale au musée de la
Marine. Ça t'intéresse?*
– *J'aimerais bien voir le musée du Cinéma. Ça
t'intéresse?*
– *Moi, j'aimerais mieux le musée des Transports.
Ça t'intéresse?*
– *Qu'est-ce qu'on va faire?... On pourrait visiter le
musée de l'Histoire de France. Ça t'intéresse?*
– *Et le musée du Cheval? J'aimerais bien le visiter.
Ça t'intéresse?*

Answers
1 f **2** d **3** g **4** h **5** e **6** a **7** b **8** c

5 **Preparation** – Point out the importance of link
phrases to make written work more interesting and
easy to follow.

6 Pupils can use the cassette as a model, and then make
up their own dialogue. Or they can use the cassette for
gap-filling, then make up their own dialogue.

COUNTER

– *Qu'est-ce qu'on va faire ce week-end?*
– *Vendredi soir il y a une fête au collège. Ça
t'intéresse?*
– *Ah oui? A quelle heure?*
– *A huit heures trente.*
– *Oui, ça m'intéresse. Et samedi matin? On
pourrait aller à la patinoire?*
– *Samedi matin? Ah non..., je dois aller au
supermarché avec mon père. On va à la patinoire
samedi après-midi?*
– *Oui, d'accord, à deux heures? Et samedi matin,
je peux aller au centre sportif avec Jérémy.*
– *Et dimanche? Qu'est-ce qu'on va faire? On va au
musée des Trains dimanche après-midi?*
– *Euh non..., je dois rester chez moi. Ma grand-
mère arrive dimanche.*

Answers
*une fête 8h30 aller à la patinoire aller au
supermarché va 2h aller au centre sportif Jérémy
va au musée des Trains rester chez moi*

D Point Langue / Atelier

Resources	Grammar
CM 5	*Aller + au / à la / à l' / aux*

Key language
Recycling of making plans for the weekend

Language learning strategies
Applying a pattern
Using context and key words as an
aid to understanding

Point Langue

This page reinforces the work of spread A with
additional practice on *au / à la / à l' / aux*.

1 **Answers**
♦ **1** *au* **2** *à la* **3** *au* **4** *aux* **5** *à l'* **6** *au* **7** *à la*

Atelier

1 Pupils should work without dictionaries.

Extra – To enhance awareness of context and
cognates – and again without dictionaries – pupils can
match up some French words drawn from the adverts
with their English equivalents. For example:
• children / lollipops / dolls / football shirts / students /
jam biscuits / a (hair) cut
• *biscuits à la confiture / étudiants / enfants / une coupe /
des maillots de foot / des sucettes / des poupées*
Answers
1 *Berthillon* **2** *Maison Citerne* **3** *Nature et Découvertes*
4 *La Boutique du Gardien de But* **5** *Françoise Marcay*
6 *Le Temps Libre* **7** *Le Temps Libre*

2 Brainstorm for ideas to help less imaginative pupils.
Allow dictionary use, but impose a limit and remind
pupils that they should use dictionaries for looking up
individual words, not whole structures. More able
pupils may, however, wish to produce full sentences, in
which case they should refer back to Ex 1 for ideas.
Pupils can also look back to Ex 1 for ideas on
addresses.

E Ça ouvre à quelle heure?

pp 82–83

Objective
Enquiring about opening hours

Resources
Cassette for BD and Ex 2 and 4
Clock and/or Unit 3 CM 2 for Ex 2
OHT (optional for Ex 6)
CM 6 and 7
Dictionaries for CM 7

Key language
Le musée, ça ouvre / ferme à quelle heure le matin / l'après-midi / le soir?
Ça ouvre / ferme à + 24-hour clock
La cathédrale, c'est ouvert le lundi?
C'est ouvert / fermé de... à..., sauf le...
Recycling of the time, time phrases and days of the week

Language learning strategies
Awareness of negatives as a clue to understanding
Giving a short presentation

Ways in
The class are on the train on their way to Paris. This leads to discussion on train departure times – using the 24-hour clock – and opening hours of Paris sights. The new language is presented as an introduction to Ex 2 and Ex 3 (see notes below).

You can introduce this spread like this: *Aujourd'hui, c'est le voyage à Paris. Pour commencer, on va écouter Grégory et Julien.*

Pupils read the BD while they listen to the cassette. Ask questions to generate language not actually provided in the BD and to reinforce understanding of question patterns. For example:
– *Où est Grégory?*
– *Il est tout seul?*
– *Qui voyage aussi avec Julien et Grégory?*
– *Qui est près de la fenêtre?*
– *Le train va où?*
– *Est-ce que c'est l'après-midi?*
– *Imaginez: pourquoi est-ce que Grégory mange?*
(BD tapescript – see Pupil's Book.)

1

Answers
All answers would be acceptable except for **c**.

2

COUNTER

Preparation – Use a clock and/or Unit 3 CM 2 for practice using the 24-hour clock.

> **1** – *Le train est à neuf heures trente-huit.*
> **2** – *Le train est à onze heures vingt-sept.*
> **3** – *Le train pour Le Mans? C'est à douze heures cinquante.*
> **4** – *Le train pour Vendôme, s'il vous plaît?*
> – *C'est à quinze heures dix-huit.*
> **5** – *Le train pour Fougères, s'il vous plaît?*
> – *Il part à... dix-sept heures quarante.*
> **6** – *Le train pour Versailles, s'il vous plaît?*
> – *Il part à seize heures quarante-cinq.*
> **7** – *Alors, le train pour Brest, voyons... il part à seize heures cinquante-cinq.*
> **8** – *Le prochain train pour Limoges, s'il vous plaît?*
> – *Vous avez un train... à... dix-neuf heures quinze.*

Answers
1 *9h38* **2** *11h27* **3** *12h50* **4** *15h18* **5** *17h40*
6 *16h45* **7** *16h55* **8** *19h15*

3

Presentation – Use a few *Paris Touristes* adverts on page 83 and gestures (*ouvert / fermé*) to illustrate the language related to opening/closing times, as indicated in the key.

Preparation – Check that pupils remember the meaning of *t.l.j.*. Ask pupils to pay particular attention to the word *sauf* in the adverts and to negative sentences in 1–10. It is not necessary to understand *été / hiver* (*zoo de Vincennes*) to do the exercise.

Answers
1 *vrai* **2** *faux; c'est fermé le mardi* **3** *vrai* **4** *vrai*
5 *faux* **6** *faux; c'est ouvert de 10h à 19h* **7** *faux; le zoo ouvre avant la tour Eiffel* **8** *faux; c'est ouvert cinq jours par semaine / c'est fermé deux jours par semaine*
9 *vrai* **10** *vrai*

4

COUNTER

Allow plenty of time for reading after listening to each item. With less able pupils, repeat the questions after the cassette if necessary.

> **1** – *La tour Eiffel, c'est ouvert le jeudi?*
> **2** – *Le musée du Sport, c'est ouvert le mercredi?*
> **3** – *On peut visiter la Cathédrale Notre Dame le week-end?*
> **4** – *On peut visiter le zoo de Vincennes tous les jours?*
> **5** – *On peut visiter le musée du Jouet le jour de Noël?*
> **6** – *On peut visiter la tour Eiffel le soir?*
> **7** – *Le château de Versailles ferme à quinze heures en octobre?*
> **8** – *Dites-moi, est-ce qu'on peut visiter le musée du Louvre tous les jours?*
> **9** – *Excusez-moi, s'il vous plaît. Je voudrais visiter la Cité des Sciences. Elle ouvre bien à 10h le matin, n'est-ce pas?*

Answers
1 *oui* **2** *non* **3** *oui* **4** *oui* **5** *non* **6** *oui* **7** *non*
8 *non* **9** *oui*

5

After a while, encourage pupils to practise without looking at the key.

6

You can reproduce the tapecript on OHT if you wish to provide visual and aural input. Most of the message, though, only uses key language except for *attention* and *les jours de fêtes*.

COUNTER

> *On peut visiter la Tour Eiffel tous les jours de 9h30 à 23h. La Cité des Sciences, c'est ouvert de 10h à 18h. Le dimanche, ça ferme à 19h... Le musée du Jouet, c'est ouvert le matin de 9h30 à midi. L'après-midi, c'est ouvert de 14h à 17h30. Attention: c'est fermé le lundi et les jours de fêtes.*

F Vous avez de la monnaie?

pp 84–85

Objective
Asking for change

Resources
Cassette for BD and Ex 2 and 4
CM 1
OHT (see **Ways in** section)

Key language
Tu as / Vous avez de la monnaie / une pièce de...?
J'ai seulement un billet de...

Je voudrais... en pièces / billets de...
Il y a une erreur.
Désolé(e). / Voilà, monsieur / madame / mademoiselle.
Recycling of numbers

Grammar
Recycling of *avoir*

Language learning strategies
Pronunciation: silent letters at the end of words

Ways in
Before the visit at the *musée de l'Homme* starts, Grégory spots a sweet machine. He asks a teacher for change. You can introduce the spread like this, showing some coins to help pupils understand: *La classe est au musée de l'Homme. Grégory voudrait acheter des bonbons. Il cherche de la monnaie.*

Use CM1 and real or fake French coins and notes to introduce French money. After a while, introduce *Tu as / Vous avez une pièce / un billet de...?* Ensure correct pronunciation of *pièces*. Ensure pupils do not mistake *monnaie* for money.

Pupils then read the BD while they listen to the cassette, then move straight onto Ex 1. (BD tapescript – see Pupil's Book.)

1

Extra — Pupils listen to these inaccurate statements about the BD and volunteer to correct them. Do this quickly to keep pupils alert. You can use intonation to indicate which words are wrong each time:
Grégory voudrait acheter des gâteaux.
Grégory parle à ses copains.
La prof écoute la classe.
La prof a un billet.
La prof n'a pas de monnaie.
Grégory veut boire.
Grégory veut une pièce de 10f.
Grégory a cinq billets de 50f.
Answer b

2

Preparation — First rehearse the prices without the cassette. Say the price of an item and offer two alternative items for pupils to choose.

During the exercise, allow sufficient time between each item for pupils to check the prices. You may prefer pupils to complete their answers with the objects afterwards. ♣ Pupils should aim to write the objects without help. ♦ Pupils can be encouraged to do the ♣ task with the help of reference materials.

COUNTER

1 –	*125f.*	7 –	*Ça fait combien?*
2 –	*750f.*		– *139f.*
3 –	*45f50.*		– *Mmm... c'est un peu cher.*
4 –	*58f50.*		
5 –	*Ça fait combien, s'il vous plaît?*	8 –	*Bon, eh bien ça vous fait 579f.*
	– *Ça fait 239f.*	9 –	*Alors attendez, cent... et cinquante francs... Voilà, 150f.*
6 –	*C'est combien, s'il vous plaît?*		
	– *375f.*		

Answers
1 e, *un poster* **2** a, *une veste* **3** c, *des chocolats*
4 h, *des chaussettes* **5** f, *un portefeuille* **6** g, *du papier à lettres* **7** b, *des boucles d'oreille* **8** d, *une montre*
9 i, *un porte-clés*

3

For an extra challenge, ask pupils to respond within a time limit, for example with pupil **A** counting up to 10 in a low voice – in French – while pupil **B** looks for an answer.

On prononce bien

COUNTER

Ecoute et répète:
    un billet   seulement   je voudrais   des pièces
    c'est ouvert   d'abord   d'accord

Preparation – Reuse CM1 to practise:
Je voudrais... en billets / pièces de...

4

COUNTER

1 –	*Je voudrais 50f en pièces de 5f, s'il vous plaît.*
2 –	*Je voudrais 200f en billets de 50f, s'il vous plaît.*
3 –	*Je voudrais 20f en pièces de 1f, s'il vous plaît.*
4 –	*Je voudrais 50c en pièces de 10c, s'il vous plaît.*
5 –	*Je voudrais 10f en pièces de 2f, s'il vous plaît.*
6 –	*J'ai seulement un billet de 50f. Vous avez des pièces de 10f?*
7 –	*J'ai un billet de 100f, et je voudrais de la monnaie. Vous avez des pièces de 10f?*
8 –	*Je voudrais 5f en pièces de 50c, s'il vous plaît.*

Answers
1 f **2** h **3** c **4** e **5** g **6** a **7** d **8** b

5

Preparation – It is worth checking the correct pronunciation of *pièces* once again.

G Au musée

pp 86–87

Objective
Enquiring about facilities at a tourist venue

Resources
Cassette for BD, Ex 1 and 3 and CM 8–9
CM 2, 8 and 9
OHT (see **Ways in** section)
Dictionaries (optional for Ex 5)

Key language
Je voudrais... billets pour adultes / enfants, s'il vous plaît.

Vous avez un tarif groupes / des dépliants?
C'est une visite guidée? / Où est la cafétéria?
Où sont les vestiaires / toilettes?
Où est-ce qu'on peut manger / acheter des souvenirs?
Recycling of directions (*près de / à gauche*, etc.)

Grammar
Est-ce que ...? / Où est-ce que ...? / Qu'est-ce que ...?

Language learning strategies
Using new language creatively

Ways in
The visit at the *musée de l'Homme* is about to start. You can introduce the spread like this: *La classe est au musée de l'Homme avec le guide. Le guide porte un uniforme. La visite va commencer, mais la classe a des questions.*

Pupils read the BD while they listen to the cassette. Use CM2 to present the new language.

1
♦ If the task is too hard, write two key words on the board before pupils listen to each cassette item, for example: *toilettes, cafétéria*.

COUNTER

1 – *Où sont les toilettes, s'il vous plaît?*
2 – *Où est la cafétéria, s'il vous plaît?*
3 – *Deux billets adultes, s'il vous plaît.*
  – *Deux adultes, oui... voilà.*
4 – *Dites-moi, c'est une visite guidée ici?*
  – *Non, non, c'est une visite libre.*
5 – *Dix billets pour enfants?*
  – *Oui. Je voudrais le tarif groupes, s'il vous plaît.*
6 – *Vous avez des dépliants, s'il vous plaît? Je fais un projet pour le collège.*
7 – *Où sont les vestiaires, s'il vous plaît?*
  – *Au fond à gauche.*
  – *On doit payer?*
  – *C'est 2f.*
8 – *Où est-ce qu'on peut acheter les souvenirs, s'il vous plaît.*
  – *Il y a un magasin devant la cafétéria.*
  – *Le magasin ferme pour le déjeuner?*
  – *Non, c'est ouvert de 9h à 17h30.*

Answers
1 c 2 f 3 h 4 b 5 d, *tarif groupes, 10 billets*
6 a, *projet pour le collège* 7 i, *au fond à gauche, 2f*
8 g, *devant la cafétéria, 9h–17h30*

2
Suggest pupils work individually, then check their answers in pairs and try again together if they disagree.

Extra – Pupils can make up a similar task on the *musée des Automates* for a partner to work out.
Answers
*Omar: 10f mère: 20f sœur: 10f frère: 20f
grand-père: 10f   TOTAL: 70f (50% de réduction le lundi!)*

3
Preparation – Give pupils time to have another read of *musée des Automates* on page 87 so as to take in as many facts as possible. First, play the cassette without a pause.

COUNTER
  – *Allô, le musée des Automates?*
  – *Oui, monsieur.*
  – *Bonjour, madame. Je voudrais visiter le musée avec ma famille. C'est ouvert tous les jours?*
  – *Euh... eh bien... tous les jours... sauf le mardi et fêtes.*
  – *C'est combien, les billets?*
  – *Les billets adultes... c'est... 40f. Et... les billets enfants... c'est... 30f.*
  – *Oui...*
  – *C'est moins cher le lundi.*
  – *Ah! Mais... je vais visiter le dimanche. Et... vous avez des réductions pour les retraités?*
  – *Des réductions pour les retraités? Non, monsieur.*
  – *Ah, et... vous avez un magasin de souvenirs?*
  – *Oui, et... c'est très joli!*
  – *Et... on peut manger?*
  – *Il y a aussi un restaurant.*
  – *Merci beaucoup, madame.*
  – *Au revoir, monsieur.*

Answers
Erreurs: Billets enfants: 30f (→ 20f)   Réductions pour les retraités: non (→ oui)   Il y a un restaurant (→ une machine-boissons)

4
Preparation – Discuss telephone routines and conventions with pupils (*Allô! Ici... / Bonjour. Je voudrais visiter le musée...* / Repeating the question to check you understood the question./Recycling of *Oui, bien sûr...*)

Pupils should recycle previous language to make up any additional information requested by their partners: *Où est la machine-boissons? A gauche, devant les vestiaires.*

5
♦ Pupils may prefer to adhere to the *musée des Automates* model and simply change the key information. ♣ Pupils should be encouraged to be more creative. They could, for example, include some whole sentences. Brainstorm on what they could add to the *musée des Automates* model.

6
For a genuine exchange, pupil **A** should ask pupil **B** questions without any knowledge of the leaflet produced by pupil **B** – apart from the nature of the museum. Should pupil **A** ask questions not addressed in pupil **B**'s leaflet, pupil **B** should improvise.

H Point Langue / Atelier

pp 88–89

Resources

Cassette for **Point Langue** Ex 2, **Atelier** Ex 1 and CM 11
CM 10 and 11
CM1 OHT (optional for CM 11 Ex 3)
CM 12, photocopied onto card and cut into individual cards
Dictionaries (optional for **Atelier** Ex 2)

Key language

Recycling of plans for a day out

Grammar

Est-ce que ...? / Où est-ce que ...? / Qu'est-ce que ...?

Language learning strategies

Applying a pattern
Learning through songs and games

Point Langue

This page provides additional practice on question forms *Est-ce que...? / Qu'est-ce que...? / Où est-ce que...?*.

1

The answers are provided on the page.

2

♣ Brainstorm on possible topics, for example home routine (meals), leisure at home and outside, shopping, school.

◆

> – Est-ce que tu vas déjeuner?
> – Oui, à midi et demi.
> – Où est-ce que tu vas manger?
> – Dans le parc.
> – Qu'est-ce que tu vas manger?
> – Des sandwichs.
> – Qu'est-ce qu'on pourrait faire ensuite?
> – On pourrait aller en ville.
> – Où est-ce qu'on peut acheter des BD?
> – Il y a un magasin rue Royale.
> – Qu'est-ce qu'on fait après le magasin?
> – Ben! On a maths à 2h!

Answers

1 d   2 e   3 a   4 b   5 f   6 c

Atelier

1

See page 4 of the introduction to the Teacher's Book for ideas about exploiting songs.

You can, for example, exploit the song through listening only before pupils look at it. Show six words or pictures (*buvette, squelette, vestiaires, tarif, monnaie, dépliants*), explain the new ones and ask pupils to identify in which order they are heard on cassette.

COUNTER

> *Où sont les vestiaires?*
> *A gauche de mon père.*
> *Et les dépliants?*
> *En face de maman.*
> *Où est la buvette?*
> *Devant les toilettes.*
> *Où est ma monnaie?*
> *Avec les billets.*
> *Regarde le squelette,*
> *Il a une grosse tête.*
> *Regarde le tarif,*
> *C'est très instructif.*
> *Ah, là, là, quel beau musée!*
> *On va bien s'amuser!*

2

Pupils may need dictionaries but should first try to do this task without help.

Answers

poterie   sculptures   squelette   préhistoire   collections   fresques

3

The aim is to train pupils to develop their awareness of cognates and near cognates and to practise matching two reading sources. Pupils can use the same museum more than once.

Answers

a 3, *musée du Cinéma*   **b** 4, *musée du Sport*   **c** 6, *musée de la Marine*   **d** 7, *musée de la Préhistoire*   **e** 7, *musée de la Préhistoire*   **f** 8, *musée des Transports*   **g** 2, *musée de l'Histoire de France*   **h** 5, *musée de Radio-France*   **i** 1, *musée du Cheval*

■ Qu'est-ce que tu vas acheter? pp 90–91

Objective
Buying souvenirs

Resources
Cassette for BD and Ex 1
Flashcards 67–71
CM 13
Grilles 5 CM for Ex 1

Key language
Qu'est-ce que tu vas acheter?
Je cherche... / Vous avez... un badge / un porte-clés /
un livre sur l'Afrique / des autocollants / des cartes postales?
C'est combien?
Il n'y a pas de badges / d'autocollants.
Recycling of personal possessions and prices

Grammar
Il n'y a pas de / d'...

Language learning strategies
Selecting the correct translation when looking up
English words

Ways in
After their visit, the class go to the *musée de l'Homme* shop. Grégory is thinking big. You can introduce this spread like this: *La visite du musée est finie, mais au musée de l'Homme il y a un magasin de souvenirs. Grégory cherche un souvenir.*

Brainstorm on souvenirs to recycle as much language as possible (*un nounours, du papier à lettres*, etc.) Use Flashcards 67–71 (see Teacher's Book introduction page 9) and realia to introduce the new key words.

Pupils then read the BD while they listen to the cassette. Afterwards, to recycle *trop* + adjectives, suggest other souvenirs and ask pupils to respond negatively, using *Non, c'est trop...* (BD tapescript – see Pupil's Book.)

1

A grid is provided on CM.

Preparation – For some writing practice, and as an easier step into the listening, ask pupils to guess and write down which two items each of the people on cassette will be asking for. The first time they listen to the cassette, pupils simply check whether their guesses were correct or not.

♦ You can simplify the task for pupils by not asking them to jot down how many of each item the people on cassette are buying.

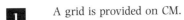

1 – *Deux badges, 14f, et... cinq cartes postales... 15f... Ça fait... 29f.*

2 – *Je voudrais le porte-clé à 17f, et... le livre sur la préhistoire à 34f.*
   – *Oui. Ça fait 51f.*

3 – *C'est combien les cartes postales?*
   – *Combien? Dix?*
   – *Non, neuf cartes postales.*
   – *Ça fait 27f.*
   – *Et les petits autocollants?*
   – *9f50.*
   – *D'accord.*
   – *36f50, s'il vous plaît.*

4 – *Je cherche des autocollants. Sur l'Afrique.*
   – *Des autocollants... Regardez, ça fait 19f50.*
   – *Et, euh... le porte-clé à 11f50.*
   – *Ça fait 31f.*

5 – *Je cherche un cadeau pour ma sœur. Tu as une idée?*
   – *Ben... un porte-clés?*
   – *Oh, non.*
   – *Ou alors... un badge? Regarde.*
   – *Un badge, 15f50? Ah, oui, d'accord. Et des cartes postales. 5 cartes postales à 15f. Elles sont jolies. Ça fait 30f50.*

6 – *Tu achètes des cartes postales?*
   – *Non, non, je prends un badge géant et un porte-clé de dinosaure.*
   – *C'est cher?*
   – *Le badge géant, ça fait 23f90. Et le porte-clés, ça fait 17f80. Donc, euh... le total... 41f70! Ça va!*

Answers
1 *2 badges (14f), 5 cartes postales (15f), total 29f*
2 *1 porte-clés (17f), 1 livre (34f), total 51f*
3 *9 cartes postales (27f), autocollants (9f50), total 36f50*
4 *autocollants (19f50), 1 porte-clés (11f50), total 31f*
5 *1 badge (15f50), 5 cartes postales (15f), total 30f50*
6 *1 badge (23f90), 1 porte-clés (17f80), total 41f70.*

2

Ask pupils to time themselves. Point out that some words need to be in the plural.

Preparation – ♣ Pupils need to look at words in brackets, examples given or abbreviations for parts of speech, and to check the gender of each word.
Answers
1 *un puzzle*   **2** *un chapeau*   **3** *des billes*   **4** *une médaille*
5 *une marionnette*   **6** *un bracelet*   **7** *un guide*
8 *des timbres*   **9** *une ceinture*   **10** *un torchon*

3

Preparation – Reuse the flashcards to present and practise *Il n'y a pas de....*

Extra – You or your pupils can improvise further statements using *Il y a / Il n'y a pas.*
Answers
1 *faux*   **2** *vrai*   **3** *faux*   **4** *faux*   **5** *faux*   **6** *vrai*
7 *vrai*   **8** *faux*

4

There are no right or wrong answers. Ask pupils to make individual choices.

5

Useful references: key pages 29, 31 and 42.

J ▽ A Paris en métro

Objective
Travelling on the underground

Resources
Cassette for BD and Ex 2 and 3
CM 14 and 15

Key language
C'est quelle station / direction pour...?
C'est...

C'est direct?
Il faut changer? Il faut changer à...
Un ticket / carnet, s'il vous plaît.

Grammar
Impersonal verbs (*Il faut / On doit*) + infinitive

Language learning strategies
Answering listening comprehension questions

Ways in
After the museum visit, the teachers are buying *métro* tickets for taking the class to the *Jardin des Plantes* for lunch. Combine your introduction to this spread directly with Ex 1, as indicated below.

1
Use the simplified map on page 92 and read out the BD – one section at a time – to explain underground travel in Paris and the route the class are going to follow:
Après la visite au musée de l'Homme, la classe va prendre le métro. Le professeur achète les tickets. Regardez le plan. La classe de Grégory est à la station Trocadéro. Le musée de l'Homme, c'est la station Trocadéro. Maintenant, regardez la BD...
Afterwards, pupils read the BD again while they listen to the cassette. (BD tapescript – see Pupil's Book.)

2
This task trains pupils to pay attention to questions as well as answers. They do not need the *métro* map for this.

Use this task to reinforce comprehension of the new language introduced in the BD. After each question, pause the cassette and ask pupils to suggest sensible answers before they actually hear the answer given on cassette.

> **COUNTER**
>
> **1** – *Pour Trocadéro, il faut changer?*
> – *Ça fait 45f.*
>
> **2** – *Un ticket, s'il vous plaît.*
> – *Non, il y a trois stations.*
>
> **3** – *Un carnet, s'il vous plaît.*
> – *Oui monsieur... Voilà.*
>
> **4** – *C'est quelle station pour la cathédrale?*
> – *C'est... la station Notre Dame.*
>
> **5** – *Trois tickets, s'il vous plaît.*
> – *Le métro ferme de midi à 14h, madame.*
>
> **6** – *C'est quelle direction pour Concorde, s'il vous plaît?*
> – *C'est une visite guidée.*
>
> **7** – *Pour aller à République, c'est direct?*
> – *A 15h30, monsieur.*
>
> **8** – *Un ticket, s'il vous plaît.*
> – *Oui, euh... vous avez de la monnaie?*

Answers
1 R   **2** R   **3** N   **4** N   **5** R   **6** R   **7** R   **8** N

3
Preparation – If pupils still have difficulty understanding how to travel on the *métro*, it is worth spending a few minutes going over a few routes in English.

Sections A and B are not related. Each one simply starts from a different métro station. For each item, ask pupils to find the simplest route (*Il faut changer une fois seulement*).
Answers
A: **1** *Nation*   **2** *Pasteur*   **3** *Porte de la Chapelle*
B: **1** *Nation*   **2** *Pigalle*   **3** *Mairie d'Issy*
♣ **1** *Porte Dauphine / Place d'Italie*   **2** *Pigalle*
   3 *Mairie d'Issy*

4

> **COUNTER**
>
> – *Deux tickets, s'il vous plaît.*
> – *Voilà, monsieur.*
> – *C'est quelle direction pour Stalingrad?*
> – *C'est... direction Nation.*
> – *Il faut changer?*
> – *Euh... oui, il faut changer à Pigalle.*
> – *Voilà une pièce de vingt francs.*
> – *Vous avez de la monnaie?*
> – *Euh... J'ai une pièce de dix francs.*
> – *Bon, ça va.*
> – *Ah, et je voudrais un dépliant sur le métro, s'il vous plaît.*
> – *Oui, regardez. C'est là-bas.*

Preparation – Check pupils understand the questions.

Answers
1 *métro / Il voyage en métro.*   **2** *deux / Il achète deux tickets.*   **3** *Stalingrad / Il veut aller à Stalingrad.*   **4** *oui / Oui, il doit changer (à Pigalle)*   **5** *20f / Il a une pièce de 20f.*   **6** *oui / Oui, il a de la monnaie (une pièce de 10f).*   **7** *dépliant / Il veut un dépliant sur le métro.*

5
Preparation – Show pupils the Ex 4 tapescript or/and play it again.

Pupils either improvise conversations, write one in full and practise it, or prepare one in cue card form. This last method is developed in more detail in Units 5–6.

K Point Langue / Atelier   pp 94–95

Resources
Cassette for **Atelier** Ex 2
CM 16 and 17

Key language
Recycling of visits to a museum and classroom routine

Grammar
Verb + infinitive

Language learning strategies
Applying a pattern
Preparing yourself for listening tasks
Using context as an aid to understanding

Point Langue

This page reviews and practises structures met so far
where two verbs are used in a row.

1

Answers
1 *7h45*   2 *Oui*   3 *Non*   4 *Non*

2

Encourage pupils to read whole sentences as an aid to
understanding.

Answers
♦ 1 *visiter*   2 *regarder*   3 *rester*   4 *boire*   5 *aller*
   6 *manger*   7 *faire*   8 *prendre*
♣ 1 *travailler*   2 *apprendre*   3 *faire*   4 *finir*   5 *regarder*
   6 *comprendre*   7 *écouter*   8 *poser*   9 *passer*

Atelier

1

Preparation – Do a recap on useful reading skills for
this type of task: starting from the task and not from
the text; starting from what you already understand;
spotting cognates; looking at parts of speech, etc. Also
point out to pupils that the words are in the order of
the text.
Answers
1 *d'abord,*   2 *au XIIe siècle*   3 *le parking*   4 *visites
libres*   5 *en langues étrangères*   6 *allemand*   7 *la vieille
ville*   8 *à pied*   9 *morceaux de faïence*

2

Before they listen to the cassette and choose ticks or
crosses, pupils check the answers to the seven

questions in the leaflet at the top of the page and write
Oui or *Non*.

COUNTER

1 –	*La cathédrale de Chartres a quel âge?*
–	*Elle est très moderne!*
2 –	*On peut aller à la cathédrale en voiture?*
–	*En voiture? C'est très difficile. Il faut prendre le bus.*
3 –	*On peut visiter la cathédrale avec un guide?*
–	*Vous avez le choix. Une visite guidée ou une visite non guidée.*
4 –	*Il y a des visites guidées tous les jours?*
–	*Vous avez des visites guidées le dimanche et le lundi.*
5 –	*Il y a des visites en anglais?*
–	*L'Office de Tourisme peut organiser des visites en anglais.*

Answers
1 ✗   2 ✗   3 ✔   4 ✗   5 ✔

L On révise

Resources
Cassette for Ex 2 and 5

Key language
Revision of Units 3–4

These tasks provide some revision of Units 3 and 4. Pupils can use them to assess their strengths and weaknesses in preparation for **Epreuve 2**. If pupils find that they need to refer back to the two units a lot while doing these tasks, they will need to revise thoroughly before doing the **Epreuve**.

First encourage pupils to scan the tasks and work out for themselves which spreads it would be useful to revise for each task.

1

Pupils make individual choices.

2

COUNTER

1 – *J'adore danser.*

2 – *J'aime regarder la télé et j'aime les programmes amusants.*

3 – *J'aime bien rester à la maison. J'aime bien aider mes parents à la maison,*

4 – *J'aime bien sortir avec les copains. J'aime bien les activités de compétition.*

5 – *Je fais la collection de fossiles, et je m'intéresse à la nature.*

6 – *J'aime aller au cinéma. La violence, ça m'amuse dans les films. J'aime bien les histoires de détectives, de crimes...*

7 – *J'aime la télé. Je m'intéresse beaucoup à la situation en France et dans d'autres pays: la politique, l'économie, etc.*

Answers
1 *(Tu peux aller à la) discothèque.* 2 *(Tu peux regarder) un film comique.* 3 *(Tu peux faire) le ménage.* 4 *le bowling / Tu peux aller au bowling.* 5 *(Tu peux visiter) un musée.* 6 *(Tu peux regarder) un film policier.* 7 *(Tu peux regarder) les informations.*

3

Pupils give their personal opinions.

4

Pupils should not use dictionaries. The aim is to recycle language.

5

Preparation – Before they hear the cassette, pupils should make predictions based on the pictures. Point out to pupils that there are eight pictures but only seven conversations.

COUNTER

1 – *Maman, je peux regarder les dessins animés?*

2 – *Tu as fini le jardin?*
– *Oui, je vais prendre une douche.*

3 – *Le film policier, ça commence à quelle heure?*

4 – *Bon, le musée, c'est bien, mais... moi, j'ai soif. Où est la cafétéria?*

5 – *Tu achètes une cravate?*
– *Oui, la rouge.*
– *C'est pour qui?*
– *C'est pour l'anniversaire de mon frère.*

6 – *Sébastien, tu as tes affaires de toilette?*
– *Oui, euh... oh, non! J'ai du dentifrice, mais j'ai oublié ma brosse à dents. Oh, zut!*

7 – *Bon, on commence la visite?*
– *Attends une minute! Les musées, c'est bien, mais... où sont les vestiaires? Et les toilettes? Et la cafétéria?*
– *Ben regarde, j'ai un dépliant. Les vestiaires, c'est... à gauche.*

Answers
1 e 2 h 3 f 4 a 5 c 6 g 7 d

6

Preparation – ♣ Brainstorm with pupils on ways of developing the topic: giving examples, justifying opinions (*parce que...*), comparing your opinions with those of others in the family, etc.

7

Preparation – Recap on useful verb structures (*On pourrait*, etc.).

Pupils may prefer to make up their own brief instead of using the picture stimulus provided.

A – Epreuve d'écoute

Exercice 1

Pupils are required to understand times in brief sentences (**A**) and in longer statements (**B**), spoken clearly, repeated, and with no interference. The first part tests performance at Level 1, the second part at Level 2.

COUNTER

> **Exemple A**
>
> – *Il est quatre heures.*
>
> **1** – *Il est sept heures.*
> **2** – *Il est huit heures.*
> **3** – *Il est minuit.*
> **4** – *Il est sept heures dix.*
> **5** – *Il est quatre heures vingt-cinq.*
> **6** – *Il est trois heures et demie.*
>
> **Exemple B**
>
> – *Je vais partir à trois heures dix.*
>
> **7** – *Le film commence à neuf heures vingt.*
> **8** – *Je vais aux magasins à onze heures et quart.*
> **9** – *Je déjeune à midi.*
> **10** – *Je vais à la piscine à sept heures moins le quart.*
> **11** – *Le train va partir à neuf heures moins cinq.*
> **12** – *Je vais arriver à Paris à quatre heures moins vingt-cinq.*

A 1 mark for each correct answer. Total 6. Pupils scoring at least 4 marks are showing some characteristics of performance at Level 1.

1 D **2** B **3** A **4** C **5** D **6** C

B 1 mark for each correct answer. Total 6. Pupils scoring at least 4 marks are showing some characteristics of performance at Level 2.

7 9.20 **8** 11.15 **9** 12.00 **10** 6.45 **11** 8.55 **12** 3.35

Exercice 2

Another test of elements of performance at Level 2 on the topic of transport.

COUNTER

> **Exemple**
>
> – *Quand je suis à Paris, je prends toujours le taxi. C'est cher mais j'aime bien le taxi.*
>
> **1** – *J'aime bien voyager par le train parce que c'est rapide.*
> **2** – *Je vais à l'école tous les jours à vélo.*
> **3** – *D'habitude je vais en ville à pied parce que ce n'est pas trop loin.*
> **4** – *Ce week-end, je vais faire une excursion en car.*
> **5** – *En général, quand on sort en famille, on prend la voiture.*
> **6** – *Chaque année nous prenons l'avion pour aller en vacances en Espagne.*

1 mark for each correct answer. Total 6. Pupils scoring at least 4 are showing some characteristics of performance at Level 2.

1 D **2** B **3** G **4** C **5** A **6** E

Exercice 3

This tests understanding of details in a short passage using familiar language, though over several topics. It tests elements of performance at Level 3.

COUNTER

> – *Voici mes projets pour le week-end. Samedi matin je vais me lever à huit heures.*
> – *Après ça, à neuf heures, pour aider ma mère, je vais faire les courses en ville.*
> – *Ensuite, à onze heures, je dois faire mes devoirs dans ma chambre.*
> – *Samedi après-midi, à deux heures, je veux aller en ville avec mes copains. On va faire du patin à glace à la patinoire.*
> – *Et samedi soir, je vais rester à la maison avec mes parents.*
> – *Dimanche, je vais sortir avec ma famille – mon père, ma mère et mon frère.*
> – *Nous allons visiter nos amis qui habitent à la montagne.*
> – *On ne prend pas le train, parce qu'il n'y a pas de gare dans notre village... donc, on va y aller en auto.*

1 mark for each correct answer. Total 7. Pupils scoring 5 or more show some characteristics of performance at Level 3.

1 D **2** C **3** A **4** D **5** C **6** C **7** A

B – Epreuve orale

Exercice I

Pupils work in pairs and take it in turns to choose two articles, 1 per role-play. They have to ask for the article and ask its price (1 mark). Then say that they only have a bank note of a certain amount (as indicated on the visual) (1 mark) 2 x 2 = 4 marks. The remaining 2 marks are given for the correct price being given for the article (by the other pupil). If teachers prefer not to assess this in a pairs situation, three items could instead be requested. Visual and verbal support is given in the example.

This test could be a test of performance at both Levels 1 and 2 depending on the utterances of the pupil. Pupils who can name the 2 items they require ("respond briefly with single words, to what they see and hear" with "pronunciation which may be approximate") are showing some characteristics of performance at Level 1. Pupils who can name the items and go on to gain at least 2 further marks by giving the further details of price and identifying the bank note, using a short phrase show some characteristics of performance at Level 2. Total 6.

Exercice 2

This test uses short verbal and visual stimuli based on opening / closing times and prices for places to visit (a swimming pool, ice rink and museum). Students choose one of the three cards and go through the conversation model in turn. Pupil **A** is assessed each time. Students should choose different cards. The test is intended to show characteristics of performance at Level 3 (brief prepared tasks of at least two or three exchanges, using visual or other cues to help them initiate and respond). Pupils who can use short phrases (mainly memorised language) to communicate on four of the five points, (e.g. *On peut nager. Ça ouvre à 9h. Ça coûte 20 francs. On va déjeuner à la cafétéria. On va en vélo.*) are showing characteristics of performance at Level 3. Pupils communicating meaning but by the use of single words in response, e.g. *vélo, cafétéria* are not showing characteristics of performance at Level 3. Pupils who can take the model, make up their own cue card and substitute words and phrases may show characteristics of performance at Level 4. Total 4.

Exercice 3

The differentiation in this exercise is again related to the outcome and characteristics of performance may be seen at different levels. Pupils pick a person and give the relevant personal details. The language focuses on household tasks, leisure activities and TV programmes. Opinions are asked for on all three areas. The tasks and cues are targeted at Level 4 (simple structured conversation of at least three or four exchanges supported by visual or other cues. As at Level 3, Level 4 includes the ability to express likes and dislikes and feelings. At Level 4, pronunciation should be generally accurate and intonation consistent.

Total 11 marks
Marks are awarded for household tasks (2) + opinions (2), preferred weekend activity (1) opinion (1) coming home time (1) TV likes (1) dislikes (1) and opinions (2). Utterances such as the following would be characteristic of Level 4:
Je fais la cuisine et je fais la vaisselle – c'est génial. Le week-end je préfère aller à la discothèque – c'est chouette.

Je dois rentrer à neuf heures et demie. J'aime regarder les dessins animés à la télévision – c'est génial. Je n'aime pas regarder les informations – ça m'énerve.

Pupils communicating on seven or more points in the above way, either taking the initiative or if preferred, responding to the teacher with ease are showing characteristics of performance at Level 4.

Teachers may wish to add bonus marks as below. These enable the amount of help/support needed from the teacher to be taken into account. Some pupils may be able to treat the exercise as a presentation and proceed unaided, whereas others may need extra support from the teacher in the form of questions. These marks also give the opportunity to reward the degree of accuracy shown by pupils.

Add bonus marks out of 3 as follows:
1 mark – pupil manages to communicate the basic messages, language is often inaccurate but the meaning of most of the messages is there. Substantial help is needed from the teacher.
2 marks – communicates all the messages despite inaccuracies. Some help from the teacher.
3 marks – communicates the messages well. Language often very accurate. Little help needed. 10 marks for communication plus 3 bonus marks. Total 13.

C – Epreuve de lecture

Exercice I

This test requires only the understanding of single words, mostly concerning personal toiletries / items needed for a weekend bag. Pupils have to match pictures of items to the appropriate words on a list. This is a test of performance at Level 1.
Total 7. Pupils scoring 5 or more marks are showing some characteristics of performance at Level 1.

1 H   **2** A   **3** B   **4** I   **5** F   **6** D   **7** C

Exercice 2

Pupils read longer items describing in simple terms types of TV programmes (from Unit 3). They have to match visuals of programme types to the descriptions. The level of language presented bridges Levels 2 and 3 but in terms of response (matching) the task is still fairly simple (Level 2), showing understanding of short phrases in familiar contexts. Total 7. Pupils scoring 5 or more marks are showing some characteristics of performance at Level 2.

1 A   **2** D   **3** E   **4** G   **5** F

Exercice 3

Pupils read extracts from young French people and the frequency with which they undertake household chores. They have to identify the tasks and the frequency of them by placing the correct symbol in the grid. As this is a new task type in the assessment section, it would be wise to check that pupils understand the rubric clearly before undertaking the test. If tasks are not specifically mentioned in the extract, pupils should place a mark in the grid as in the example. 4 marks are available on the grid for a total of 9 correct boxes – marks are awarded on a sliding scale as shown below. There are also 2 final marks available for gist comprehension based on who does the most / least tasks. Total = 6 marks. This is a test of performance at Level 3 (pupils show understanding of short texts which are printed or word processed). They identify and note main points. Pupils scoring 4 or more marks are showing characteristics of performance at Level 3.

Astrid (*Exemple*)	✔✔	✗	–	–	–
Paul	✔✔	✗	✔	✔	–
Sylvie	–	–	–	✔	✔
Charlotte	✗	✔	✗	–	–

8 – 9 boxes = 4 marks
5 – 7 boxes = 3 marks
3 – 4 boxes = 2 marks
1 – 2 boxes = 1 mark
Qui fait le plus? = Paul (1 mark)
Qui fait le moins? = Charlotte (1 mark)

Exercice 4
Pupils read a longer, denser text. The language featured focuses on that needed to describe invitations (outings) and also tests comprehension of the modal verbs in this context. Comprehension of main points, details and opinions is necessary to perform well on this test. These are all characteristics of performance at Level 4. Pupils are also showing some understanding in terms of reformulation and paraphrasing on questions requiring sentence completions based on verbal multiple choice. Total 7. Pupils scoring 5 or more marks are showing characteristics of performance at Level 4.

1 *en ville* **2** *au parc* **3** *aller à la piscine* **4** *en car*
5 *peut* **6** *doit* **7** *travailler*

D – Epreuve écrite

Exercice 1
Pupils are asked to copy single familiar words correctly. At the same time, they are matching the words with the appropriate pictures. The exercise tests elements of performance at Level 1.

1 mark for each correctly matched and copied word. $1/2$ mark if any answer incorrectly matched but correctly copied. In any one answer, deduct $1/2$ mark for any accent error. Total 8. Pupils scoring at least 6 marks are showing characteristics of performance at Level 1.

1 *brosse à dents* **2** *dentifrice* **3** *porte-monnaie*
4 *porte-feuille* **5** *parapluie* **6** *argent* **7** *télécarte*
8 *casquette*

Exercice 2
Pupils are asked to write short sentences from memory. It tests elements of performance at Level 2. Spelling can be approximate. Pupils are asked to write a time as well, but this can be accepted in the form of figures. Note that a choice can be made from a number of phrases and times.

1 mark if a correct phrase used, with a time, spelt with reasonable accuracy.

$1/2$ mark if a correct phrase used but with poor accuracy and/or if time missing.

Tolerate gender errors. Total 4. Pupils scoring at least 3 marks are showing some characteristics of performance at Level 2.
Je fais la vaisselle. Je fais la cuisine. Je fais le ménage. Je fais le / du jardinage. Je fais le / mon lit. Je fais ma / la chambre.
Do not penalise if the same time is used in each.

Exercice 3
In this exercise, pupils write short phrases from memory and also copy phrases. It therefore includes elements of performance at Levels 2 and 3.

2 marks if sentence written with reasonable accuracy, containing one of illustrated activities + one *petite expression*.

1 mark if accuracy is limited and/or part of sentence missing.
$1/2$ mark if evidence of some knowledge of required vocabulary.

Total 8. Pupils scoring at least 6 marks are showing some characteristics of performance at Level 3. The Level 2 and Level 3 elements could be assessed separately; if 3 or more of the 4 *expressions* were correctly copied, pupils would be showing characteristics of performance at Level 2.

Exercice 4
This exercise tests a particular grammar point covered during the preceding unit. Pupils write a few short sentences from memory. The exercise tests elements of performance at Level 3.

1 mark for each sentence. Total 5. Pupils scoring at least $3 1/2$ marks are showing some characteristics of performance at Level 3.

Award 1 mark if the sentence uses the correct vocabulary and is spelt with a reasonable degree of accuracy (i.e. can be understood) and uses the correct form of *à*.

Award $1/2$ mark if there is doubt as to meaning or if the form of *à* is incorrect.

0 marks if incorrect word for place. Accent errors can be ignored.

1 *Je vais à la piscine.*
2 *Je vais à l'église.*
3 *Je vais aux magasins/au magasin.*
4 *Je vais au cinéma.*
5 *Je vais à l'école.*

CAMARADES 2	OVERVIEW – UNITE 5 – LES AVENTURES DE GREGORY			NATIONAL CURRICULUM	
Topics/Objectives	Key language	Grammar	Strategies	PoS coverage	AoE
A **Vive la liberté!** Background information on La Villette			Reading: using context, key words and awareness of cognates and near cognates as an aid to understanding	1 f, g, i 2 a, j 3 c, d, e 4 a	CE
B **Tu viens avec nous?** Giving, accepting and refusing invitations	*Tu viens (vous venez) au cinéma / à la piscine avec moi (nous)? En métro / A pied / Avec mes parents. Je ne sais pas. D'accord, je vais / on vient avec toi (vous). Désolé(e), je vais / on va chez Jenny / en ville.* Recycling of places of entertainment/transport	Present tense of *venir*	Improving conversational skills: providing details, arguments, explanations and suggestions	1 a, c, d, f, h, i 2 a, d, e, g, h, i, k, n 3 b, e, f, g	BC
C **Vous allez où?** Arranging to meet someone	*Je vais... / Tu vas... / Vous allez... / On va... où? ...au cinéma? Quand? Dans cinq minutes / A 3h. Bon, alors, rendez-vous au ... à ...h.* Recycling of places of entertainment and the time	Present tense of *aller* Recycling of *venir*	Pronunciation: *-u / -ou* Checking work with a partner Working in pairs	1 a, c, d, h, i, j, k 2 a, d, e, f, h, i, k, l 3 b, c, f, g	BC
D **Point Langue** **Atelier**	Recycling of invitations and arranging to meet Recycling of numbers	Present tense of *aller* and *venir*	Applying a pattern Learning through play	1 a, b, c, d, g, i 2 b, d 3 f 4 a	BC
E **C'était bien?** Saying what you did on a day out	*C'était comment, ton après-midi? C'était bien, la Géode? Oui, c'était chouette / pas mal. Bof, pas génial. / Non, c'était nul. J'ai été au parc / chez John / avec Habib. J'ai regardé / visité / écouté / mangé / travaillé / acheté...*	Perfect tense: regular *-er* verbs with *j'ai...*	Pronunciation: *-ai / -é* Writing from notes	1 a, c, d, g, h, i, j 2 a, d, e, f, h, i, j 3 b, c, g	B
F **Qu'est-ce que tu as fait?** Saying what you did on a day out	*Qu'est-ce que tu as fait? Hier / Mardi dernier... j'ai pris des photos / j'ai bu un coca / j'ai fait une promenade / j'ai vu la Géode / j'ai perdu ma veste. Tu as (visité...)? (Est-ce que) Tu as (mangé...)?*	Perfect tense with *j'ai / tu:* regular *-er* verbs + some irregular verbs	Looking up irregular forms in the dictionary	1 a, c, d, g, h, i, j, k 2 a, d, e, i, j 3 d, f, g	BC

CAMARADES 2	OVERVIEW – UNITE 5 – LES AVENTURES DE GREGORY		Cont.	NATIONAL CURRICULUM	
	Topics/Objectives	Key language	Grammar	Strategies	PoS coverage	AoE

	Topics/Objectives	Key language	Grammar	Strategies	PoS coverage	AoE
G	**La Porte de Pantin** Finding your way	*Le métro, s'il vous plaît? C'est tout droit. C'est la première / deuxième / troisième rue à droite / gauche. C'est avant / après / devant... le commissariat / le marché / la librairie / la pharmacie ... puis sur la gauche / droite* Recycling of places in town		Learning through play	1 a, c, d, g, h 2 a, b, d, e 3 c, g 4 a	C
H	**Point Langue Atelier**		Perfect tense: *j'ai... / tu as...*	Applying a pattern	1 a, c, g, i 2 a, i 3 e, f 4 a	C
I	**On rentre à Chartres** Buying train tickets	*Un aller simple / aller-retour pour... s'il vous plaît. C'est combien? Il y a un train à quelle heure pour...? Le train arrive à... à quelle heure? Il y a un wagon-restaurant? C'est quel quai? Quai numéro...* Recycling of numbers and 24-hour clock		Pronunciation: familiar cognates and near cognates Learning full sentences by heart Awareness of sequencing	1 a, c, g, h 2 a, d, e, f, g, j, l 3 b	C
J	**Les aventures de Grégory** Describing what someone else did	*Le prof a cherché... Il a contacté la police. Annie a fini la visite. Elle a attendu 20 minutes.*	Perfect tense with *il / elle a...* Recycling of past participles	Using context as an aid to understanding	1 a, c, d, g, h, i, j 2 a, e, i, j, k 3 b, c, d, e, f, g	BC
K	**C'était génial!** Saying what someone else did on a day out	*Tu as /Il a /Elle a... voyagé comment? / ... mangé où? / ... bu quoi? / ... visité le zoo quand? / ... pris le car à quelle heure? ... payé combien? / ... voyagé avec qui? On a... (acheté des souvenirs).* Recycling of key question words	Perfect tense with *on a...* Recycling of past participles	Using spider webs for writing or speaking	1 a, c, d. h, j 2 a, d, e, g, i, k 3 c. f, g	BC
L	**Point Langue Atelier**		Perfect tense singular of *avoir* verbs	Learning verbs Learning through rap	1 a, c, d, g, j 2 i, n 3 a, b, f	BC

99

IT Opportunities

CORE ACTIVITIES

Text manipulation

Spreads E–F

Produce a model text, something like the one below, in which a young person writes about a day out:

Samedi j'ai été à Paris avec mon ami Patrick. A neuf heures on a visité le zoo de Vincennes. J'ai préféré les tigres et les lions, mais Patrick a préféré les serpents et les éléphants. Dans le zoo j'ai pris des photos et j'ai acheté des posters pour ma chambre. Ensuite on a déjeuné dans un parc et à deux heures on a été au musée du Sport. C'était chouette! A six heures et demie on a pris le train pour Chartres. Dans le train j'ai écouté mon walkman et j'ai lu des magazines. On a été à la gare de Chartres à huit heures et j'ai été chez moi à huit heures vingt.

Encourage pupils to identify all the verbs used in the *passé composé*. Then ask them to emulate the model by producing their own account of a day out, either on paper or in a word processor.

Word processing – guided writing

Spread L

Create and save the following set of nonsense answers to activity 2:

Mon père a vu un coca.
L'après-midi j'ai parlé du bateau.
A Paris on a bu en métro.
J'ai visité des photos.
On a perdu le Planétarium.
Finalement, j'ai fait une casquette.
Dans le bateau, j'ai été une souris.
Mon père a acheté avec les visiteurs.

Pupils replace each past participle with the appropriate one from the list in the box.

Presentation

Spread L (i)

Pupils produce a reference sheet of all the past participles that they can find in the unit. They begin by entering and saving the past participles in a word processor. They then devise a way of sorting them into groups for easy reference. For example, one pupil might group by word endings whilst another might group by perceived usefulness. Each group is then presented in a different font or colour. When complete, the reference sheets are printed out and put into the pupils' exercise books/folders.

Spread L (ii)

Pupils continue the rap choosing from the following past participles: *visité, contacté, écouté, lu, pris, perdu, payé, regardé, vu, fait.* They then present the rap with the past participles emphasised, for example in a bigger font size, in bold, in italics or in a different colour. If a multi-media package is being used, the rap could be recorded and played back as part of the presentation.

ADDITIONAL ACTIVITIES

Word processing – extended writing

Spread B

Pupils work in pairs to write and then act out dialogues similar to activity 6B. Settings could include:
à la piscine   à la discothèque   au zoo   au parc
au bowling   au centre de loisirs   chez moi

The Internet

Spread A

Type *Cite des Sciences* or *Cinaxe* into a search engine. Find pictures and information in both French and English about prices and opening times. Your search may give you access to unofficial sites in addition to the official *Parc de la Villette* site (currently listed as *www.parisnet.com/french/city/musees/villette.htm#cite_metiers*).

Spread I

Type *SNCF* into a search engine. Find pictures and information in both French and English about French Railways. Your search will give you access to unofficial sites as well as to the official SNCF site (currently listed as *www.sncf.fr/indexe.htm*). You may be able to find timetable information about trains from Paris to Chartres.

Copymasters

The *présentation* and the *grilles* copymasters should be used as indicated.
The other copymasters (worksheets and vocabulary lists) should be used with or after the spread indicated.

Pupil's Book Spread	Corresponding Copymaster
A	22–23 *Glossaire*
B	–
C	5–6 *On écoute; Grilles 6*
D	7 *Grammaire*
E	1 *Présentation*
F	2 *Présentation; 8–9 On lit*
G	3 *Présentation; 10 Feuille complémentaire 1; 11 On s'amuse*
H	12 *Grammaire; 13 Que sais-tu?*
I	14 *Feuille complémentaire 1; Grilles 6*
J	15–16 *On écrit*
K	4 *Présentation; 17–18 On parle*
L	19 *Grammaire; 20 Plaisir de lire; 21 Que sais-tu?*

Notes to accompany Copymasters

Feuilles 1–4
Presentation sheets designed to practise the perfect tense (Feuilles 1, 2 and 4) and language connected with directions (Feuille 3).

Feuilles 5–6 On écoute
These two CMs provide additional listening practice about topic 1. Both ♦ and ♣ tasks are on CM 5. The realia for both levels is on CM 6.

Ex 1 – There is a different tapescript for ♦ and ♣. The rubric and the grid, however, are identical.

♦ Feuille 5

1 – Rendez-vous sous la Cabane des Robinson à 10 heures et demie.

2 – Rendez-vous au 'Pirates of the Caribbean' à 11 heures et quart.

3 – Rendez-vous à Star Tours à 11 heures moins le quart.

4 – Rendez-vous à Indiana Jones et le Temple du Péril à 2 heures et demie.

5 – On va au 'Phantom Manor'? C'est super, il y a des automates.
   – D'accord! A quelle heure?
   – Rendez-vous au 'Manor' à 3 heures vingt.

6 – Moi, je vais aller au Visionarium avec Frédérique. C'est un cinéma. J'ai rendez-vous avec Frédérique devant le Visionarium à midi et demi.

7 – On va au 'Labyrinth'?
   – D'accord, mais cet après-midi.
   – Alors, rendez-vous au 'Labyrinth' à 4 heures moins dix.

♣ Feuille 6

1 – Ah, regarde le plan! Il y a une cabane, c'est comme dans Robinson Crusoë.
   – Ah oui, dans des branches.
   – Alors on va à la cabane?
   – Bon, d'accord. On se donne rendez-vous à 10 heures et demie.
   – 11 heures et quart? Oui, ça va.

2 – Qu'est-ce que c'est, que ça?
   – C'est une forteresse, non?
   – Ah oui, c'est pour les pirates. On va visiter?
   – Ouais, d'accord. A onze heures et quart, ça va?

3 – Regarde, qu'est-ce que c'est que ce château, là?
   – C'est une forteresse.
   – Ah oui, et il y a des pirates qui attaquent la forteresse.
   – C'est amusant, ça! On se donne rendez-vous à 11 heures?
   – Euh... ben, 11 heures et quart. C'est plus facile pour moi.

4 – Dis, tu viens voir la Star Tours avec moi, non?
   – C'est, ça s'appelle Star Tours, c'est un voyage spatial en simulation.
   – Bon, ben on pourrait y aller vers 2 heures et demie?
   – Ben oui, d'accord.

5 – Les fantômes, ça te fait peur?
   – Pourquoi?
   – Regarde le manoir, là. Il y a des automates fantômes.
   – Mais non, ça ne me fait pas peur!
   – Allez, rendez-vous à 3 heures vingt. Ça te va?
   – Ahhh! Moi, j'ai peur!!!

6 – Il y a un cinéma avec des effets spéciaux, là. Ça t'intéresse?
   – Où ça? Ah, oui, le Visionarium, c'est ça?
   – Oui, il y a des films avec des dessins animés et des acteurs, des vrais acteurs. On pourrait y aller à 2 heures et quart?
   – Oh non, à midi et demi, avant le déjeuner.
   – Oui, d'accord. Bonne idée.

7 – Qu'est-ce que c'est, que ça? C'est Alice?
   – Oui, il y a un labyrinthe avec Alice, le château de la reine, le chat...
   – C'est amusant ça. On y va?
   – Oui, à 4 heures moins dix, c'est possible pour toi?
   – Oui, d'accord. Rendez-vous à 4 heures moins dix.

Answers

♦ **1** e, 10h30 **2** f, 11h15 **3** c, 10h45 **4** d, 2h30
   5 g, 3h20 **6** i, 12h30 **7** a, 3h50
♣ **1** e, 10h30 **2** f, 11h15 **3** f, 11h15 **4** c, 2h30
   5 g, 3h20 **6** i, 12h30 **7** a, 3h50

Ex 2 – Here again, ♦ and ♣ have different recorded material but the rubric, grid and answers are identical.

Extra – The map on CM 6 can be exploited further for listening or speaking purposes. For example: pupil **A** gives directions and pupil **B** guesses where (s)he is going; pupils use the map to discuss and agree on a programme of visits for the day.

♦ Feuille 5

1 – Tu viens chez Paul?
   – Chez Paul? Désolé, j'ai des devoirs.

2 – Tu viens chez Julie?
   – Chez Julie? Désolée, je vais chez ma grand-mère.

3 – On va à la patinoire?
   – D'accord, mais à quelle heure?
   – A une heure et demie.

4 – Tu viens au musée?
   – Au musée? C'est bien?
   – Euh... oui.
   – Désolée, je vais en ville avec ma mère.

5 – On va à la piscine?
   – Je ne sais pas, j'ai des devoirs.
   – Oh, écoute!
   – D'accord, mais à trois heures.

6 – Tu viens à la fête avec moi?
   – Il y a une fête?
   – Oui, à mon collège.
   – Désolé, je vais travailler avec mon père.

♣ Feuille 6

1 – *Dis, j'aimerais bien sortir cet après-midi. Tu viens avec moi?*

– *C'est après-midi? Qu'est-ce que tu veux faire?*

– *Tu viens chez Paul avec moi? On pourrait jouer aux cartes.*

– *Et les devoirs? La géo? Et les maths pour demain? On a cinq exercices! Non, je ne peux pas!*

2 – *Tu fais tes devoirs cet après-midi?*

– *Non, pourquoi?*

– *Parce que j'aimerais bien aller chez Julie. Tu viens avec moi?*

– *C'est qui?*

– *C'est la sœur de Sébastien.*

– *Ah... euh... non, je vais chez ma grand-mère.*

3 – *Ton match finit à quelle heure cet après-midi?*

– *Mon match? C'est ce matin.*

– *Alors viens à la patinoire cet après-midi.*

– *Avec toi?*

– *Ben oui, bien sûr!*

– *Je vais déjeuner chez moi, mais... rendez-vous à une heure et demie?*

– *D'accord. Bonne chance pour le match!*

4 – *Il y a une exposition d'objets africains au musée. Ça t'intéresse? Tu viens avec moi?*

– *Bof, moi, tu sais, les musées...*

– *Mais écoute! C'est très intéressant pour le projet en géographie!*

– *Moi, j'ai un CD-rom pour le projet.*

– *Allez, viens!*

– *Ah ben zut! Désolé, je vais en ville avec ma mère cet après-midi. Alors le musée, impossible!*

5 – *Ça t'intéresse d'aller à la piscine avec moi?*

– *Ah, je ne sais pas. Ce n'est pas facile, tu sais. J'ai beaucoup de devoirs en ce moment.*

– *Oh, écoute, fais un effort!*

– *Bon, je viens avec toi, mais à 3 heures seulement. Avant 3 heures, c'est impossible.*

6 – *Alors, tu vas venir à la fête avec moi?*

– *Une fête? Mais où?*

– *C'est à mon collège. Et ma classe organise une loterie.*

– *Oh, moi, les fêtes... Et c'est quand?*

– *C'est demain après-midi.*

– *Ah ben, demain, je ne peux pas. Le samedi après-midi, je travaille toujours avec mon père.*

Answers ♦ and ♣

1 *Chez Paul / – / Jouer aux cartes chez Paul; devoirs de géo et maths*

2 *Chez Julie / – / Va chez sa grand-mère / Julie: sœur de Sébastien*

3 *A la patinoire / 1h30 / – / Match le matin; le garçon va déjeuner chez soi*

4 *Au musée / – / a un CD-rom + va en ville avec sa mère / Objets africains au musée; pour le projet en géographie*

5 *A la piscine / 3h00 / – / Fille a beaucoup de devoirs*

6 *A la fête / – / Travaille / Fête au collège; classe organise loterie; garçon travaille avec son père le samedi après-midi.*

Feuille 7 Grammaire

This CM provides more practice on *aller* and *venir*.

Ex 1 ♦ – The cards are for playing dominoes. It is best to print the dominoes onto card. They can be laminated.

Ex 2 ♣ ***Extra*** – Pupils can make up a few items of their own for a partner to practise.
Answers
1 *On vient / Nous venons*   **2** *je vais*   **3** *je viens*
4 *on va/nous allons*   **5** *on vient/nous venons*
6 *on vient/nous venons*

Feuilles 8–9 On lit

These two CMs provide additional practice of reading material in the perfect tense with *j'ai...* and *tu as...* The two CMs can easily be used concurrently. Go through the ♦ CM 8 rubrics with the pupils while the other pupils make a start on ♣ CM 9 on their own. The use of dictionaries should not be permitted.

Feuille 8 ♦

Ex 1 – You can provide the words on card to save pupils from having to copy the words. This, however, means that each phrase can only be used once.

Extra – Pupils read their partner's sentences to check how many they have in common.

Ex 2
Answers
1 *V*   **2** *V*   **3** *F*   **4** *V*   **5** *F*   **6** *V*   **7** *F*   **8** *F*   **9** *F*   **10** *V*

Feuille 9 ♣
Ex 1
Answers
1 *F*   **2** *F*   **3** *V*   **4** *V*   **5** *V*   **6** *F*   **7** *F*   **8** *V*   **9** *F*   **10** *V*

Ex 2 – Decide whether or not you want answers in full sentences.
Answers
1 *(Elle est) toute seule.*   **2** *(Elle a vu Jeannine) samedi matin.*   **3** *Ludivine (a réparé le vélo).*   **4** *(Elles ont déjeuné) dans une petite cafétéria.*   **5** *(Parce qu') elle n'aime pas la science-fiction et la violence.*   **6** *Ludivine et ses parents (ont préparé le dîner).*

Feuille 10
See Spread G notes for how to use

Feuille 11 On s'amuse
Ex 1 – The aim of this exercise is to train pupils to listen for specific words, which is an important prelude to listening for meaning.

Extra – Give pupils a copy of the incomplete tapescript for gap filling.

– Oh, regarde la publicité!

– Qu'est-ce que c'est?

– C'est pour la piscine Arc-en-ciel. La première visite, 7f seulement.

– La piscine Arc-en-ciel. C'est où?

– C'est rue Victor Hugo, devant la pharmacie.

– Il y a une pharmacie?

– Oui, c'est facile. D'abord tu passes devant la pâtisserie et tu trouves la pharmacie à gauche et la piscine à droite.

– D'accord. On va aller à la piscine mercredi? On prend le bus?

– Pour la piscine? Non, on y va à pied. Rendez-vous devant la pâtisserie.

– Et n'oublie pas la publicité!

– La publicité? Pourquoi?

– La réduction pour la piscine.

Ex 2 – _Preparation_ - Ask pupils to read the song, with or without the cassette. Explain anything they might not understand through action only.

Pupils may prefer rap to singing, in which case they should make up a rap rhythm of their own.

Extra – Here is a choice of three games that use the 18 pictures from CM1, cut into cards.

Réflexes (1 jeu de cartes, 4/5 joueurs)
A: Tu es le maître du jeu. Montre les 18 cartes sur la table. Dis une phrase.
Exemple: J'ai visité un musée.
Qui trouve la carte en premier? Un point.
A: Continue. Dis une autre phrase.

Loto (1 jeu de cartes)
Choisis 5 cartes.
Ecoute le professeur et joue au loto avec tes cartes.

Devinettes (1 jeu de cartes, 2 joueurs)
A: Choisis une carte.
B: Devine la carte. Pose des questions.
Exemple:
B: Tu as acheté quelque chose?
A: Non.
B: Tu as visité quelque chose?
A: Oui.
B: Tu as visité Disneyland?

Feuille 12 Grammaire
This CM provides additional practice on the perfect tense.

Ex 1

1 J'ai mangé.
2 Je travaille.
3 Tu écoutes?
4 Tu as travaillé?
5 J'ai regardé un feuilleton.
6 Je fais la vaisselle.
7 Tu as fait le ménage?
8 Je regarde toujours les informations.
9 J'ai vu Michel en ville.
10 Tu vas au bowling tous les samedis?
11 Tu bois de la bière? Tu as quel âge?
12 J'ai visité la cathédrale avec ma classe.

Answers
1 PA 2 PR 3 PR 4 PA 5 PA 6 PR 7 PA 8 PR
9 PA 10 PR 11 PR 12 PA

Ex 2 – ♦ You can give pupils a choice of two verb forms (present/past) each time.
Answers
1 je fais 2 j'ai perdu 3 as fait 4 J'ai été 5 as joué
6 as été 7 Je vais 8 j'ai vu

Ex 3 – Suggest a scoring system to enhance motivation: one point per quick, accurate answer.

Feuille 13 Que sais-tu?
This CM offers some revision of topics 1 and 2.

Ex 1

– Sophie, tu viens au cybercafé avec moi?

– Au cybercafé?

– Oui, ça ouvre dans deux jours. Tu viens samedi?

– Ben... je ne sais pas...

– Oh, écoute, viens!

– Samedi matin, c'est impossible. Je vais au club des Jeunes.

– Et samedi après-midi?

– Bon, d'accord. On y va à pied?

– Non, c'est assez loin. On y va en métro.

– Rendez-vous devant le café?

– Euh... ben, j'ai une idée. Non, je viens chez toi à 2 heures et demie. D'accord?

– D'accord!

Answers
1 Vrai 2 Faux 3 Vrai 4 Faux 5 Vrai 6 Vrai
7 Faux

Ex 2
Answers
1 as mangé / as acheté; ai mangé / ai acheté
2 as voyagé; ai voyagé 3 as pris; ai cheté
4 as vu / as visité; ai fait

Ex 3
Answers
1 Vrai 2 Faux 3 Faux 4 Faux 5 Faux 6 Vrai

Feuilles 15–16 On écrit
These two CMs provide additional writing practice using the perfect tense. They can easily be used concurrently. Both the ♦ and the ♣ task are on CM 15. CM 16 provides the realia to be used for the two tasks.

Ex 1 – You can suggest pupils work in pairs. Instead, they can work on their own then do peer checking before finalising their answers.

Answers
♦ **1** *fait, chien* **2** *acheté, pâtisserie* **3** *été, son, près*
 4 *perdu* **5** *regardé* **6** *été* **7** *trouvé, photo*
 8 *commissariat* **9** *vu, avec*

Ex 2 ♣ *Preparation* – Brainstorm on other useful link words. Minimise dictionary use by suggesting, for example, that pupils should not look up more than five words. Encourage the use of Pupil's Book for reference purposes.

As with ♦, you can suggest pupils work in pairs or suggest they work on their own and have their work checked by another pupil. Provide a checking brief for accuracy (verb endings, adjectival endings, genders, plurals, punctuation, use of capitals, etc.) and for fluency and variety (link words, longer sentences, variety of vocabulary). You may like to teach *il était* + adjective (*fatigué*, etc.) for description of mood, as an extension of *c'était*, taught in topic 2.

Feuilles 17–18 On parle
These two CMs provide additional speaking practice about travelling by train and narrating past events.

Answers
A *combien*   **B** *345f*   A *wagon-restaurant* **B** 6
A *quelle*   **B** *13h36* A *arrive*   **B** *17h58*
A *quai*   **B** *Quai (...) 5*

Feuille 17 ♦ Feuille 18 ♣
Ex 1 **Extra** – Pupils can practise further, using details of their own choosing.

Ex 2 – Either give a time limit or a number of points to be reached. Point out that pupils can start their sentences with *Mon frère / Ma copine* etc. To prevent accusations of cheating, suggest Pupil **A** ticks in pencil the phrases (s)he chooses.

Feuille 19 Grammaire
This CM provides additional practice on the perfect tense.

You can explain the task like this:
Découpez les cartes. L'objectif: faire des phrases avec six éléments: quand? Qui? Un verbe au passé composé (deux cartes); un objet; où? Exemple: Hier / ma sœur / a / vu / un clown / à la patinoire.

Preparation – Pupils classify the cards into the six categories.

Point out the importance of the link between the subject and the correct part of *avoir*.

Feuille 20 Plaisir de lire
Preparation – The aim here is to read for pleasure and not to 'dissect' the articles. Let pupils browse through the articles at leisure before they do the task. Discourage dictionary use, as the number of cognates/near cognates used should provide sufficient clues.

After the corrections, give pupils the opportunity to ask questions about any points of interest to them that they did not quite understand, but do not exploit these articles in too much detail.

Answers
Les barbus ... août 1967   Les kidnappeurs ... septembre 1961   Des gobelins ... 21 août 1955   Chef ... 18 avril 1961   Le silence ... 24 juin 1947   Le Vénusien ... 20 novembre 1952

Feuille 21 Que sais-tu?
This CM provides some revision of topic 3.

1	– *C'est une visite guidée?*
2	– *Où est-ce qu'on achète les billets?*
3	– *On peut manger quelque chose ici?*
4	– *Non, non, je voudrais un aller simple.*
5	– *On va arriver à quelle heure?*
6	– *Où sont les toilettes?*
7	– *Ça ferme à quelle heure?*
8	– *Il y a un wagon-restaurant?*
9	– *Il y a un train à quelle heure?*
10	– *On peut acheter des souvenirs?*

Answers
Ex 1: **1** M **2** T+M **3** T+M **4** T **5** T **6** T+M
    7 M **8** T **9** T **10** M
Ex 2: **1** *avant Noël* **2** *car* **3** *8h30* **4** *tapisserie*
    5 *dans le car* **6** *promenade en ville / magasins*
    7 *T-shirt* **8** *couleur (vert)* **9** *magasins / shopping*

A Vive la liberté! pp 98–99

Objective
Background information on La Villette

Language learning strategies
Reading: using context, key words and awareness of cognates and near cognates as an aid to understanding

Resources
Cassette for Ex 2
OHT (optional for Ex 1)
CM 22–23 for reference throughout Unit 5

Ways in
Grégory's class are still in Paris. In the afternoon, they go to La Villette on the outskirts of Paris, a highly popular recreational park with a cultural objective. Some of the attractions described in this spread are part of *la Cité des Sciences et de l'Industrie*, one of the main flagships of La Villette.

This spread introduces some of the attractions frequently referred to in Unit 5. There is no key language.

You can introduce the spread like this:
Le voyage à Paris continue. L'après-midi, après le déjeuner dans le parc, la classe de Grégory va à La Villette. On va lire une brochure sur La Villette.

1
Pupils should not use dictionaries. The aim here is to practise reading skills (awareness of parts of speech, context, etc.).

Pupils can try to do the matching first, then read the brochure for confirmation of their answers through context.

Answers
1 c   2 e   3 a   4 f   5 d   6 b

Extra – To encourage scanning and skimming, put the box below on OHT. Speed is important: *Regarde A–I très vite et trouve les paragraphes. Exemple 1C... Tu finis en ... minutes.*

1	Un écran de cinéma de 360°.
2	Un pilotage d'hélicoptère.
3	Un concert.
4	Des documentaires vidéo.
5	Un spectacle sur le cosmos.
6	Une exposition sur l'énergie.
7	Les voyages interplanétaires.
8	Des robots.

Answers
1 c *la Géode*   2 h *la Techno Cité*
3 d *La Cité de la Musique*   4 f *La Médiathèque*
5 a *Le Planétarium*   6 i *Explora*
7 b *La Station spatiale*   8 g *L'Inventorium*

2
Preparation – Make sure pupils understand the written statements and know that some of them are not accurate. Tell them that the statements on the cassette are all correct.

Pupils can either make notes from what they hear, then compare their notes with the written statements, or directly compare what they hear with the statements without making notes.

Extra – ♣ Ask pupils to correct the false statements.

COUNTER

> **1** – *Le Parc de la Villette, c'est où?*
>   – *Au nord-est de Paris.*
> **2** – *C'est ancien?*
>   – *Non, c'est très moderne.*
> **3** – *On y va comment?*
>   – *En bus, en voiture ou en métro.*
> **4** – *C'est ouvert tous les jours?*
>   – *Oui, sauf le lundi.*
> **5** – *Ça ouvre à quelle heure?*
>   – *Du mardi au samedi, c'est ouvert de 10h à 18h. Le dimanche, c'est ouvert de 10h à 19h.*
> **6** – *C'est cher?*
>   – *Il y a des réductions pour les enfants.*

Answers
1 *faux (au nord-est)*   2 *vrai*   3 *vrai*
4 *faux (fermé le lundi)*   5 *faux (19h)*   6 *vrai*

3
The aim here is to encourage pupils to read the brochure in more detail and to help them memorise some information about the attractions, which are referred to frequently in the rest of the unit.

B Tu viens avec nous?

pp 100–101

Objective
Giving, accepting and refusing invitations

Resources
Cassette for BD and Ex 1, 3 and 6

Key language
Tu viens / Vous venez au cinéma / à la piscine avec moi / nous?
Comment? En métro / A pied / Avec mes parents.
Je ne sais pas.

D'accord, je viens / on viens... avec toi / vous.
Désolé(e), je vais / on va... chez Jenny / en ville.
Recycling of places of entertainment and means of transport

Grammar
Present tense of *venir*

Language learning strategies
Improving conversational skills: providing details, arguments, explanations and suggestions

---

Ways in
Each pupil in Grégory's class is deciding which of the attractions to visit in La Villette. Grégory can't make up his mind. The new language here is essentially grammar (present tense of *venir* and *aller*). As is customary in **Camarades**, this spread practises only the parts of the verbs which are needed for the purpose of the spread while the **Point Langue** on page 104 and the accompanying CM7 present and practise all the singular forms (♦) or the whole paradigm (♣).

You can introduce the spread like this:
On est à La Villette. Les copains de Grégory choisissent un programme pour l'après-midi. Grégory hésite. Il aimerait bien tout visiter.

Pupils then read the BD while they listen to the cassette. (BD tapescript – see Pupil's Book.)

1

Preparation – Tell pupils about useful clues on the cassette: use of *oui /non / d'accord / désolé* and use of place names from La Villette.

Extra – To focus attention on some of the key language and emphasise sound discrimination, give pupils the phrases *avec moi / avec toi / avec nous / avec vous*, play the cassette again and ask pupils to tick the phrases whenever they hear them. The same can be done with *je viens / tu viens / je vais / tu vas*.

COUNTER

1 – *Je vais au Planétarium. Tu viens avec moi?*
   – *Au Planétarium? D'accord, je viens avec toi.*
2 – *Je vais à la Station spatiale. Vous venez avec moi?*
   – *D'accord, on vient avec toi.*
3 – *Qu'est-ce que vous faites?*
   – *On va à l'Inventorium. Tu viens avec nous?*
   – *Ah, désolée, je vais à la Médiathèque.*
4 – *Tu viens à la Médiathèque avec moi?*
   – *Je ne sais pas... Non, je vais à la Cité de la Musique. La Médiathèque, c'est nul!*
5 – *Qu'est-ce que vous faites, madame?*
   – *Moi? Je vais au Cinaxe. Et toi, tu viens?*
   – *Ah, moi, je vais à la Géode avec Jean-Paul.*
6 – *Je vais à la Techno Cité. Vous venez?*
   – *Oh ben, non! Viens à l'exposition Explora avec nous!*
   – *Désolée, Damien, je préfère aller à la Techno Cité.*
7 – *Explora, c'est pas mal, je pense.*
   – *Mais non! Tu viens à la Géode?*
   – *Ben... et Explora?*
   – *Il est 4h! Explora, c'est une exposition: c'est long!*
   – *Bon, d'accord, je viens avec vous.*

Answers
1 *oui* 2 *oui* 3 *non* 4 *non* 5 *non* 6 *non* 7 *oui*

2

This reinforces knowledge of *tu viens / je viens / je vais / d'accord / désolé / avec toi / avec moi.*

3

Preparation – Revise means of transport using Flashcards 62–66 and add *en métro / à pied*. Some pupils may remember *à pied*, used twice in reading tasks in previous units. You can also guide pupils regarding the destinations by revising place names.
♦ To make this task easier still, you can provide the list of destinations in the wrong order for multiple choice.

COUNTER

1 – *On va comment au cinéma? En bus?*
   – *Oh non, en métro. C'est plus rapide.*
   – *En métro? D'accord.*
2 – *Tu viens à la boulangerie?*
   – *D'accord. En vélo?*
   – *Mais non, à pied! Je n'ai pas de vélo.*
3 – *Maman, tu vas en Espagne jeudi?*
   – *Oui, pour le travail.*
   – *En train?*
   – *Non, en avion, c'est plus confortable!*
4 – *Vous allez à la patinoire?*
   – *Oui, en bus.*
   – *Mais non, il pleut. Venez en voiture.*
   – *En voiture? D'accord, merci!*
5 – *Vite, Amandine! On va au bowling.*
   – *Il est 3h15?? On y va en métro?*
   – *Mais non, on y va à pied! C'est à 300m.*
6 – *Tu vas où cet après-midi?*
   – *A la piscine, avec Lucie.*
   – *En vélo?*
   – *Ben... Lucie n'a pas de vélo. On peut aller en voiture avec toi?*
   – *Bon, d'accord.*

Answers
1 e *cinéma, plus rapide* 2 d, *boulangerie, pas de vélo*
3 c, *Espagne, plus confortable* 4 a, *patinoire, il pleut*
5 d, *bowling, 300m* 6 a, *piscine, pas de vélo*

4

Encourage pupils to do this without help, then to use the key afterwards for checking.

Answers
1 *en voiture* 2 *en avion* 3 *à pied* 4 *en car*
5 *en métro* 6 *en bus* 7 *en train* 8 *en vélo*

5

Preparation – Emphasise the link between question and answer as an aid to selecting the correct words.

You can ask pupils to hide the multiple-choice words and use context only.

Answers

1 *toi* **2** *Désolé(e)* **3** *je viens* **4** *vous* **5** *venez* **6** *vous*

6

After pupils have read the dialogues once, go through the strategy box with them and ask them to find in **Conversation B** examples of the suggestions given in the box.

Preparation – ♦ At the productive stage, brainstorm with pupils about which elements from **Conversation B** can be changed.

Conversation A

— *Je vais au cinéma. Tu viens?*

— *A quelle heure?*

— *A 4h15.*

— *Non. Je vais en ville.*

— *Non. Tu viens avec moi?*

— *Non.*

Conversation B

— *Je vais au cinéma cet après-midi. Tu viens avec moi, Julien?*

— *Ah? Au cinéma? A quelle heure?*

— *A 4h15. Au Cinéma Royal. Il y a un film policier. C'est génial!*

— *Je suis désolé, Mélanie, mais je dois aller en ville.*

— *C'est un film policier, tu sais.*

— *Oui, mais je vais avec ma mère. Je dois acheter un pantalon. Tu pourrais inviter Pascal?*

— *Ah, oui, d'accord. Bonne idée!*

— *Au revoir!*

C Vous allez où?

pp 102–103

Objective
Arranging to meet someone

Resources
Cassette for BD, Ex 1 and 2 and CM 5–6
Clock and/or Unit 3 CM 2
CM 5 and 6
Grilles 6 CM (optional for Ex 1)

Key language
Je vais...
Tu vas... / Vous allez... / On va... où? / ... au cinéma?

Quand? Dans cinq minutes / A 3h.
Bon, alors, rendez-vous au... à... h.
Recycling of places of entertainment and the time

Grammar
Present tense of *aller*
Recycling of *venir*

Language learning strategies
Pronunciation: *-u / -ou*
Checking work with a partner
Writing in pairs

Ways in

The pupils are about to start their visits. You can
introduce the spread like this:
*Un garçon et sa copine vont visiter la Géode. Mais il y a
un petit problème...*

Pupils read the BD while they listen to the cassette.
(BD tapescript – see Pupil's Book.) Ask a few questions
to check understanding and recycle question forms and
useful verb forms:
Qu'est-ce que le garçon va visiter?
Il voudrait visiter avec qui?, etc.

1

Preparation – Explain the meaning of *rendez-vous* and
revise the time using a clock and/or Unit 3 CM 2.
Revise *devant / derrière* etc.

COUNTER

> **1** – *Rendez-vous à... trois heures et demie?*
>   – *Trois heures et demie? Où?*
>   – *Devant le Cinaxe.*
> **2** – *Rendez-vous à quelle heure?*
>   – *A... trois heures et quart.*
>   – *Où?*
>   – *Devant la Station spatiale?*
> **3** – *Julien, tu vas où?*
>   – *Je vais à la Cité de la Musique.*
>   – *Alors, rendez-vous à quatre heures moins le quart?*
>   – *A quatre heures moins le quart? Oui, mais où?*
>   – *Devant la cafétéria?*
> **4** – *Je vais à la Géode. Et toi?*
>   – *A l'Inventorium. Rendez-vous dans... une heure
>   et demie?*
>   – *Dans une heure et demie? Donc à... 4h?*
>   – *Oui, rendez-vous à 4h. Devant l'Inventorium.*
> **5** – *Allez, vite, vite!*
>   – *Pourquoi?*
>   – *J'ai rendez-vous.*
>   – *Tu as rendez-vous? Quand?*
>   – *Dans dix minutes. A quatre heures moins vingt.*
>   – *Ah bon? Avec qui?*
>   – *Avec Patrick. Derrière le Planétarium.*
> **6** – *On va à la Techno Cité?*
>   – *Ben... non, je ne peux pas. J'ai rendez-vous avec
>   Sophie et Frédéric.*
>   – *Pourquoi?*
>   – *On va à la cafétéria.*
>   – *Je peux aller avec vous?*
>   – *Oui! On a rendez-vous à quatre heures moins dix
>   en face de la Géode.*

Answers
1 *3h30, devant le Cinaxe* **2** *3h15, devant la Station
spatiale* **3** *3h45, devant la cafétéria* **4** *4h, devant
l'Inventorium* **5** *3h40, derrière le Planétarium*
6 *3h50 en face de la Géode*

2

Preparation – Point out to pupils that the pictures
follow a logical sequence as stimulus for a dialogue,
unlike the cassette.

COUNTER

> **1** *Désolée, je vais chez le dentiste.*
> **2** *Tu vas où à midi?*
> **3** *A 3h30.*
> **4** *A quelle heure?*
> **5** *Je vais au parc.*
> **6** *Alors, rendez-vous à 4h?*
> **7** *D'accord!*
> **8** *Tu viens à la piscine cet après-midi?*

Answers
Listening: **1** d **2** a **3** f **4** e **5** b **6** g **7** h **8** c

On prononce bien

COUNTER

> *Ecoute:*
>   *-u   -ou   tu vas où?*
> *Répète:*
>   *-u   -ou   tu vas où?   rendez-vous où?*
>   *douze minutes   une douche   un bus rouge*
>   *une bouteille   où est la cuisine?*

3

Both 1–5 and a–e are in the wrong order. To do the
first part of the task, pupils simply need to work out
which answer makes sense with which question.

You can simplify the second part of the task by giving
pupils the correct order for items 1–5, thus making
this a copying task instead.
Answers
3–b–2–d–5–a–1–e–4–c

4

Pupils can either adapt the messages from Ex 3
(different place, time, etc.) or be more creative.

Extra – Pupils cut out and jumble up their messages
for a partner to put in a correct sequence. Depending
on the nature of the messages, there may be more
than one correct sequence.

D Point Langue / Atelier   pp 104–105

Resources
Cassette for Atelier Ex 2
Scissors for CM 7
CM 7 printed on card

Key language
Recycling of invitations and arranging to meet
Recycling of numbers

Grammar
Present tense of *aller* and *venir*

Language learning strategies
Applying a pattern
Learning through play

Point Langue

This page complements Spreads B and C by providing additional practice on the present tense of *venir* and *aller*.

Introduction – Point out that in English one talks about 'coming and going'. In French, it is the other way round.

COUNTER

> *Je vais, je viens,*
> *Le travail, ce n'est pas bien.*
> *Tu vas, tu viens,*
> *Le travail, ce n'est pas sain.*
> *Il va, il vient,*
> *Et il dort de moins en moins.*
> *Nous allons, nous venons,*
> *Le travail, ce n'est pas bon.*
> *Vous allez, vous venez,*
> *Et vous êtes très fatigués.*
> *Ils vont, ils viennent,*
> *Vive la fin de la semaine!*

1 The ♦ task only practises singular forms. In the ♣ task, pupils should be encouraged to use both singular and plural forms.

COUNTER

> – *Tu viens avec moi?*
> – *Tu vas où?*
> – *Je vais à l'Inventorium.*
> – *Moi aussi! Je viens avec vous.*
> – *Bon! Je vais au Cinaxe!*
> – *Le prof aussi va au Cinaxe. Salut!*
> – *Alors, on va au Cinaxe, Zoë?*
> – *Euh... non, j'ai changé d'idée.*

Answers
♦ **1** *viens* **2** *vas* **3** *vais* **4** *viens* **5** *vais* **6** *va* **7** *va*

Atelier

1 ***Preparation*** – Brainstorm about possible answers to the board game questions.

2 ***Preparation*** – Do some number revision: tens and hundreds. You can simplify the task by providing the answers in the wrong order for multiple choice, possibly adding one or two numbers not on cassette. Instead, you can provide a choice of two numbers for each item.

COUNTER

> *La Villette en chiffres.*
> *La Médiathèque est très grande. On trouve 500 journaux et magazines.*
> *A la Médiathèque, on trouve aussi 300 logiciels.*
> *Au cinéma de la Géode, il y a 400 places.*
> *A la Géode, une caméra pèse 50 kilos.*
> *Le système de projection est très moderne.*
> *Il pèse 2 tonnes.*
> *Un film, c'est très cher. Pour un film de 30 minutes, il faut 3 kilomètres de pellicule.*

Answers
1 500 **2** 300 **3** 400 **4** 50 **5** 2 **6** 3

E C'était bien?

Objective
Saying what you did on a day out

Resources
Cassette for BD and Ex 1 and 3
CM 1
OHT (see **Ways in** section)

Key language
C'était comment, ton après-midi? C'était bien, la Géode?

Oui, c'était chouette / pas mal. Bof, pas génial. / Non, c'était nul.
J'ai été au parc / chez John / avec Habib.
J'ai regardé / visité / écouté / mangé / travaillé / acheté...

Grammar
Perfect tense: regular -*er* verbs with *j'ai...*

Language learning strategies
Pronunciation: -*ai* / -*é*
Writing from notes

Ways in
The class meet again and share their experiences. You can introduce the spread like this: *L'après-midi à La Villette est fini. La classe donne des opinions sur La Villette.*

Use CM 1 on OHT to introduce the verb forms. Pupils then read the BD while they listen to the cassette. Use the cassette for repetition practice.

Preparation – Use the pictures to practise opinions with *c'était*.

COUNTER

1 – *C'était comment, le Cinaxe?*
  – *Ah, c'était génial! C'était un film sur les pilotes d'avions.*
2 – *La cafétéria, c'était bien?*
  – *Oui, c'était bien! Et pas très cher!*
3 – *L'aquarium, c'était bien?*
  – *C'était nul! Moi, je préfère les zoos.*
4 – *C'était comment, la Techno cité?*
  – *C'était pas mal, mais je préfère le musée de l'Homme.*
5 – *Tu as été à la Station spatiale?*
  – *Moi? Oui, avec Julien.*
  – *C'était comment?*
  – *Ah! C'était vraiment excellent!*
6 – *Tu as été à la Cité de la musique?*
  – *Ben, oui! Moi, la musique, euh...*
  – *C'était bien?*
  – *Ben... pas génial. Il n'y a pas de concerts en semaine. Seulement le samedi et le dimanche.*
7 – *Tu as été où?*
  – *J'ai été à Explora.*
  – *Explora? Qu'est-ce que c'est?*
  – *Ben c'est... l'exposition sur le... sur l'univers.*
  – *C'était bien?*
  – *Bof, oui et non. C'était bien pour le projet, mais c'était un peu ennuyeux.*

Answers
1 *Cinaxe* 😊 2 *cafétéria* 😊 3 *Aquarium* 😦

4 *Techno cité* 😐 5 *Station spatiale* 😊

6 *Cité de la Musique* 😐 7 *Explora* 😐

2

Extra – Pupil **A** reads out one of the sentences. Pupil **B** – with book closed – responds with the appropriate facial expression and with *ouais / bof / nul.*

3

Preparation – ♦ Tell pupils that it is only the verbs – not the other detail – that matters here. Use the pictures to rehearse the verbs before you start.

COUNTER

1 – *C'était bien, le week-end?*
  – *Oui, pas mal, j'ai acheté un jeu vidéo.*
2 – *Salut, Magalie. C'était bien, ton week-end?*
  – *Bof, comme ci, comme ça. J'ai travaillé samedi.*
3 – *Ah, Ahmed, c'était bien, ton anniversaire?*
  – *Ah, ouais! Le soir, j'ai mangé au restaurant avec ma famille.*
4 – *C'était bien, le cours de musique?*
  – *Le cours de musique? Bof, on a écouté un disque. Du piano.*
5 – *Et donc, euh... tu as été à la patinoire?*
  – *La patinoire? Non, c'est fermé le lundi!*
  – *Ah bon?*
  – *Ben oui! Alors j'ai été chez Max.*
6 – *Vous avez passé un bon week-end?*
  – *Oui, merci. J'ai visité la Tour Eiffel avec la famille.*
  – *Ah, c'est bien!*
  – *Oui, mais c'est fatigant!*
7 – *Tu as été chez Ludivine samedi soir!*
  – *Moi? Non, non...*
  – *Si! Tu as été chez Ludivine!*
  – *Non, non! J'ai... j'ai regardé la télé.*
  – *Qu'est-ce que tu as regardé?*
  – *Ben, euh... je... je ne sais pas, j'ai... j'ai oublié.*

Answers
1 d *(jeu vidéo)* **2** c *(samedi; bof)* **3** b *(restaurant avec famille)* **4** g *(disque, piano)* **5** f *(Max)* **6** e *(Tour Eiffel)* **7** a *(oublié)*

4

Preparation – Ask pupils to use only the verbs from the key in their answers. Do some whole-class practice before children start working in pairs.

5

Answers
♦ **1** *travaillé* **2** *visité* **3** *acheté* **4** *regardé* **5** *mangé* **6** *écouté* ♣ **1** *faux – J'ai été à la gare en car.* **2** *faux – J'ai visité avec un guide.* **3** *faux – J'ai acheté un cadeau / une surprise pour grand-père.* **4** *faux – J'ai déjeuné dans le parc.* **5** *vrai* **6** *vrai*

6

Samedi matin, j'ai été au collège. A midi et demi, j'ai été en ville. J'ai mangé un hamburger. Samedi après-midi, j'ai été à la patinoire avec Marc. Ensuite, j'ai acheté un poster pour ma chambre. J'ai été à la maison à sept heures. Samedi soir, j'ai regardé un film policier à la télé. A neuf heures et demie, j'ai été dans ma chambre et j'ai écouté des CD.

F Qu'est-ce que tu as fait?   pp 108–109

Objective
Saying what you did on a day out

Resources
Cassette for BD and Ex 1
CM 2, 8 and 9 (CM 8 can be copied onto card)
Dictionaries (optional for Ex 3)
OHT (see **Ways in** section)

Key language
Qu'est-ce que tu as fait?

Hier / Mardi dernier,... j'ai pris des photos / j'ai bu un coca / j'ai fait une promenade / j'ai vu la Géode / j'ai perdu ma veste
Tu as ... (visité ...)? (Est-ce que) Tu as... (mangé...)?
Recycling of past participles (Spread E)

Grammar
Perfect tense with *j'ai / tu*: regular -er verbs + some irregular verbs

Language learning strategies
Looking up irregular verb forms in the dictionary

Ways in
Before the class leave La Villette, a girl suddenly starts to panic: she has lost her jacket. You can introduce the spread like this: *A La Villette, c'est la panique! Une fille a un problème.*

Pupils read the BD while they listen to the cassette. Ask them to use the visuals and the context to work out the meaning of the new verbs in the perfect tense, then improvise a quick check from French (you) into English (pupils), then the other way round. You can then use CM 2 – which can be made into an OHT – for further presentation and practice work. (BD tapescript – see Pupil's Book.)

1   COUNTER

– *J'ai perdu mon portefeuille!*
– *Qu'est-ce que tu as fait cet après-midi?*
– *J'ai vu un film... à la Géode...*
– *Un film? Et ensuite?*
– *Ensuite? Euh... j'ai pris des photos.*
– *Des photos?*
– *Oui, devant le Planétarium...*
– *Et ensuite?*
– *Ben, j'ai... j'ai fait du bateau avec Hayoon...*
– *Du bateau? Et... après?*
– *Après le bateau, j'ai bu un coca.*
– *Un coca? Au café?*
– *Oui, et j'ai fait des dessins pour mon projet.*
– *Des dessins? C'est bien.*
– *Mon portefeuille! Il est au café!*

Answers
1 e, d, c, a, b

2 Pupils should only use verbs in the perfect presented in Spreads E and F. ♣ Pupils practise the use of *tu as...* in the perfect tense in their written notes.

3 Pupils should translate the verbs without dictionaries as much as possible, using the context and their knowledge of verbs in the infinitive or the present tense to deduce meaning.
Answers
hier = yesterday *dernier* = last *j'ai ouvert* = I opened *j'ai couru* = I ran *j'ai mis* = I put *tu as reçu* = you received *j'ai lu* = I read *j'ai appris* = I learnt *tu as attendu* = you waited
1 Daniel **2** Daniel **3** Anouk **4** Daniel **5** Anouk

4 Pupils should reuse verbs from Spreads E and F only. ♣ In addition to key verbs, pupils can reuse verbs from Ex 3.

G La Porte de Pantin? pp 110–111

Objective
Finding your way

Resources
Cassette for BD, Ex 1 and 5 and CM 11
Flashcards 72–75
CM 3, 10 and 11
OHT (see **Ways in** section)
Town map (optional for Ex 6)
CM 11 tapescript (optional)
CM 1 card pictures (optional – see CM 11 notes)

Key language
Le métro, s'il vous plaît? C'est tout droit
C'est la première / deuxième / troisième rue à droite / gauche.
C'est avant / après / devant... le commissariat / le marché /
la librairie / la pharmacie.
... puis; ... sur la gauche / droite
Recycling of places in town

Language learning strategies
Learning through play

Ways in
The class are now on their way home, but one teacher
has had to stay behind to wait for Grégory. You can
introduce the spread like this: *La classe va prendre le train
et rentrer à la maison, mais un prof reste à La Villette.
Pourquoi?*

Use CM 3 – which can be made into an OHT – to
introduce directions. Also practise with pupils moving
round the classroom if possible.

Pupils then read the BD while they listen to the cassette.
Ask pupils to generate as many statements as possible
about the BD. To motivate them, give them a
challenging target number of statements to reach as a
whole class, for example fifteen: – *C'est Grégory.* / –
Grégory est à La Villette. / – *Grégory n'est pas avec la
classe.* etc.
(BD tapescript – see Pupil's Book.)

1

COUNTER

1 – *C'est tout droit, puis la deuxième rue à gauche, et
la troisième rue à gauche. Je répète. Tout droit, la
deuxième à gauche et la troisième à gauche.*

2 – *C'est la première rue à droite, et encore la
première rue à droite. Je répète. La première à
droite, et la première à droite.*

3 – *C'est tout droit, et la deuxième rue à droite, puis
la première rue à gauche. Je répète. Tout droit, la
deuxième à droite et la première à gauche.*

4 – *C'est tout droit. Ensuite, c'est la deuxième rue à
droite, et c'est tout droit. Je répète. Tout droit, la
deuxième à droite, et vous continuez tout droit.*

5 – *C'est tout droit. Ensuite, c'est la deuxième rue à
gauche, et la première rue à droite. Je répète. Tout
droit, la deuxième à gauche, et la première à droite.*

6 – *C'est tout droit. Je répète. Vous allez tout droit.*

7 – *C'est la première rue à gauche, hein, puis la
deuxième rue à droite. Je répète. La première à
gauche et la deuxième à droite.*

8 – *C'est la première rue à droite, puis c'est tout droit!
Je répète. La première à droite, et c'est tout droit.*

Answers
1 e 2 o 3 d 4 i 5 b 6 c 7 j 8 p
Oskarrr a quatre objets seulement. (screw driver missing)

2

♦ Encourage pupils to follow the map with their finger.

3

Answers
C'est tout droit, la première rue à gauche, puis la deuxième rue à gauche.
C'est tout droit, la première rue à gauche, puis la première rue à droite.
C'est tout droit, la deuxième rue à gauche, puis la deuxième rue à droite.
C'est tout droit, la deuxième rue à droite, puis la première rue à gauche.
C'est tout droit, la deuxième rue à droite, puis la première rue à droite.

4

Pupils need CM 10 for this task.

Preparation – Use Flashcards 72–75 to teach the new
place names. Check pupils remember the other place
names used on the maps.

After completing their maps, pupils should say the
directions to the places they have spotted back to their
partners to check they have found the correct places.

5

Pupils need CM 10 again for this task.

Preparation – Pupils who did not complete Ex 4 or
made mistakes need to complete their maps accurately to
do this task. Point out to pupils that one place is used
twice.

COUNTER

1 – *C'est la première rue à gauche. C'est sur la
droite.*

2 – *C'est la première rue à droite puis la première
rue à gauche. C'est sur la droite.*

3 – *C'est la première rue à droite, et c'est sur la
gauche, en face du cinéma.*

4 – *Alors... c'est tout droit, euh... la deuxième rue à
gauche, et... la première rue à droite. C'est sur la
droite.*

5 – *C'est la troisième rue à droite. Oui, c'est ça. La
troisième à droite. Et... c'est sur la gauche.*

6 – *Eh bien, attendez... C'est la... deuxième rue à
gauche, oui, c'est ça, et... la troisième rue à
droite. Et ensuite, c'est tout droit!*

7 – *Eh bien... c'est la... première rue à droite, vous
allez devant la patinoire et le cinéma, et... c'est
la première rue à gauche.*

8 – *Bon, allez à gauche, la... la première rue à
gauche. Ensuite, vous continuez... entre la
boulangerie et la boucherie, et c'est tout droit.*

Answers
1 *la boucherie* 2 *le café/la cafétéria* 3 *la pharmacie*
4 *le commissariat* 5 *la librairie* 6 *le métro/la station de
métro* 7 *le café/la cafétéria* 8 *le collège*

6

The Humanities department may have a simplified map
of your town/village which the whole class could use.

H Point Langue / Atelier   pp 112–113

Resources
Cassette for **Point Langue** Ex 1 and for CM 12 and 13
CM 12 and 13
Card for **Atelier**

Grammar
Perfect tense: *j'ai... / Tu as...*

Language learning strategies
Applying a pattern

Point Langue

This page provides additional practice on the forms of
the perfect tense addressed so far.

1

After the reading and before the listening, tell pupils
that the interview does not duplicate sentences 1–5
word for word.

COUNTER

> **1** – *Yannick, bienvenue à Désirs et Réalité.*
> – *Bonjour.*
> – *Yannick, tu as 14 ans. Tu as décidé d'être astronaute. Pourquoi?*
> – *Un jour, j'ai été à la Cité des Sciences: sensationnel!*
>
> **2** – *Qu'est-ce que tu as vu exactement?*
> – *J'ai commencé avec le Planétarium, et puis... ensuite, j'ai visité la Station spatiale.*
> – *Qu'est-ce que tu as préféré?*
> – *La Station spatiale.*
>
> **3** – *Tu as préféré la Station spatiale? Pourquoi?*
> – *J'ai... j'ai lu de l'information sur les voyages dans l'espace. C'était intéressant.*
>
> **4** – *Tu as pris beaucoup de notes pendant ta visite?*
> – *Oui, mais pas beaucoup, parce que j'ai acheté deux livres, un livre sur Ariane et la biographie d'un astronaute. En plus, j'ai pris plus de cinquante photos.*
>
> **5** – *Tu as déjà voyagé en avion?*
> – *En avion, non. En hélicoptère, oui.*
> – *Eh bien, Yannick, une surprise. Dimanche, tu vas faire un voyage Paris-New York en Concorde.*

Answers
a *ai décidé* **b** *ai été* **c** *ai vu/visité* **d** *ai préféré*
e *ai lu* **f** *ai pris* **g** *ai acheté* **h** *ai pris* **i** *ai voyagé*

2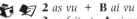

Answers
1 *as décidé* + **C** *ai décidé, ai visité*
2 *as vu* + **B** *ai vu*
3 *as fait* + **A** *ai préparé, ai inventé*

Atelier

Encourage pupils to work out the rubrics for the two
games on their own.

Coin lecture can be used simply for reading for pleasure.
To give this a purpose, ask pupils to copy the article
headings in order of interest and in order of difficulty.
For further exploitation, improvise some *On parle de...*
sentences and ask pupils to spot the correct article as
quickly as possible. For example:
On parle d'un voyage sur une planète différente.
On parle d'une construction très longue.

1 On rentre à Chartres

pp 114–115

Objective
Buying train tickets

Resources
Cassette for BD and Ex 1 and 3
Flashcards 76–81
CM 14
Grilles 6 CM for Ex 3

Key language
Un aller simple / aller-retour pour..., s'il vous plaît
C'est combien?

Il y a un train à quelle heure pour...?
Le train arrive à... à quelle heure?
Il y a un wagon-restaurant?
C'est quel quai?
Quai numéro...
Recycling of numbers and 24-hour clock

Language learning strategies
Pronunciation: familiar cognates and near cognates
Learning full sentences by heart
Awareness of sequencing

Ways in
Grégory and his teacher are having to get back to
Chartres on their own. They are at the train station in
Paris. You can introduce the spread like this:
*Grégory et son prof sont à la gare à Paris. Ils vont rentrer
à Chartres tout seuls.*

Use Flashcards 76–81 to introduce the key language.
Pupils then read the BD while they listen to the
cassette. Next, ask pupils to use the BD to complete
your sentences: *Grégory et le prof sont à... / Le prof
achète... / Il y a un train à... / Le train est au quai... /
Le train va arriver à... / On peut manger dans le... /
Le voyage n'est pas très long: seulement... (41 minutes!)*
(BD tapescript – see Pupil's Book.)

1 This task is meant to develop awareness of context –
useful when pupils have to draw conclusions.

1	*Un aller simple, s'il vous plaît.*
2	*C'est quel quai?*
3	*Il y a un train à quelle heure?*
4	*J'ai perdu mes sandwichs!*
5	*Le commissariat, s'il vous plaît?*
6	*Il y a un wagon-restaurant?*
7	*Rendez-vous à trois heures.*
8	*Le train arrive à Chartres à quelle heure?*
9	*Un aller-retour, s'il vous plaît.*
10	*C'est le quai numéro 8.*

Answers
1 ✔ f 2 ✔ e 3 ✔ a 4 ✗ 5 ✗ 6 ✔ d 7 ✗
8 ✔ c 9 ✔ b 10 ✔ g

2 Encourage pupils to reuse this method regularly for
learning and revision purposes.

3 A grid is provided on CM.

Preparation – ♣ Tell pupils that the extra detail is
heard at the end of each conversation.

1 – *Un aller simple pour Orléans, s'il vous plaît.*
– *85f, monsieur.*
– *Il y a un wagon-restaurant?*
– *Oui, bien sûr.*
– *Il y a un train à quelle heure?*
– *A 21h35.*
– *21h35. Et il arrive à quelle heure?*
– *Il arrive à 22h28.*

– *C'est quel quai?*
– *Quai numéro 6.*
– *Où sont les toilettes, s'il vous plaît?*
– *Là-bas, à gauche.*
2 – *Un aller simple pour Le Mans, s'il vous plaît.*
– *148f, madame.*
– *Il y a un wagon-restaurant?*
– *Oui, bien sûr.*
– *Il y a un train à quelle heure?*
– *A 20h55.*
– *20h55. Et il arrive à quelle heure?*
– *Il arrive à 21h32.*
– *C'est quel quai?*
– *Quai numéro 9.*
– *Je voudrais acheter des magazines. Il y a un
kiosque?*
– *Oui, regardez. Le kiosque est en face du café.*
3 – *Un aller-retour pour Dreux, s'il vous plaît.*
– *Oui, ça vous fait 118f.*
– *Il y a un wagon-restaurant?*
– *Ah, non, non, non, pas dans le train pour Dreux.*
– *Il y a un train à quelle heure?*
– *Il y a un train à 22h40. Et... il arrive à Dreux
à 23h15.*
– *C'est quel quai?*
– *Euh, voyons... c'est le numéro 4.*
– *Excusez-moi, vous avez de la monnaie pour la
machine à snack?*
4 – *Excusez-moi. Un aller-retour pour Toulouse, s'il
vous plaît.*
– *Oui... Ça fait 563f.*
– *On peut manger dans le train?*
– *Oui, bien sûr!*
– *Il y a un train à 23h46, c'est ça?*
– *Oui, c'est ça, 23h46.*
– *Il arrive à Toulouse à quelle heure?*
– *Euh... demain matin... à 5h21.*
– *Et c'est le quai...*
– *Quai 2, madame.*
– *Oh, euh... je voudrais une place près de la
fenêtre.*

Answers
1 *a 85f   b 21h35   c 6   extra: toilettes à gauche*
2 *d aller simple   e oui   f 21h32   extra: kiosque
(magazines) en face du café*
3 *g 118f   h 22h40   i 4   extra: monnaie pour machine
à snack*
4 *j aller-retour   k oui   l 5h21   extra: place près de la
fenêtre*

4 Pupils should jot down the information they gather,
then report back to their partners in speaking at the
end to check it is correct.

5 ♦ Pupils need CM 14. ♣ Pupils should use context and
awareness of sequencing instead. They can use CM 14
after they have completed the task, for double checking
only.
Answers
*Samedi et... / Dimanche soir,... / J'ai été à la gare... /
J'ai trouvé... / J'ai pris le train... / Arrivé à Dijon,... /
Pour une chambre,... / Le week-end prochain,...*

◻ Les aventures de Grégory

pp 116–117

Objective
Describing what someone else did

Resources
Cassette for BD and Ex 1
CM 15 and 16
Dictionaries optional for CM 15

Key language
Le prof a cherché...

Il a contacté la police.
Annie a fini la visite.
Elle a attendu 20 minutes.

Grammar
Perfect tense with *il a... / elle a...*
Recycling of past participles

Language learning strategies
Using context as an aid to understanding

Ways in
Grégory is in the headteacher's office. One of his
teachers is reporting his misadventure in Paris the
previous day. You can introduce the spread like this:
*Le voyage à Paris est fini. Grégory est au collège. Il est
avec un prof et avec Madame Adam, la directrice* (explain
directeur / directrice by using your school headteacher
as an example).

There is little new language in this spread. Apart from
a few past participles only met receptively in topic 2,
the emphasis is on the perfect tense with *il / elle a...*

Pupils read the BD while they listen to the cassette.
Make sure pupils understand the verbs, and emphasise
the use of *chercher* without preposition for 'to look for'.
(BD tapescript – see Pupil's Book.)

Answers
1 c, *Médiathèque très moderne* 2 f, *n'aime pas beaucoup
le prof* 3 d, *copain préféré* 4 a, *c'était bien* 5 i, *film
intéressant* 6 j, *super* 7 b, *c'est long* 8 g, *tout seul:
dommage* 9 h, *sympa(s)* 10 e, *dommage*

2

Extra – Pupils describe as many of the pictures as
they can entirely from memory. They compete in pairs
and get one point per correct item.

3

♦ **Preparation** – Point out the use of *d'abord / ensuite /
après / finalement* as a reminder of good sequencing.

♣ **Preparation** – The words are listed chronologically.
Point out use of context and awareness of parts of
speech as reading clues.
Answers
♦ *D'abord... / Il a visité... / Ensuite... / A la station... /
C'était bien... / Après... / Il a trouvé... / Finalement...*
♣ 1 *pour commencer* 2 *en plus* 3 *fusées*
4 *Malheureusement* 5 *c'est dommage* 6 *crustacés*
7 *groupes scolaires* 8 *trop tard*

4

Pupils should write in the third person. ♦ Pupils can
use 1–8 from Ex 3 as a model.

1

COUNTER

1 – *Alors, Grégory, qu'est-ce qu'il a fait?*

– *D'abord, Grégory a été à la Médiathèque avec les
profs. C'est une médiathèque très moderne.*

2 – *Il a été à la Médiathèque avec les profs?*

– *Oui, mais après dix minutes, il a fini sa visite. Il
n'aime pas beaucoup Monsieur Besse.*

3 – *Ah oui, et alors?*

– *Ben, il a cherché Thierry, mais sans succès!
Thierry, c'est son copain préféré.*

4 – *Sans succès? Et après?*

– *Après, il a été à la Station spatiale, pour voir...*

– *La Station spatiale? Oui, c'était bien.*

5 – *Oui, mais Thierry a été au Cinaxe avec Anaïs. Ils
ont regardé un film intéressant sur la planète Mars.*

6 – *Alors, euh... il a pris des photos à la Station
spatiale.*

– *Ah oui, j'ai vu son appareil-photo. Il est super!*

7 – *Ensuite, il a attendu vingt minutes.*

– *Oh, vingt minutes, c'est long!*

8 – *Finalement, il a visité l'aquarium, tout seul...*

– *Oh, c'est dommage!*

9 – *Après, il a contacté un gardienne...*

– *Un gardien? Ah, oui, ils sont très sympas, les
gardiens.*

10 – *...mais il a perdu le groupe. Complètement perdu!*

– *Oh, c'est dommage! Et... aïe, aïe, aïe, les
professeurs!!!*

K C'était génial! pp 118–119

Objective
Saying what someone else did on a day out

Resources
Cassette for BD and Ex 1 and 4
CM 4, 17 and 18
OHT (see Ways in section)

Key language
Tu as / Il a / Elle a... voyagé comment?/ ... mangé où? /
... bu quoi? / ... visité le zoo quand? / ... pris le car à quelle heure? ... payé

combien? / ... voyagé avec qui?
On a... (acheté des souvenirs)
Recycling of key question words

Grammar
Perfect tense with *on a...*
Recycling of past participles

Language learning strategies
Using spider webs for writing and speaking

Ways in
The headteacher explains that every *classe de 5ᵉ* went on a different trip. The various accounts of those trips provide an opportunity for recycling the perfect tense forms practised so far. There is little new language, but a useful recap on question forms, using the informal structures often used in speaking. You can introduce the spread like this: *Au collège de Grégory, il y a cinq classes de 5ᵉ différentes: la 5ᵉ1, la 5ᵉ2, la 5ᵉ...* (let pupils continue). *Grégory est en 5ᵉ2. La classe de Grégory a été à Paris, mais les autres classes ont fait des voyages différents.*

Pupils read the BD while they listen to the cassette. Afterwards, use CM 4 – which can be made into an OHT – to practise the question forms in the perfect tense. (BD tapescript – see Pupil's Book.)

1 ***Preparation*** – Start from the pictures and generate as much language as possible. If necessary, start from individual words, then ask for sentences. Make sure this includes some use of the perfect tense:

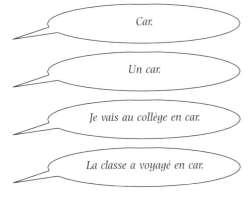

Car.

Un car.

Je vais au collège en car.

La classe a voyagé en car.

Items 5–9 are more difficult.

COUNTER

> **1** – *Assan, qu'est-ce que tu as fait?*
> – *J'ai fait du camping.*
>
> **2** – *Qu'est-ce que tu as fait, Mathilde?*
> – *J'ai fait une promenade à pied.*
>
> **3** – *Et toi, Romain, qu'est-ce que tu as fait?*
> – *J'ai fait de l'équitation.*
>
> **4** – *Sylvia, tu a été où?*
> – *J'ai été à la fête foraine et au parc safari.*

> **5** – *Nous, on a été à la campagne en train. Après, on a fait une promenade et on a été à la plage.*
>
> **6** – *La campagne, la nature, c'est super. Mais je n'aime pas beaucoup les promenades à pied, donc le camping, pour moi, c'était idéal. Et puis, j'aime bien voyager en vélo.*
>
> **7** – *Moi, j'aime beaucoup les animaux. Alors, le voyage, c'était super. Plus tard, j'aimerais bien travailler dans une ferme, moi aussi.*
>
> **8** – *J'ai été au parc safari, j'adore les animaux. J'ai une collection de magazines d'animaux, des animaux sauvages. J'aime surtout les lions et les baleines.*
>
> **9** – *Bon, les activités, le sport, ça va, c'était bien. Mais le déjeuner à la cantine: pouahhh! Dégoûtant!*

Answers
1 5ᵉ4 **2** 5ᵉ5 **3** 5ᵉ1 **4** 5ᵉ3 **5** 5ᵉ5 **6** 5ᵉ4
7 5ᵉ4 **8** 5ᵉ3 **9** 5ᵉ1

2 ♦ ***Preparation*** – Rehearse the key question words again if necessary.

♣ Make sure pupils do not attempt to use plural forms in the perfect tense. *On* can of course be used for 'we', as in the example. Encourage a mixture of *J'ai... / On a... / Paul a...* Point out that, as in the present tense, verb forms with *on, il* and *elle* in the perfect tense are identical.

Answers
♦ **1** e **2** a **3** g **4** b **5** c **6** d **7** f

3 Suggest pupils answer within five seconds (♦) or ten seconds (♣) to score a point.

4 ***Preparation*** – Check pupils understand the columns headings for dialogue 1. The items are chronological.

The second part of the tasks is aimed at familiarising pupils with spider diagrams. Explain that the four items are related: the beginning of the dialogue about lions, etc. is merely a warm-up.

COUNTER

Dialogue 1

- *Tu as fait un voyage? Tu as été où?*
- *J'ai été au zoo.*
- *Au zoo? Tu as été au zoo avec qui?*
- *Avec ma classe.*
- *Avec ta classe. Et tu as été au zoo quand?*
- *Quand? Euh... lundi.*
- *Tu as été au zoo comment? En train?*
- *Non, non, en car.*
- *Et tu as pris le car à quelle heure?*
- *Le car? Euh... à... 8h15 le matin.*
- *C'était bien?*
- *Ouais, ça va, c'était amusant.*

Dialogue 2

- *Alors, tu a vu quoi au zoo?*
- *Ben... des animaux! Des lions, des tigres, des girafes...*
- *Quand? Le matin?*
- *Oui, oui, le matin. Et l'après-midi, j'ai regardé les pingouins.*
- *Tu as regardé les pingouins avec qui? Avec la classe?*
- *Toute la classe, non. Avec Isabelle et Cédric.*
- *Et les pingouins, c'était bien?*
- *Oui, c'était super!*

Answers
Dialogue 1: **1** *zoo, en car, amusant, lundi, 8h15*
Dialogue 2: **1** *vrai* **2** *vrai* **3** *vrai* **4** *faux*

5

The aim is for pupils to learn how to plan their work. The difference between ♦ and ♣ is purely in terms of quantity.

Make sure pupils work in two steps, first devising diagrams, then using them as a guide for writing their dialogues.

COUNTER

- *Tu as acheté des souvenirs? Qu'est-ce que tu as acheté?*
- *Oh, des autocollants, c'est tout. C'est cher au zoo!*
- *Tu as acheté des autocollants pour qui?*
- *Ben... pour mon frère!*
- *Ah oui?*
- *Ben oui, il aime les animaux.*
- *Tu as payé combien?*
- *J'ai payé 25f.*

L Point Langue / Atelier

Resources
Cassette for CM 21
CM 19 printed on card
Scissors for CM 19
CM 20 and 21

Grammar
Perfect tense singular of *avoir* verbs

Language learning strategies
Learning verbs
Learning through rap

Point Langue

This page provides additional practice of the perfect tense singular for the verbs addressed so far.

Answers
tu as fini   j'ai mangé   tu as contacté   il a acheté

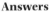

♣ Preparation – To encourage pupils to build up their reference skills, ask them to browse through the whole of Unit 5 to find useful models.

Answers
♦ **1** *A Paris, on a voyagé en métro.* **2** *On a visité le Planétarium.* **3** *J'ai pris des photos.* **4** *Mon père a bu un coca.* **5** *L'après-midi, j'ai fait du bateau.* **6** *Dans le bateau, j'ai vu une souris.* **7** *Mon père a parlé avec des visiteurs.* **8** *Finalement, j'ai acheté une casquette.*

Atelier

1 **Preparation –** Give pupils a free choice within a time limit. Ask them to read through all the rubrics in silence, then ask them to help each other clear any comprehension problems. Intervene as little as possible.

2 Pupils can do collaborative writing. Encourage them to learn their raps by heart – maybe a few lines each – and to create a rhythm. Give pupils the opportunity to perform, possibly in the presence of a jury (sixth formers, other teachers, French assistants, etc.).

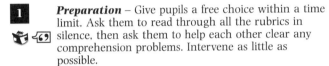

CAMARADES 2	OVERVIEW – UNITE 6 – L'ECOLE EST FINIE!			NATIONAL CURRICULUM	
Topics/Objectives	Key language	Grammar	Strategies	PoS coverage	AoE
A **Tu as combien en maths?** Discussing school reports	*Qu'est-ce que tu as en... (maths)? J'ai D / 12 sur 20 / excellent / bien / assez bien / «travail sérieux» / «a des difficultés» / «fait des progrès» / «fait des efforts» / «doit faire des efforts» / «doit écouter en classe».* Recycling of school subjects		Comparing two reading sources	1 a, c, d, g, h, i, j 2 a, d, e, j 4 a	A
B **Mon bilan scolaire** Talking about your school work this year	*Tu as bien / beaucoup travaillé en...? Tu as un problème en...? J'ai bien travaillé en... Je n'ai pas beaucoup travaillé en... J'ai (beaucoup) révisé en... J'ai (bien) fait mes devoirs en... J'ai (beaucoup) bavardé. J'ai (souvent) oublié mes... J'ai trouvé... facile / difficile.*	Perfect tense negative: *Je n'ai pas...* Recycling of perfect tense forms from Unit 5	Comparing two written sources	1 a, c, f, g, h, i 2 a, d, e, h, i, j, k, l 3 f	A
C **J'ai beaucoup aidé!** Talking about extra-curricular activities done this year	*Tu as fait des activités au collège? Tu as été dans l'équipe de netball? J'ai été dans l'équipe de... J'ai été au club de... J'ai fait douze matchs de... J'ai gagné une compétition de... J'ai aidé à la bibliothèque / pour la fête. J'ai joué dans Bugsy Malone. Je n'ai pas fait d'activités cette année.*	Recycling of perfect tense	Making notes from what you hear Planning written work	1 a, c, d, g, h, i, i 2 a, d, e, h, i, j, k, l 3 f	A
D **Point Langue Atelier**	Recycling of what you have done at school this year	Perfect tense: *J'ai... / Je n'ai pas... Tu as... / Tu n'as pas...*	Preparing and delivering an oral presentation	1 a, d, f, h, j 2 a, h, i, k, l 3 c, d, f, g	A
E **Il n'a pas travaillé** Describing someone else's school achievements	*Il (Elle) a (assez) travaillé? Il (Elle) a / n'a pas (bien) fait ses devoirs. Il (Elle) a/n'a pas (bien/assez) révisé. Il (Elle) a/n'a pas écouté en classe. Il (Elle) a / n'a pas bavardé en... Il (Elle) a / n'a pas (trop) regardé la télé.* Recycling of school subjects	Perfect tense negative: *Il / Elle n'a pas...*	Learning through poems	1 a, c, d, g, h, i 2 a, i, k 3 a, e, f	A
F **Et l'année prochaine?** Making resolutions for the next school year	*Tu vas aller en quelle classe l'année prochaine? Je vais aller en 4ᵉ3. Tu vas beaucoup travailler en... / à la maison? Je vais bien faire mes devoirs en... Je vais mieux réviser / écouter / écrire. Je vais bien / mieux apprendre mes maths / moins regarder la télé / moins sortir.*	Recycling of immediate future	Pronunciation: liaisons	1 a, c, f, g, h, i, k 2 a, d, e, f, i, k 3 b, c, g	A

CAMARADES 2		OVERVIEW – UNITE 6 – L'ECOLE EST FINIE!		Cont.	NATIONAL CURRICULUM	
	Topics/Objectives	Key language	Grammar	Strategies	PoS coverage	AoE
G	**Tu vas travailler cet été?** Saying what you are going to do this summer or this weekend	*Tu vas travailler cet été / ce week-end? Je vais / Je dois faire le jardin de ma grand-mère / faire le ménage / laver la voiture de mes parents / garder mon petit frère / faire les courses / aller en vacances / sortir avec les copains. Je ne vais pas travailler.*	How to express the English possessive **'s** in French	Pronunciation: *-in / -ain / -aim / -un / -ien* Making notes while listening Learning sounds through poems	1 a, c, d, f, g, h, i, j, k 2 a, d, e, f, h, i, l 3 a, c, f, g	A
H	**Point Langue Atelier**	Recycling of school work and summer activities	Awareness of past and future	Comparing reading sources	1 g, i 2 a, i, j, n 3 e, f	A
I	**Tu vas aller en vacances?** Making holiday plans	*Qu'est-ce qu'on va / tu vas faire cet été? Tu vas (On va) aller en vacances? Je vais... / J'aimerais mieux... / On pourrait... aller à la montagne (mer / campagne) / aller en Espagne / faire des barbecues (promenades) / nager / bronzer. Oui, bonne idée. Oh, non! Ce n'est pas drôle!*		Making notes from what you hear Speaking from notes	1 a, c, d, f, g, h, i 2 a, d, e, g, h, i, l 3 c, g	BE
J	**On va partir comment?** Holiday plans: discussing dates, travel and accommodation	*On va / Tu vas partir quand? On va / Tu vas aller où? On va / Tu vas partir comment? Je vais partir le + date. On va aller dans un camping / hôtel / gîte. J'aimerais bien aller... chez Julie / les grands-parents... en voiture / bateau / avion. Recycling of dates*		Planning written work using spider diagrams	1 a, c, d, g, h, i, j, k 2 a, d, e, i, j, l, n 3 b, c, g	BE
K	**Point Langue Atelier**	Recycling of planning future events	Overview of question forms	Reading for personal interest and enjoyment	1 d, g, h, i, j 2 a, j, l 3 f	BE

121

IT Opportunities

CORE ACTIVITIES

Text manipulation

Spreads B, C and F

Produce a model text in the first person in which a pupil writes about:

- what (s)he has done at school (e.g. *cette année j'ai bien travaillé en maths mais j'ai beaucoup parlé en histoire*)
- how (s)he has helped at school and/or contributed to extra-curricular activities (e.g. *j'ai aidé pour la fête, j'ai été dans l'équipe de foot*)
- resolutions for next year (e.g. *l'année prochaine je vais mieux écouter et moins bavarder en géo*)

After work has taken place at the computer, time could be spent on rapid question – answer work related to the text. This could take the form of:

- spelling words (not as a test, but to check how much has been retained)
- teacher reading part of a sentence and pupils predicting the rest
- teacher demonstrating, from a copy of the text on the OHP, good language use (e.g. how two simple sentences are joined by *et*; use of negatives)
- asking pupils to identify specific points of language (e.g. all the different verbs in the text)
- asking pupils to explain a point of language (e.g. why is *devoirs* spelt with an *s* at the end?)

Teachers should then have clear strategies for encouraging pupils to emulate the model on which they have been working. For example, a "parallel" text to the model could be provided (supported perhaps by key word/picture prompts) as well as clear guidance related to the use of support material.

Word processing – guided writing

Spread H

Create and save a file in which the first eight questions of Exercise 2 are presented, followed by the eight answers in a different order. In the answers the phrases: *tout seul   des chaussures   en voiture chez Jérémy   une casquette   ma cousine   en ville en avion* are highlighted.

Pupils use "cut and paste" techniques to place the answers below the appropriate questions. They then replace the highlighted phrases with others that will make sense.

A similar file can also be made for the second, more difficult set of questions and answers, with the following phrases highlighted: *au restaurant   le musée du Sport   mes sciences   à la Cité des Sciences   au snack-bar   mon anglais   à la gare   une heure   à 9h34*.

Presentation

Spread A

Pupils use features such as fonts, tables, borders and shading to design and write their own end-of-year school report. As well as a good design, the task should require pupils to use a wide range range of vocabulary and phrases, such as those found on pages 122–123. An alternative task could be to design and write a report on their teachers!

ADDITIONAL ACTIVITIES

Word processing – extended writing

Spreads I–J

Pupils use support materials from the Pupil's Book to write about a forthcoming holiday by expanding the following prompts: *vacances / mer / France / parents, copain / voiture, bateau / gîte / partir 31/7 / rentrer 16/8 nager, bronzer, faire des barbecues etc.*

An alternative task could be to describe a teacher's forthcoming holiday in the third person.

Database

The database activity for this unit provides opportunities to explore pupils' performance in school in relation to their habits concerning television and homework. The information found could provide additional interest in terms of gender difference.

As in Unit 3, teachers and pupils will need to be familiar with basic data-handling terminology as well as the need for precision and consistency in data entry.

Conduct a pupil survey, in the form of a simple and carefully constructed multiple choice questionnaire:

- gender – *M* or *F*
- how many hours the pupil watches television per week
- how many hours the pupil spends on homework per week
- whether the pupil has a television in his/her room – *oui* or *non*

You can make the survey across the whole year group rather than across one class only. In this way the information found will have more credibility. In addition, the potential of the database to organise large amounts of information at a speed that could not be achieved manually, will be apparent.

Enter data consistently and accurately against the fields of:

- *sexe* (alpha-numeric)
- *telheures* (numeric)
- *devheures* (numeric)
- *chambre* (alpha-numeric)

Pupils interrogate the database to find specific information (e.g. the proportion of pupils who have a television in their room, the average time spent on homework) as well as significant gender differences in the areas investigated. It may also be possible to investigate hypotheses such as "the more time pupils spend watching television, the less time they spend on homework".

Show pupils effective ways of reporting back the information they have gathered. This could be done by teaching specific items of language such as *par semaine* (e.g. *cinq personnes regardent plus de 30 heures de télévision par semaine*) or *la plupart* (e.g. *la plupart des garçons ont un téléviseur dans la chambre*), as well as further reinforcing the use of *plus* and *moins* (e.g. *les filles font moins de devoirs que les garçons*) from Unit 1.

Copymasters

The *présentation* and the *grilles* worksheets should be used as indicated.
The other copymasters (worksheets and vocabulary lists) should be used with or after the spread indicated.

Pupil's Book Spread	Corresponding Copymaster
A	20–21 *Glossaire*
B	1 *Présentation*
C	2 *Présentation*; 3–4 *On lit*
D	5 *Grammaire*
E	6 *On s'amuse*; 7–8 *On écoute*; *Grilles 6*
F	–
G	9 *Plaisir de lire*
H	10 *Grammaire*; 11 *Que sais-tu?*
I	12–13 *On écoute*
J	14–15 *On parle*
K	16 *Grammaire*; 17 *Que sais-tu?*; 18–19 *On révise*

Notes to accompany Copymasters (CMs)

Feuilles 1–2
These two **Presentation Sheets** introduce the language needed for talking about school performance and extra-curricular activities in the past year.

Feuilles 3–4 On lit
These two CMs provide additional reading practice about topic 1. They can easily be used concurrently: go through the rubrics with the pupils working on CM3 ♦ while pupils working on CM4 ♣ begin unaided.

Feuille 3 ♦
Answers
Ex 1: **1** P   **2** P   **3** N   **4** N   **5** P   **6** N   **7** N   **8** P
9 P   **10** N   **11** P   **12** N
Ex 2: *Aider les profs: classer des livres / fermer les fenêtres / porter le magnétophone / donner les cahiers à la classe*
Aider pour une fête: préparer un stand / faire un poster publicité / décorer des ballons / organiser une loterie
Faire du sport: gagner un match / gagner une médaille / faire une compétition / organiser une équipe

Feuille 4 ♣
Answers
Ex 1: **1** E   **2** D   **3** A   **4** F   **5** B   **6** G   **7** C
Ex 2: **1** *Non*   **2** *anglais*   **3** *musique*   **4** *maths*
5 *géographie et technologie*   **6** *géographie*   **7** *non*
8 *histoire*

Feuille 5 Grammaire
This CM complements the work of **Point Langue** on negative sentences in the perfect tense.
Answers
Ex 1: *Colonne 1: J'ai révisé tous les soirs. Je n'ai pas bavardé. J'ai bien écrit. Je n'ai pas trop regardé la télé. J'ai appris mon vocabulaire.*
Colonne 2: Je n'ai pas écouté. J'ai oublié mes cahiers. Je n'ai pas trouvé mes livres. Je n'ai pas fini l'exercice. J'ai perdu mon sac.

Feuille 6 On s'amuse
See the introduction to the Teacher's Book (page 4) for ideas on exploiting songs.

> – *Mireille a bien travaillé?*
> – *Mais non, regardez son carnet!*
> – *Elle a bien appris ses maths?*
> – *Non, elle n'a pas appris ses maths!*
> – *Elle a écouté en classe?*
> – *Non, elle a bavardé, hélas!*
> – *Elle a fait tous ses devoirs?*
> – *Ah non, mais elle a joué très tard.*
> – *Elle a lu trop de BD?*
> – *Oui, et elle n'a pas révisé.*
> – *Elle n'est pas très motivée?*
> – *C'est dommage, elle va redoubler!*

Answers
travaillé maths classe devoirs BD révisé

Feuilles 7–8 On écrit
These two CMs provide additional writing practice about evaluating someone's school work. They can easily be used concurrently. Go through the rubrics with the pupils working on CM7 ♦ while pupils working on CM8 ♣ begin unaided. Then check pupils understand the CM 8 rubrics.

Answers
Français: a fait des efforts   Maths: a fait des efforts / a des problèmes   Anglais: a fait des efforts / a très bien travaillé   Histoire: a mieux travaillé / n'est pas rapide   Géographie: a bien travaillé à la maison / a très bien travaillé   Sciences: n'est pas rapide / a trop parlé   Dessin: a mieux travaillé / a fait des efforts   Musique: n'as pas bien écouté / a mieux travaillé   Technologie: n'est pas rapide   Informatique: n'est pas rapide / n'a pas fait assez d'efforts   Sport: a très bien travaillé

Feuille 9 Plaisir de lire
Ask pupils to underline in each paragraph the elements that enabled them to select the answers.

Extra – Pupils can write a report for a character of their choice.

Answers
1 D *Tintin* **2** E *Astérix* **3** B *Obélix* **4** C *Monsieur Bean* **5** A *Popeye*

Feuille 10 Grammaire
This CM takes **Point Langue** one step further by providing discrimination tasks about the past, the present and the future.
Answers
Ex 1

Passé	*Présent*	*Futur*
La semaine dernière	*Quelquefois*	*Demain matin*
	Normalement	*Mercredi prochain*
Hier soir	*Souvent*	*Dans trois jours*

Ex 3
1 *allons* **2** *a acheté / a vu / a perdu...* **3** *travaille...*
4 *a fait* **5** *vais travailler* **6** *va aller*

Feuille 11 Que sais-tu?
This CM provides some revision of topics 1 and 2.

Ex 1

1 – *Tu as bien travaillé en anglais?*
  – *En anglais? J'ai beaucoup bavardé.*
2 – *Tu as bien travaillé en technologie?*
  – *En techno? J'ai fait des efforts et j'ai fait des progrès.*
3 – *Tu as bien travaillé en dessin?*
  – *En dessin? Ben... je n'ai pas beaucoup écouté.*
4 – *Tu as bien travaillé en histoire?*
  – *En histoire? Regarde: j'ai 18 sur 20.*
5 – *Qu'est-ce que tu as en informatique?*
  – *En informatique? J'ai: «Très motivé, excellents résultats».*
6 – *Et toi, en français, ça va?*
  – *Ben, en français, j'ai eu des difficultés avec le travail écrit.*
7 – *Tu as fait des progrès en sport?*
  – *En sport? J'ai gagné la compétition d'athlétisme.*

Answers
1 G **2** K **3** B **4** F **5** H **6** C **7** A

1 ☹ 2 ☺ 3 ☹ 4 ☺
5 ☺ 6 ☹ 7 ☺

Ex 2 – Pupils may wish to write more than one sentence for each number. More able pupils can try to complete 1–6 with phrases of their own making.

Ex 3 – Have a minimum of five pupils per group. Pupils who make a mistake are out of the game. The only pupil left is the winner.

Feuilles 12–13 On écoute
These two CMs provide additional listening practice on holiday plans.

Feuille 12 ♦

Ex 1

1 – *Tu vas rester à la maison?*
2 – *Tu vas aller en Espagne?*
3 – *Tu vas voyager avec qui?*
4 – *Vous allez voyager en avion?*
5 – *Tu vas aller à la mer?*
6 – *Qu'est-ce que tu vas faire?*
7 – *C'est nul!*

Answers
1 c **2** e **3** a **4** f **5** d **6** g **7** b

Ex 2

A – *Tu vas aller en Espagne cet été?*
  – *Cet été? Non, je vais aller en Ecosse.*
B – *C'est bien, l'Ecosse?*
  – *Je ne sais pas. Je n'ai jamais été en Ecosse.*
  – *Et l'Espagne, tu aimes ça?*
  – *Ah, oui, c'est génial!*
C – *Ma sœur a visité l'Ecosse l'année dernière. Elle aime la nature?*
  – *Et toi?*
  – *Moi, je préfère la ville, les discos, les copains...*
D – *Tu vas en Ecosse avec ta famille?*
  – *Avec ma famille et Coralie, ma cousine.*
  – *Elle est sympa?*
  – *Coralie? Elle est nulle! Elle m'énerve.*

Answers
A 2 B 4 C 5 D 7

Feuille 13 ♦

Ex 1

1 – *Tu vas voyager cet été?*
2 – *Je vais à la mer avec les copains cet après-midi. Tu viens avec nous?*
3 – *Qu'est-ce ta famille va faire cet été?*
4 – *On pourrait faire un barbecue dimanche. Ça t'intéresse?*
5 – *Tu vas aller en vacances à la campagne? Pourquoi?*
6 – *Tu aimes bien bronzer, toi?*
7 – *Tu vas travailler? Pourquoi?*

Answers
1 g **2** e **3** b **4** h **5** a **6** f **7** c

Ex 2

Extra – For written practice, ask pupils to turn their notes into full sentences.

1 – *Qu'est-ce que tu vas faire cet été?*

– *Moi, cet été, j'aimerais bien aller en Espagne, mais mes parents préfèrent aller en Ecosse. Donc on va aller en Ecosse.*

– *En Ecosse?*

– *Oui. On a été en Espagne l'année dernière, et... c'était fabuleux!*

– *Et l'Ecosse, c'est bien aussi?*

– *L'Ecosse? Ben... je ne sais pas, moi. Je n'ai jamais été en Ecosse.*

– *Ah bon?*

– *Ma sœur, oui. Elle a fait un voyage scolaire en Ecosse, dans les montagnes, et elle a trouvé ça génial.*

2 – *En général, la nature ne m'intéresse pas beaucoup. Moi, je préfère la ville... les activités bruyantes... sortir en ville avec les copains... Mais en Ecosse, on va aller dans un village de vacances, avec des activités organisées. J'aimerais bien trouver une petite copine sympa! Mon frère a une copine, Christine, mais elle bavarde toujours: elle est vraiment fatigante!*

Answers
1 *non* **2** *oui* **3** *non* **4** *oui* **5** *sa sœur* **6** *la ville* **7** *il aime les activités bruyantes / sortir en ville avec les copains* **8** *une (petite) copine (sympa)* **9** *la copine de son frère* **10** *elle bavarde toujours*

Feuilles 14–15 On parle
These two CMs provide additional speaking practice about all the topic areas covered in Unit 6. The nature of the task is identical for CM 14 (♦) and for CM 15 (♣), so it is possible for all pupils to work together. The only difference is that the stimulus provided on CM 14 is more detailed.

Preparation – Rehearse the questions with the class. This is easier to do if you show the CM or CMs on the OHP.

Point out to pupils that once they have had a *oui* (or *non*) answer to a question, there is no need to write *oui* (or *non*) in the question box more than once if other pupils later give the same answer.

Feuille 16 Grammaire
This CM provides advice and practice on the different ways of translating the English possessive **'s** into French.

Ex 1 – **Answers**
1 *chez* **2** *à la* **3** *de* **4** *à l'* **5** *chez le* **6** *de* **7** *du* **8** *chez le*

Ex 2 – **Answers**
1 *On va/Nous allons à la boulangerie.* **2** *Elle est chez ma cousine.* **3** *Désolée, je vais chez mes grands-parents.* **4** *On va à la pâtisserie?* **5** *Non, c'est le chat de ma grand-mère.* **6** *Non, c'est le pull de mon frère.* **7** *Non, il va chez le dentiste.* **8** *Je dois aller à la boucherie.* **9** *Non, je vais chez mon (petit) copain.*

Feuille 17 Que sais-tu?
This CM provides some revision tasks on topic 3.

Ex 1
Answers
1 a, c **2** b, c **3** a, c **4** b, c **5** a, c **6** b, c

Ex 2 *Preparation* – Give pupils some thinking time, but do not allow them to make notes, as they are meant to practise semi-improvisation.

Extra – Pupils can then do this as a written task.

Feuille 18–19 On révise
These two copymasters provide some revision tasks on Units 5 and 6 prior to Epreuve 3 or 4. Pupils need both sheets at the same time, as the realia for Ex 4 (CM 18) appears on CM 19.

Ex 1
Answers
1 C **2** B **3** A **4** D

Ex 2

Allô? C'est Aurélie. Tu viens à Chartres avec moi le 23 juillet? On pourrait voyager en car. Alors, voici mon idée. Rendez-vous chez moi à 8h45. A Chartres, le matin, on pourrait faire du shopping. A midi, on pourrait manger dans un restaurant fast-food avec mon copain Jean-Marc. Il habite à Chartres. L'après-midi, on pourrait aller à la patinoire et au cinéma. Le soir, on pourrait rentrer à Dreux entre 8h et 8h30 et on pourrait dîner chez moi. Ça t'intéresse?

Answers
1 *23 juillet* **2** *car* **3** *8h45, Aurélie* **4** *shopping* **5** *restaurant fast-food* **6** *patinoire, cinéma* **7** *8h00 et 8h30* **8** *chez Aurélie*

Ex 3

– *Deux billets euh... aller-retour pour Chartres, s'il vous plaît.*

– *Deux aller-retour...*

– *Il y a un car à 8h15?*

– *Non, non. A 8h30.*

– *On arrive à Chartres à quelle heure?*

– *A... 9h20. Voilà. Ça fait 114f.*

– *114f... Et... c'est quel car?*

– *Le numéro 48.*

– *Merci!*

– *Pas de quoi, mademoiselle.*

Answers
1 b **2** b **3** a **4** b **5** a

Ex 4
Answers
1 B **2** C **3** A **4** F **5** D **6** E
Passé: 2, 3, 4 Futur: 1, 5, 6

Ex 5 – ♦ You can suggest pupils write short individual sentences instead, reusing familiar verbs in the perfect tense with *j'ai*. Provide a verb list to choose from and suggest a target number of sentences.

♣ Advise pupils to include opinions using *c'était...*

Ex 6 – Decide whether you want pupils to work from a full script or from notes/cue cards.

A Tu as combien en maths?

pp 122–123

Objective
Discussing school reports

Resources
Cassette for BD and Ex 2 and 4
CM 20–21 for reference throughout Unit 6

Key language
Qu'est-ce que tu as en... (maths)?

J'ai D / 12 sur 20 / excellent / bien / assez bien / «travail sérieux» / «a des difficultés» / «fait des progrès» / «fait des efforts» / «doit faire des efforts» / «doit écouter en classe»
Recycling of school subjects

Language learning strategies
Comparing two reading sources

Ways in
This unit focuses on taking stock of the school year and on making holiday plans.

In this spread, the 5ᵉ 2 are given their school reports. You can introduce this spread like this: *La classe a bien travaillé? Thierry et ses copains ont des bons résultats? Le prof donne les bulletins scolaires.*

The new language is introduced through reading comprehension tasks. First, pupils read the BD while they listen to the cassette. (BD tapescript – see Pupil's Book.)

1 It is better if pupils work without dictionaries. ♦ You can make the task simpler for pupils by asking them to copy only their statements under each category. Explain that school work in France is frequently marked out of twenty. Make sure pupils understand the use of the commas.

Extra – To encourage fast reading – and (♦) to give pupils a chance to look at Thierry's report before Ex 2 – ask pupils to spot which comments appear in both reports. You can also improvise a quick revision of subjects and numbers:

Valérie, dessin.

Sept sur vingt!

Teacher | **Pupils**

2

COUNTER

Extra – Ask for answers in full sentences: *Numéro 1: Valérie a 12 en francais, pas 11.*

> 1 – *En français, j'ai 11.*
> 2 – *En histoire, j'ai 11,5.*
> 3 – *En maths, j'ai 8,5.*
> 4 – *En technologie, j'ai 11.*
> 5 – *Qu'est-ce que tu as en dessin?*
>   *– En dessin? Oh, là, là! J'ai 5.*
> 6 – *Qu'est-ce que tu as en géographie?*
>   *– En géographie? J'ai, euh... 11,5.*
> 7 – *Et en sport, qu'est-ce que tu as?*
>   *– Oh, en sport, ça va. J'ai 17. 17 sur 20.*
> 8 – *Et en anglais, ça va?*
>   *– Bof, j'ai... j'ai 9,5 sur 20.*
> 9 – *Tu as bien travaillé en technologie.*
>   *– Ben, euh... oui et non... j'ai 13 sur 20.*
> 10– *Et en musique, tu as un bon résultat?*
>   *– Euh, j'ai oublié... Ah, j'ai 14,5. Ça va.*
> 11– *Et en sciences? Qu'est-ce que tu as en sciences?*
>   *– Ah, pas mal, les sciences! J'ai 15,5 sur 20.*

Answers
1 11 – F (12)   **2** 11,5 – V   **3** 8,5 – V   **4** 11 – V
5 5 F (7)   **6** 11,5 – F (6)   **7** 17 – V   **8** 9,5 – F (8,5)
9 13 – F (11)   **10** 14,5 – V   **11** 15 – F (12)

♣ The approach is meant to make pupils look more carefully at the question forms.

Extra – Reuse the question forms to improvise further statements about the two school reports.
Answers
1 B   **2** A   **3** B   **4** A   **5** A   **6** A   **7** C   **8** A

4
♦ You can simplify this task by asking pupils simply to jot down the subjects the first time they hear the cassette.

> 1 – *En français, tu dois bien écouter.*
> 2 – *En maths, bravo, tu travailles bien.*
> 3 – *En anglais, tu dois bien faire tes devoirs.*
> 4 – *Ça va bien en histoire. Tu aimes ça?*
> 5 – *Tu as des problèmes en géographie?*
> 6 – *En sciences, tu dois travailler aussi à la maison.*
> 7 – *Ça va bien la musique, maintenant. 14,5? Bravo!*
> 8 – *Comment ça va, le sport? Ah! Tu as fait des progrès en basket!*

Answers
1 V   **2** T   **3** V   **4** T   **5** V   **6** V   **7** V   **8** T

5 Pupils should compare by reporting back on the notes they made in speaking, not by looking at each other's notes.

6 Pupils can express their agreement or disagreement with their partners' comments simply with ticks and crosses. The main purpose here is to write for an audience.

B Mon bilan scolaire

pp 124–125

Objective
Talking about your school work this year

Resources
CM 1
OHT (see **Ways in** section)
Cassette for BD and Ex 2

Key language
Tu as bien / beaucoup travaillé en...?
Tu as un problème en...?
J'ai bien travaillé en... / Je n'ai pas beaucoup travaillé en... /
J'ai (beaucoup) révisé en... / J'ai (bien) fait mes devoirs en... /
J'ai (beaucoup) bavardé / J'ai (souvent) oublié mes... / J'ai trouvé...
facile / difficile.
Recycling of school subjects

Grammar
Perfect tense negative: *Je n'ai pas...*
Recycling of perfect tense forms from Unit 5

Language learning strategies
Comparing two written sources

Ways in
Valérie is unhappy with her school report. She discusses it with her grandfather. You can introduce this spread like this: *Le bulletin scolaire de Valérie n'est pas génial. Valérie parle avec son grand-père.*

Pupils read the BD while they listen to the cassette. (BD tapescript – see Pupil's Book.)

Use CM 1 – which you can make into an OHT – to introduce the key language with *j'ai... / je n'ai pas....*

1
Extra – Improvise some statements along the same lines and ask pupils to put their hands up or say *Moi aussi* if the statements apply to them.

2 **COUNTER**

1 – *Ça va, le français?*
  – *Oh, en français, j'ai travaillé beaucoup, mais c'est difficile!*
2 – *Toi, tu as bien travaillé en dessin?*
  – *En dessin? Je n'ai pas beaucoup travaillé, mais c'est facile, le dessin.*
3 – *Tu as beaucoup travaillé en anglais?*
  – *En anglais? Je n'ai pas fait mes devoirs. J'ai 5 sur 20.*
4 – *Et les sciences, ça va, toi?*
  – *Ah, en sciences, j'ai fait des devoirs trois fois par semaine! J'ai 17!*
5 – *Qu'est-ce que tu as en géo?*
  – *Ben... j'ai 9.*
  – *9 sur 20?*
  – *Ben oui! J'ai beaucoup bavardé avec Julien.*
6 – *Tu as 6 en maths?*
  – *Ouais. Oh, là, là, mes parents!*
  – *6 sur 20? Mais pourquoi?*
  – *J'ai souvent oublié mon cahier.*
  – *A la maison?*
  – *Ouais.*
7 – *Qu'est-ce que tu as en musique?*
  – *Regarde!*
  – *Ah! Mais c'est génial!*
  – *Ah, mais j'ai beaucoup révisé, tu sais!*

Answers
1 *français, oui – difficile* **2** *dessin, non – facile* **3** *anglais, non – 5* **4** *sciences, oui – devoirs* **5** *géographie, non – bavardé* **6** *maths, non – cahier* **7** *musique, oui – révisé*

Extra task – This task does not figure in the Pupil's Book.

Choisis deux matières (♦) ou quatre matières (♣).
Pour chaque matière, pose la question à un maximum de personnes:

Tu as beaucoup travaillé en...?

Ecris les résultats dans une grille:

	Oui	Bof	Non
Maths	✔	✔✔✔✔	✔✔

3
Pupils can use the key to vary the question forms. For example:

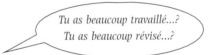
Tu as beaucoup travaillé...?
Tu as beaucoup révisé...?

Suggest that pupils miss a turn when they fall on *Départ.*

4
♣ Tell pupils whether you would like them to correct the inaccurate statements using *je* or *il*.
Answers
♦ *Musique, français, sport, techno.*
♣ *Musique (J'ai/Il a fait des efforts.) Français (Je n'ai/Il n'a pas bien écrit, et j'ai/il a écouté en classe.) Sport (J'ai/Il a trouvé l'athlétisme difficile.) Technologie (J'ai/Il a très bien travaillé.)*

5
Ask pupils to answer in full sentences. ♣ Ask pupils to provide as much detail as possible, using link words such as *et / mais.*

C J'ai beaucoup aidé!   pp 126–127

Objective
Talking about extra-curricular activities done this year

Resources
CM 2, 3 and 4
OHT (see **Ways in** section)
Cassette for BD and Ex 2 and 4

Key language
Tu as fait des activités au collège?
Tu as été dans l'équipe de netball?
J'ai été dans l'équipe de... / J'ai été au club de... / J'ai fait douze

matchs de... / J'ai gagné une compétition de... /
J'ai aidé à la bibliothèque / pour la fête. / J'ai joué dans Bugsy Malone. /
Je n'ai pas fait d'activités cette année.
Recycling of sports and school subjects

Grammar
Recycling of perfect tense

Language learning strategies
Making notes from what you hear
Planning written work

Ways in
Valérie's grandfather is trying to cheer her up by pointing out her extra-curricular achievements at school this year. You can introduce this spread like this: *Valérie a des problèmes en classe, mais elle a beaucoup aidé le collège et les profs. Ça aussi, c'est important.*

Pupils read the BD while they listen to the cassette. Check that pupils understand *aidé* and elicit the meaning of *course à pied* through action.
(BD tapescript – see Pupil's Book.)

Use CM 2 – which you can make into an OHT – to present the new language.

1

Preparation – Warn pupils to be careful about negative sentences.

Answers
1 V   2 F   3 ?   4 ?   5 V   6 F   7 V

2

> 1 – *Thierry, tu as fait des activités au collège cette année?*
> – *Euh... oui, j'ai été au club d'informatique.*
> 2 – *Grégory, tu as fait des activités cette année?*
> – *Oui, j'ai aidé pour la fête de Noël.*
> 3 – *Et toi, tu as fait des activités, Ludivine?*
> – *Moi? J'ai fait des compétitions d'athlétisme.*
> 4 – *Et toi, Julien? Tu as aidé les profs?*
> – *Oui, j'ai aidé à la bibliothèque.*
> 5 – *Tu as été à un club cette année?*
> – *Oui, j'ai été au club de musique.*
> 6 – *Tu as aidé pour la fête?*
> – *Non, je n'ai pas fait d'activités.*
> 7 – *Et toi, tu as fait des activités?*
> – *A Noël, j'ai joué dans Peter Pan.*

Answers
1 h   2 d   3 c   4 a   5 b   6 g   7 e

3

Preparation – To prevent accusations of cheating, ask pupils to jot down secretly the letter of the picture they are selecting.

Extra task – This task does not figure in the Pupil's Book.

Frédéric a fait combien d'activités cette année? Ecoute et écris les activités.

Preparation – Warn pupils that there are some distractors.

> – *Frédéric, tu as bien travaillé cette année?*
> – *Oui, ça va.*
> – *Et tu as fait beaucoup d'activités?*
> – *Ben... j'ai fait du sport.*
> – *Tu as fait du sport?*
> – *Oui, euh... J'ai été dans l'équipe de foot.*
> – *Ah, dans l'équipe de foot. Et tu as fait de l'athlétisme aussi?*
> – *Ben... non. Le jeudi soir, j'ai aidé M. Lebrun.*
> – *Tu as aidé M. Lebrun?*
> – *Oui, euh...*
> – *Ah, à la bibliothèque?*
> – *Oui, oui, à la bibliothèque.*
> – *Tu as fait de la musique?*
> – *Ah, non. Moi, je préfère le dessin. J'ai été au club de dessin.*
> – *Au club de dessin?*
> – *Oui, j'aime bien ça.*

Answers
sport (*équipe de foot*)   bibliothèque (*aidé M. Lebrun*)
club de dessin

Extra task – Give pupils some copying practice and reinforce the verb structures at the same time by providing sentences with the past participles missing. Pupils should copy and complete the sentences without looking at the key. Provide a list of the missing past participles (all from the key).

4

Preparation – Explain that for better time management pupils should start from statements 1–7 and not from the texts. Warn pupils about distractors, and ask them to pay attention to negative phrases in the statements and in the letters.
Answers
1 M   2 G   3 M   4 G   5 G   6 M   7 M

5
Pupils who have not taken part in many extra-curricular activities can write some negative sentences.

D Point Langue / Atelier   pp 128–129

Resources
CM 5
Cassette for **Atelier** Ex 1

Key language
Recycling of what you have done at school this year

Grammar
Perfect tense: *J'ai... / Je n'ai pas... / Tu as... / Tu n'as pas...*

Language learning strategies
Preparing and delivering an oral presentation

Point Langue

This page provides additional practice of negative sentences in the perfect tense.

1

Extra – Do some speed drill practice to help pupils memorise the negative forms. When you say a positive sentence, pupils instantly make it negative, and vice-versa.

Answers
Positif: J'ai vu.   J'ai oublié.
Négatif: Tu n'as pas vu.   Je n'ai pas fait.

2

Answers
♦ **1** b   **2** d   **3** f   **4** h   **5** g   **6** e

Atelier

Preparation – Pupils should do this task in two stages. They should only try to identify the correct circles after they have finished making notes from the cassette.

1

COUNTER

- *Moustafa!*
- *Moustafa, qu'est-ce que tu as fait cette année?*
- *J'ai été au club de sciences... euh... j'ai fait de la natation... et puis ... j'ai aidé à préparer la fête... et... j'ai joué au foot.*
- *Au...?*
- *Au football.*

- *Julie!*
- *Julie, qu'est-ce que tu as fait cette année?*
- *J'ai... aidé pour la fête ... et... euh... j'ai été au club de sciences... puis... j'ai été au club de musique... et... j'ai joué dans Peter Pan.*

- *Jérémy!*
- *Jérémy, qu'est-ce que tu as fait cette année au collège?*
- *Au collège? J'ai fait de la gymnastique... euh... et... j'ai été au club de sciences... et aussi... euh... j'ai... j'ai joué dans Peter Pan... et j'ai... aidé pour la fête, pour la loterie.*

- *Catherine!*
- *Catherine, tu as fait des activités au collège cette année?*
- *Oui, j'ai fait de la natation... j'ai été au club de musique... puis... euh... j'ai... j'ai fait de la gymnastique... et... j'ai aidé à la fête.*

Answers
Cercle 1 = Catherine   **Cercle 2** = Moustafa
Cercle 3 = Jérémy

2

Although the statements include unfamiliar language, pupils should work without dictionaries so as to practise effective reading skills.
Answers
1 d   **2** f   **3** e   **4** a   **5** c   **6** b

3

Pupils can reproduce their *aide-mémoire* on OHT and use this as support to make their presentations to the class. Presentations can be made to a group or recorded instead.

E Il n'a pas travaillé?

pp 130-131

Objective
Describing someone else's school achievements

Resources
Cassette for BD, Ex 1, 3 and 6 and CM 6
CM 6, 7 and 8
Grilles 6 CM (optional for Ex 1)

Key language
Il (Elle) a (assez) travaillé?

Il (Elle) a / n'a pas (bien) fait ses devoirs.
Il (Elle) a / n'a pas... (bien/assez) révisé / écouté en classe / bavardé en... / (trop) regardé la télé.
Recycling of school subjects

Grammar
Perfect tense negative: *Il n'a pas... / Elle n'a pas...*

Language learning strategies
Learning through poems

Ways in
The school reports have not gone down well in every household. Here, Sébastien is in the headteacher's office with his dad. You can introduce this spread like this: *Sébastien est dans la classe de Valérie et Thierry. Il n'a pas très bien travaillé. Il est au collège avec son père et avec la directrice.*

There is little new language on this spread. The main aim is to recycle verbs from topic 1 in the perfect tense using *il / elle*. Pupils can read the BD while they listen to the cassette. (BD tapescript – see Pupil's Book.)

1

A grid is provided on CM.

Preparation – This task practises categorisation. Point out to pupils that they will not necessarily hear the words listed at the top of the grid.

Extra – Pupils can listen again and note more detail (e.g. subject) writing *P* for *positif* or *N* for *négatif*.

COUNTER
> 1 – *En maths, Sébastien a bien écouté en classe.*
> 2 – *En sciences, Sébastien n'a pas bien fait ses devoirs.*
> 3 – *En histoire, il a bien écouté en classe.*
> 4 – *Il n'a pas beaucoup révisé sa géographie.*
> 5 – *Sébastien a beaucoup aidé au club de foot.*
> 6 – *Cette année, il n'a pas fait ses devoirs d'anglais.*
> 7 – *Sébastien est très sympa. Il m'a beaucoup aidé pour la fête de Noël.*
> 8 – *Sébastien? Ah... c'est un problème, Sébastien. Il a beaucoup bavardé en dessin cette année.*
> 9 – *En informatique? Ah, c'est dommage! Il a oublié de réviser. Hein, Sébastien, tu n'as pas beaucoup révisé pour l'examen?*
> 10 – *En technologie, Sébastien doit faire des efforts! Cette année, il a oublié de faire ses devoirs. Très souvent!*

Answers
1 *discipline* 2 *devoirs* 3 *discipline* 4 *révisions*
5 *sports et loisirs* 6 *devoirs* 7 *sports et loisirs*
8 *discipline* 9 *révisions* 10 *devoirs*

2

Extra – For straightforward writing practice, pupils can change the positive sentences into negative ones, and vice versa.
Answers
1 a 2 h 3 d 4 e 5 b 6 g 7 c 8 f

Extra task – This task does not figure in the Pupil's Book.

La directrice rend visite à la classe. Ecoute la cassette. Fais correspondre 1–8 et les dessins a–h de l'exercice 2.

COUNTER
> 1 – *Qu'est-ce qu'il a, ce garçon? Une mauvaise note?*
>   – *Oui, il n'a pas révisé.*
> 2 – *Et cette élève? Elle a trop bavardé?*
>   – *Elle n'écoute pas, elle n'écoute jamais! Elle a beaucoup parlé ce matin!*
> 3 – *Ben alors, ça ne va pas?*
>   – *Il a mangé trop de chocolat pour son anniversaire, je crois.*
> 4 – *Mais, Gaëtan, il est 9h30!*
>   – *Excusez-moi, j'ai oublié l'heure, et le bus n'a pas attendu! J'ai pris mon vélo.*
> 5 – *Regarde Patricia? Ça ne va pas?*
>   – *Elle a trop regardé la télé hier soir.*
> 6 – *Qu'est-ce que tu as? Ça ne va pas?*
>   – *Ben... j'ai froid. J'ai oublié ma veste dans le bus.*
> 7 – *Fabien! Enfin! Qu'est-ce que tu fais sous la table?*
>   – *Il a regardé un film d'horreur hier soir à la télé!*
> 8 – *Mais... bravo, Philippe! Tu as fait des progrès!*
>   – *Ouais, 20 sur 20!*
>   – *Ah, il a bien révisé!*

Answers
1 g 2 c 3 a 4 h 5 f 6 d 7 e 8 b

3

After a few minutes, pupils can challenge each other further: **A**: *Montre un dessin.* **B**: *Dis une phrase pour décrire le dessin.*

4

Preparation – Suggest pupils first attempt the task without looking at the multiple choice words.

Extra – Give pupils a few more minutes to read the letter again, then ask them to re-tell as many facts as they can from memory.
Answers
1 *peut* 2 *fini* 3 *ai* 4 *appris* 5 *travaillé* 6 *beaucoup*
7 *a* 8 *n'a pas* 9 *oublié* 10 *chez*

Preparation – First ask pupils to read the poem silently. They can look up *boulot* and *interros* in the glossary. Check if they can guess the meaning of *jusqu'à*.

5

Use the poem to practise reading aloud. To help pupils memorise the song, show it on the OHP and gradually cover more and more of the text. Pupils can also copy the poem, cut out each line and reorder it against the clock. They can make the poem into a rap.
(Tapescript – see Pupil's Book.)

F Et l'année prochaine? pp 132–133

Objective
Making resolutions for the next school year

Resources
Cassette for BD and Ex 1

Key language
Tu vas aller en quelle classe l'année prochaine? Je vais aller en 4^e3.
Tu vas beaucoup travailler en... / à la maison?
Je vais bien faire mes devoirs en....
Je vais mieux réviser / écouter / écrire.

Je vais bien / mieux apprendre mes maths / moins regarder la télé / moins sortir.
Je ne vais pas bavarder en...
Recycling of school subjects and school work

Grammar
Recycling of immediate future

Language learning strategies
Pronunciation: liaisons

Ways in
Valérie and Sébastien are chatting about next year. Will they remain in the same class? This spread contains little new language. Instead, it reuses many of the verbs used so far in this unit to talk about good resolutions for next year. You can introduce this spread like this: *Valérie et Sébastien sont en 5^e2, avec Thierry, Ludivine, Grégory et tous les copains. Mais... en septembre? Surprise!*

Pupils then read the BD while they listen to the cassette. Revise the French school year system if necessary and explain that pupils are generally in the same class for all subjects. (BD tapescript – see Pupil's Book.)

Answers
4^e1: Cyril, Delphine 4^e2: Nadir, Rodolphe 4^e3: Fatima, Rachida 4^e4: Céline, Ahmet, Aurélie, Patrick

 2

COUNTER

Preparation – Rehearse pronunciation of *quatrieme*.

> **Ecoute la différence:**
>
> *vais:* *Je vais aller en 4^e3.*
> *bien:* *Tu vas bien apprendre.*
> *des:* *Elle va faire des efforts.*
> *dois:* *Je dois écouter.*
>
> **Répète:**
>
> *Je vais bien écouter.*
> *Je dois apprendre mes maths.*
> *Je vais faire des efforts.*
> *Je vais arriver à l'heure.*
> *Tu dois écouter en classe.*
> *Elle écoute en anglais.*

Extra task – This task does not figure in the Pupil's Book.

C'est une bonne décision pour bien travailler?

Oui → dessine

Non → dessine

COUNTER

> 1 *Je vais moins écouter en histoire.*
> 2 *Je vais bien réviser en maths.*
> 3 *Elle va moins regarder la télé.*
> 4 *Il ne va pas bavarder en classe.*
> 5 *J'ai l'impression que tu ne vas pas beaucoup travailler en vacances.*
> 6 *L'année prochaine, c'est sûr, c'est décidé: je vais mieux faire mes devoirs.*
> 7 *Elle est toujours très bavarde. Je suis pessimiste. Elle ne va pas bien écouter en classe.*
> 8 *Le collège? C'est nul! Et les devoirs, ça m'énerve. Alors moi, l'année prochaine, je vais sortir tous les soirs.*

 1

COUNTER

> 1 – *Nadir, tu vas aller en quelle classe l'année prochaine?*
>   – *Je vais aller en 4^e2.*
> 2 – *Aurélie, tu vas aller en quelle classe l'année prochaine?*
>   – *Je vais aller en 4^e4.*
> 3 – *Fatima, tu vas aller en quelle classe l'année prochaine?*
>   – *Je vais aller en 4^e3.*
> 4 – *Rodolphe, tu vas aller en quelle classe l'année prochaine?*
>   – *Je vais aller en 4^e2, avec Nadir.*
> 5 – *Céline, tu vas aller en quelle classe l'année prochaine?*
>   – *Je vais aller en 4^e4.*
> 6 – *Et Cyril, il va aller en quelle classe?*
>   – *Cyril? Il va aller en 4^e1.*
> 7 – *Rachida va aller en 4^e4?*
>   – *Rachida? Non, elle va aller en 4^e3.*
> 8 – *C'est super! Ahmet va aller dans ma classe!*
>   – *Ahmet?*
>   – *Oui, il va aller en 4^e4.*
> 9 – *Patrick, tu vas aller en classe avec Ahmet?*
>   – *Non, je vais aller en 4^e4, avec Aurélie.*
> 10 – *Et toi, Delphine? Tu vas aller où?*
>   – *Moi? Je vais être avec Cyril.*
>   – *En quelle classe?*
>   – *En 4^e1.*

Answers

1 ☹ 2 ☺ 3 ☺ 4 ☺

5 ☹ 6 ☺ 7 ☹ 8 ☹

3

Preparation – Do number **1** with pupils to put them on the right track.

Answers

1 *moins manger* **2** *mieux travailler* **3** *moins parler*
4 *moins boire* **5** *mieux écrire* **6** *moins regarder*
7 *Je ne vais pas oublier mes cahiers.*

4

Pupils should keep a record of how many questions they ask in total to obtain five positive answers. The pupil who asks the least questions wins.

5

Encourage peer checking before pupils finalise their work. ♦ Pupils can lift phrases directly from the key, rather than writing about a wider range of school subjects. ♣ Pupils should aim at writing longer sentences, using link words and justifying their decisions with *parce que*, for example.

G Tu vas travailler cet été?   pp 134–135

Objective

Saying what you are going to do this summer or this weekend

Resources

Flashcards 82–87
Cassette for BD and Ex 2, 4, 5 and 6
Dictionaries (optional for Ex 7)
CM 9

Key language

Tu vas travailler cet été / ce week-end?
Je vais / Je dois faire le jardin de ma grand-mère / faire le ménage /

laver la voiture de mes parents / garder mon petit frère / faire les courses / aller en vacances / sortir avec les copains.
Je ne vais pas travailler.

Grammar

How to express the English possessive 's in French

Language learning strategies

Pronunciation: *-in / -ain / -aim*
Making notes while listening
Learning sounds through poems

Ways in

The class can now look forward to the holidays. Valérie is keen to hear about Sébastien's plans for the summer. You can introduce this spread like this: *En mai, on travaille. En juin, on travaille (...). Mais en août? On va au collège? Non! C'est les vacances* (emphasise the word *vacances*). *Valérie parle des vacances avec Sébastien.*

Use Flashcards 82–87 to introduce the new language. See Teacher's Book introduction page 4 on ideas for using flashcards.

1

Extra – Ask pupils to hide the BD and their answers and to repeat the task, this time with the cassette. (BD tapescript – see Pupil's Book.)

Answers

1 b **2** c **3** e **4** f **5** a **6** d

2

COUNTER

Preparation – Tell pupils that the information on cassette is provided in the same order as on the graph.

> *Voici les résultats de l'enquête pour la classe de 5ᵉ2. Ce week-end, 7 personnes vont laver la voiture des parents; 11 personnes vont faire le ménage; 7 personnes vont faire les courses; 6 personnes vont garder un petit frère ou une petite sœur; 2 personnes vont faire le jardin; et 9 personnes ne vont pas travailler.*
>
> *Voici les résultats de l'enquête pour la classe de 5ᵉ3. Ce week-end, 3 personnes vont faire le jardin; 5 personnes vont garder un petit frère ou une petite sœur; 7 personnes vont faire le ménage; 11 personnes vont faire les courses; 1 personne va laver la voiture; et 12 personnes ne vont pas travailler.*

Answers

5ᵉ2: Erreurs: ménage (15 personnes)   pas travailler
    (9 personnes)
5ᵉ3: jardin: 3   garder frère/sœur: 5   ménage: 7
    courses: 11   voiture: 1   pas travailler: 12

3

Preparation – Pupils should use the question from the key to initiate each exchange. Suggest they prepare a grid to record their peers' responses before producing a graph.

On prononce bien

COUNTER

> **Ecoute:**
>   *jardin train brun bien*
>
> **Ecoute et répète:**
>   *le jardin un dessin un magasin ce matin*
>   *mes copains un train j'ai faim demain*
>   *c'est bien c'est combien? je viens un village*
>   *ancien*

4

This complements the pronunciation work that has just been carried out.

Preparation – Ask pupils to spot all the words containing the *in* sound.

Extra – Pupils can either learn this by heart or make up a mini poem of their own, reusing words from the pronunciation box or others they know that contain the same sound.

COUNTER

> *Un chien, c'est bien*
> *Deux chiens, tout bruns*
> *Trois chiens, copains*
> *Quatre chiens, j'ai faim!*

5

Preparation – Let pupils listen to the whole dialogue once just for the feel of it before they read the rubric. Once they look at what to do, point out that all the statements are false. Give pupils time to take in the statements – looking particularly at the words in bold – before they listen again. Ask pupils to make brief notes only while they listen, then give them time to write full sentences.

COUNTER

> – *Magalie, tu veux sortir demain?*
> – *Demain? Ben écoute, Max, euh... non, le samedi, je dois travailler.*
> – *Travailler? Qu'est-ce que tu vas faire, Magalie?*
> – *Je vais laver la voiture de ma mère et je dois garder mon cousin.*
> – *Demain après-midi?*
> – *Non, non, demain matin.*
> – *On peut aller en ville demain après-midi? A la cafétéria?*

> – Ah! Ben, alors d'accord, mais après 4h. L'après-midi, je vais faire le jardin de ma grand-mère.
> – Elle habite où, ta grand-mère?
> – Rue Lecourbe.
> – Ecoute, rendez-vous chez ta grand-mère à 4h, d'accord?
> – Bon, ben... oui, oui, ça ira. Mais je dois rentrer à la maison à 6h30.

Answers

1 *Max invite Magalie.* **2** *Max invite Magalie pour samedi.* **3** *Magalie doit garder son cousin.* **4** *Magalie va faire le jardin de sa grand-mère.* **5** *Sa grand-mère habite rue Lecourbe.* **6** *Max donne rendez-vous chez la grand-mère de Magalie.* **7** *Magalie doit rentrer à 6h30.*

6 *Preparation* – Point out that there are no right or wrong answers.

For the listening part, give pupils time to read each statement again before they hear Sébastien's opinion. Pupils can simply put ticks or crosses next to their L/T answers.

COUNTER

> **1** – *Je n'aime pas les animaux. Promener le chien, oh, c'est ennuyeux!*
> **2** – *Aider dans le jardin, c'est super. J'adore ça.*
> **3** – *Faire la cuisine, c'est difficile et ce n'est pas amusant. Ça m'énerve.*
> **4** – *J'adore ma petite sœur, et j'aime bien faire des promenades avec elle.*
> **5** – *La mécanique, ça m'intéresse beaucoup, et les copains aussi. C'est mon loisir préféré.*
> **6** – *J'adore Disneyland, la Cité des Sciences... mais les petites fêtes, ça ne m'intéresse pas. Et aller au collège le week-end? Ça, c'est embêtant.*
> **7** – *Caroline a des problèmes avec ses parents parce qu'elle ne fait jamais sa chambre. Je vais l'aider. C'est sympa parce que c'est ma copine, et faire la chambre à deux, c'est plus facile.*
> **8** – *Je n'aime pas beaucoup le collège, mais le shopping, ça m'amuse beaucoup. J'adore regarder dans les magasins, choisir... Et l'argent? C'est ma mère! En plus, il y a une collection de stylos très jolis dans les magasins en ce moment.*

7 *Preparation* – Brainstorm about possible activities not contained in the key but which pupils are able to express in French. Restrict dictionary use. Remind pupils of useful time phrases: *La première semaine / Tous les samedis / Le dimanche matin / De temps en temps.*

H Point Langue / Atelier

pp 136–137

Resources
CM 10 and 11
Cassette for CM 11

Key language
Recycling of school work and summer activities

Grammar
Awareness of past and future

Language learning strategies
Comparing reading sources

Point Langue

This page complements topics 1 and 2 by practising recognition of verbs in the past and the future.

1

Answers
Passé: 2, 4, 6
Futur: 1, 3, 5, 7, 8

2

Answers
♦ **1** d **2** g **3** a **4** f **5** h **6** c **7** b **8** e
♣ **1** b **2** e **3** f **4** a **5** c **6** g **7** d **8** i **9** h

Atelier

1

Answers
1 Dominique **2** Jo **3** Chris **4** Ginny

2

Ask pupils to jot down the clues that give the answers away. The cassette should only be used afterwards.

COUNTER

1 – *Tu as quel âge?*
   – *13 ans.*
   – *Tu as des problèmes au collège?*
   – *Oui, parce que je n'aime pas les maths. Je ne veux pas faire maths. Je veux choisir. Je préfère la danse et le dessin.*
2 – *Tu es assez timide?*
   – *Oui, et je n'aime pas ma classe. Je suis assez petit, et ils sont très grands et très sportifs.*
   – *Tu n'aimes pas le sport?*
   – *Non.*
3 – *Ça ne va pas en classe?*
   – *Ben, non! Je parle trop! Alors les punitions, oh, là, là!...*
   – *Mais... les profs sont sympas?*
   – *Non, ils me détestent!*
4 – *Tu travailles bien au collège?*
   – *Oui, oui, le collège, ça va.*
   – *Alors, le problème...?*
   – *Le problème, c'est ma famille.*
   – *Pourquoi?*
   – *Parce que j'ai trois petits frères, et je ne peux pas beaucoup sortir.*

Answers
1 *Jo: fille (indépendante)* **2** *Dominique: garçon (petit)*
3 *Ginny: garçon (bavard, poli, sûr)* **4** *Chris: fille (travailleuse)*

3

Answers
Chris: e or i (or b!) Dominique: d or h Jo: f (or a!)
Ginny: c (or g!)

Unité 6

L'école est finie!

1 Tu vas aller en vacances?

pp 138–139

Objective
Making holiday plans

Resources
Flashcards 87–92
Cassette for BD, Ex 2 and CM 12–13
Card and scissors for Ex 4
CM 12 and 13

Key language
Qu'est-ce qu'on va / tu vas faire cet été?

Tu vas / On va aller en vacances?
Je vais... / On va... / J'aimerais mieux... / On pourrait...
... aller à la montagne / mer / campagne
... aller en Espagne
... faire des barbecues / promenades
... nager / bronzer
Oui, bonne idée / Oh, non! Ce n'est pas drôle!

Language learning strategies
Making notes from what you hear
Speaking from notes

Ways in
Valérie's family are discussing what they could do for the holiday. You can introduce this spread like this: *La famille de Valérie fait des projets de vacances. Mais il y a des opinions différentes dans la famille, et la décision est difficile.*

Use Flashcards 87–92 to introduce the new language (see Teacher's Book introduction on how to use Flashcards). The BD is exploited in Ex 1.

Pupils read the BD while they listen to the cassette.

1
This can be done in two phases. First, pupils carry out the task purely as a reading task. After the corrections, ask pupils to cover the BD and their answers and to repeat the task with the cassette.
(BD tapescript – see Pupil's Book.)

Answers
1 d 2 a 3 f 4 c 5 g 6 b 7 h 8 e

2

COUNTER

1 – Ce week-end, je vais aller à la campagne. On va faire un barbecue.
2 – Samedi, je vais aller à la mer. Je vais nager avec mon père.
3 – Moi, je vais aller à la campagne.
   – Quand?
   – En juillet. On va faire des promenades.
4 – Et toi? Tu vas aller en vancances?
   – Oui. Je vais bronzer! Je vais aller à la mer!
   – Quand? En juillet?
   – Non, en août.
5 – Tu vas aller à la mer?
   – Non. A la montagne. Et je vais bronzer!
   – Quand?
   – On va aller en vacances le 15 juillet.
6 – Tu vas aller en Espagne?
   – Oui, on va aller à la mer.
   – Quand?
   – Le 5 août, pour deux semaines.

Answers
1 g, b, *week-end* 2 d, a, *samedi* 3 g, c, *juillet* 4 e, d, *août* 5 f, e, *15 juillet* 6 h, d, *5 août (deux semaines)*

3
One of the aims here is for pupils to use awareness of cognates and near cognates to cope with unfamiliar language.

4
Preparation – Pupils prepare six cards each, as indicated. Pupils **A** and **B** pick a card at random from their packs. If Pupil **B**'s card is identical to Pupil **A**'s, **B** answers Pupil **A** positively. Otherwise, (s)he suggests the activity on his/her card.

5
Preparation – Warn pupils that this is a long conversation. To familiarise pupils with uninterrupted passages, do not allow for any pauses. Instead, allow pupils to hear the passage as many times as they need to. Warn them that a lot of the language they will hear is key language.

COUNTER

– Alors? On va aller à la campagne? En Italie?
– Oh... La campagne, ce n'est pas drôle!
– Ben... on pourrait faire des barbecues à la campagne...
– A la maison aussi, on peut faire des barbecues!
– On pourrait aller en Espagne! En Espagne, il fait beau... ce n'est pas cher...
– Ah ouais! On pourrait nager, on pourrait bronzer. On pourrait faire des promenades... des barbecues...
– Il fait chaud en Espagne! Je préfère l'Ecosse.
– Mais... c'est le soleil! C'est les vacances!
– Alors, c'est d'accord pour l'Espagne?
– Bon, moi, ça va...
– Alors, c'est d'accord!

Answers
Espagne (il fait beau; pas cher; nager; bronzer; promenades; barbecues; soleil)

6
Preparation – Ask pupils to identify which phrases from the model dialogue can be adapted. Pupils can reuse their cards from Ex 4 and create new ones if needed.

COUNTER

– Qu'est-ce qu'on va faire cet été?
– On pourrait aller à la mer?
– Oh, non! Je n'aime pas nager! On va à la montagne? En Ecosse?
– A la montagne? Pourquoi?
– J'aimerais bien faire des promenades.
– Moi, j'aimerais mieux bronzer.
– On peut bronzer à la montagne!
– Bon, d'accord.

▮ On va partir comment?

pp 140–141

Objective
Holiday plans: discussing dates, travel and accommodation

Resources
Flashcards 93–96
Cassette for BD and Ex 1 and 4
CM 14 and 15
OHTs (optional for CM 14 and 15)

Key language
On va / Tu vas partir quand?

On va / Tu vas aller où?
On va / Tu vas partir comment?
Je vais partir le + date
On va aller dans un camping/ hôtel / gîte
J'aimerais bien aller... chez Julie / les grands-parents
... en voiture / bateau / avion.
Recycling of dates

Language learning strategies
Planning work using spider diagrams

Ways in
Valérie and her family are now discussing how to travel for their holiday. You can introduce this spread like this: *C'est décidé! Valérie et sa famille vont aller en vacances en Espagne. Mais... ils vont voyager comment? Et ils vont aller où exactement? Encore des décisions difficiles.*

Use Flashcards 93–96 to introduce the new language (see Teacher's Book introduction page 4 for ways of using Flashcards).

Pupils can then read the BD while they listen to the cassette. Improvise 'quick-fire' questions which pupils should answer with/without the BD:

Le petit frère de Valérie voudrait voyager comment?

(BD tapescript – see Pupil's Book.)

1

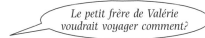

1 – *J'aimerais bien aller dans un camping. On pourrait partir en voiture.*

2 – *J'aimerais bien aller dans un hôtel. On pourrait partir en avion.*

3 – *Moi, j'aimerais bien aller dans un gîte. On pourrait partir en voiture.*

4 – *On pourrait aller chez grand-père et grand-mère. Ils ont une maison en Espagne. On pourrait partir en bateau?*

5 – *On pourrait partir en bateau, et aller dans un camping à la mer.*

6 – *Allô? C'est l'oncle Arthur! Je vous invite! Vous pouvez venir en voiture?*

Answers
1 a, f **2** b, g **3** d, f **4** e, h **5** h, a **6** c, f

2

Preparation – Pupils could prepare a grid with the key words (*hôtel*, *voiture*, etc.) as column headings. Ask pupils to memorise the questions prior to carrying out their interviews.

3
For added motivation, suggest pupils score a point for each question they ask. The pupil with the lowest score wins.

4

Preparation – Check pupils know how many days there are in each month.

1 – *Je vais aller en vacances le 20 juillet. Je vais partir deux semaines.*

2 – *Je vais aller en vacances le 3 septembre. Je vais partir une semaine.*

3 – *Je vais aller en vacances le 15 juin. Je vais partir dix jours.*

4 – *Je vais aller en vacances le 15 juillet. Je vais partir une semaine.*

5 – *Je vais partir en vacances le 1er août. Je vais partir trois semaines.*

6 – *Je vais partir en vacances le 13 juillet. Je vais partir 5 jours.*

7 – *Je vais partir en vacances le 2 août. Je vais partir un mois.*

Answers
1 3 août **2** 10 septembre **3** 25 juin **4** 22 juillet
5 22 août **6** 18 juillet **7** 2 septembre
Le numéro 3 va finir les vacances en premier

Extra task – This task does not figure in the Pupil's Book.

Travaillez à deux. Faites des phrases sur les vacances.
A: Ecris un mot. On
B: Ajoute un mot. On va
A: Ajoute un mot. On va aller
Qui fait la phrase la plus longue dans la classe?

5

Preparation – Advise pupils to start from 1–8 rather than from the letter. Ask them to watch carefully whether the verbs are in the past or the future, both in 1–8 and in the letter.
Answers
1 faux **2** vrai **3** faux **4** vrai **5** vrai **6** faux
7 vrai **8** faux

6

Pupils can describe real or fictional holiday plans.

K Point Langue / Atelier

Resources
CM 16, 17, 18 and 19
Cassette for **Atelier** Ex 2 and CM 18

Key language
Recycling of planning future events

Grammar
Overview of question forms

Language learning strategies
Reading for personal interest and enjoyment

Point Langue

This page provides a recap on question forms practised in **Camarades 2**.

1

Extra – Pupils can practise further, either hiding 1-6 or a-f.

Answers
1 e **2** c **3** f **4** a **5** d **6** b

2

Extra – Both ♦ and ♣ pupils make up their own answers.

Answers
♦ **1** d **2** b **3** a **4** f **5** c **6** e
♣ **1** *Qu'est-ce que tu vas faire cet été?* **2** *Tu vas partir quand?* **3** *Tu vas partir / aller en vacances avec qui?*
4 *Tu vas / Vous allez aller ou?* **5** *Qu'est-ce que tu vas / vous allez faire?* **6** *Tu vas / Vous allez rentrer quand?*

Atelier

1

Preparation – Ask pupils to look up *gratuit / autoroute / aires de repos* in the **Camarades 2** Pupil's Book glossary. Restrict – or ban – dictionary use. If pupils do not understand a particular word, they should ask themselves if that word prevents them from understanding the overall context. If they forget the meaning of a familiar word, they should look through the Pupil's Book or ask a friend for help rather than using a dictionary.

2

Preparation – Warn pupils that they will hear an uninterrupted dialogue. Do not pause when playing the cassette, but allow pupils to listen several times.

> – *Monsieur?*
> – *Je regarde... je cherche un livre... une brochure... des dépliants... je ne sais pas.*
> – *Qu'est-ce qui vous intéresse?*
> – *Je ... c'est pour les vacances.*
> – *C'est pour des vacances en famille?*
> – *En famille? Non, non, euh... c'est pour moi. Je voudrais trouver une activité différente, intéressante...*
> – *Le sport, ça vous intéresse?*
> – *Le sport? Euh... non, pas vraiment...*
> – *Vous cherchez des activités à Paris?*
> – *A Paris? Non, non, je préfère la campagne...*
> – *Eh bien, regardez, j'ai une brochure intéressante ici...*

Answer
Idée A

3

Preparation – Ask pupils to look up *plage* in the Pupil's Book glossary.

Encourage pupils to reuse phrases from *Idées Vacances*. If pupils prepare a ***publicité-radio***, emphasise the need to sound convincing.

A – Epreuve d'écoute

Exercice 1

Pupils are asked to identify the main points in short instructions given at near normal speed but with some distortion and with each item repeated. The exercise tests elements of performance at Level 3.

COUNTER

> **Exemple**
>
> – Le train pour Marseille est au quai numéro trois. Ce train va partir à neuf heures dix. Il va arriver à Marseille à onze heures quinze.
>
> **1** – Le train rapide pour Paris est au quai numéro deux. Ce train va partir à six heures vingt. Il va arriver à Paris à huit heures cinq.
>
> **2** – Le train pour Bordeaux est au quai numéro quatre. Ce train va partir à sept heures quinze. Il va arriver à Bordeaux à dix heures quarante.
>
> **3** – Le train pour Lyon Perrache se trouve au quai numéro un. Il va partir à treize heures et il va arriver à Lyon à seize heures trente.

1 mark for each correct answer. Total 9. Pupils scoring at least 7 marks are showing some characteristics of performance at Level 3.

1 2 6h20 8h05
2 4 7h15 10h40
3 1 13h/1h 16h30/4h30

Exercice 2

This tests understanding of a longer passage from which pupils identify the main points. The dialogue is spoken at near normal speed. Elements of performance at Level 4 are tested.

COUNTER

> **Exemple**
>
> – Michel. Qu'est-ce que tu as fait le week-end dernier?
> – Alors, samedi après-midi, j'ai visité le musée, mais ce n'était pas très intéressant!
>
> **1** – Et toi, Mélanie?
> – Ben, samedi soir, j'ai été au cinéma avec mon copain. C'était bien.
>
> **2** – Grégory. Qu'est-ce que tu as fait, toi?
> – Pas grande chose. J'ai été dans un café... et j'ai bu trop de limonade, je pense!
>
> **3** – Et Lucie. Qu'est-ce que tu as fait?
> – Samedi, j'ai déjeuné chez Mc.Do avec ma famille. J'ai mangé un hamburger.
>
> **4** – Frédéric – dis-moi ce que tu as fait le week-end.
> – Moi, j'ai travaillé dans le jardin. J'aime bien faire du jardinage, tu vois.
>
> **5** – Et toi, Virginie?
> – Moi aussi, j'ai travaillé, mais c'était du travail scolaire. J'ai lu un très long livre – c'était formidable.
>
> **6** – Julien. Qu'as-tu fait?
> – J'ai été en ville et j'ai acheté un livre à la librairie.
>
> **7** – Et Nadine?
> – Moi aussi, j'ai été en ville. J'ai rencontré mon petit ami.
>
> **8** – Fabien. Qu'as-tu fait?
> – Tu sais bien que j'aime le dessin, n'est-ce pas? Alors j'ai beaucoup dessiné ce week-end.
>
> **9** – Et toi finalement, Isabelle.
> – Moi, j'ai fait une longue promenade à la campagne. C'était vraiment bien!
> – Merci, mes amis!

1 mark for each correct answer. Total 9. Pupils scoring at least 7 marks are showing some characteristics of performance at Level 4.

1 F **2** I **3** C **4** D **5** K **6** A **7** E **8** H **9** J

Exercice 3

In this exercise, pupils' understanding of familiar language in simple sentences within a longer passage is tested. They identify the main points in a text spoken at near normal speed and past tense actions are included. This is an exercise testing elements of performance at Level 4, moving towards Level 5.

COUNTER

> Salut! C'est Sophie! Je téléphone pour t'inviter à sortir ce soir. Tu veux venir au théâtre avec moi? Un ticket, ça fait quarante francs. Rendez-vous à sept heures et demie? Tu peux venir devant la gare. Le théâtre va finir à dix heures et quart, je pense. Après ça, on peut aller au café si tu veux. On va aller au café du collège. C'est assez loin du théâtre, mais on doit y aller à pied parce qu'il n'y a pas d'autobus à cette heure-là et le taxi est trop cher.

1 mark for each correct answer. Total 7. Pupils scoring at least 5 marks are showing some characteristics of performance at Level 5.

1 théâtre **2** 40 francs **3** 7h30 **4** gare
5 10h15 **6** café **7** à pied

B – Epreuve orale

Exercice 1
Pupils point to four destinations/forms of transport, using the model, say where they are going and how. They respond with short phrases using the model and cue as support. Their pronunciation may be approximate. Total 4.

Exercice 2
This exercise features two mini role-plays of two or three exchanges based on the GCSE format of visually cued role plays. Pupils have to initiate and respond using the visuals for support. Pupils choose 1a+1b or 2a+2b. The **A** role only is assessed. Weaker pupils carrying out the **B** role could have their part written on OHT.

This is a test of performance at Level 3. Award 1 mark per item successfully communicated. Ensure that pupils are familiar with interpreting the visuals before starting so that elements such as *Quand / A quelle heure* are not missed from the cue. Pupils gaining a total of 4 or 5 marks are showing characteristics of performance at Level 3. Total 5.

Exercice 3
This is a test in which pupils may show evidence of performance at different levels. The exercise aims to test the pupil's ability to use the perfect tense in a school context. The conversation is simple and structured and supported by visual cues. The **B** role only is assessed. Pupils who communicate the message on at least four of the five points but who do not show an awareness of appropriate tense use are showing characteristics of performance at Level 4. Pupils who communicate at least four of the messages and who try to make use of the perfect tense show some characteristics of performance at Level 5. Total 5.

Exercice 4
Pupils who communicate the message on at least six of the eight points as shown in the illustration, but who do not show an awareness of appropriate tense use show some characteristics of performance at Level 4. Pupils who can communicate six of the eight points and who try to make use of *aller* + the infinitive or who develop the situation show some characteristics of performance at Level 5.

Teachers may wish to add bonus marks as below. These enable the amount of help/support needed from the teacher to be taken into account. Some pupils may be able to treat the exercise as a presentation and proceed unaided, whereas others may need extra support from the teacher in the form of questions. These marks also give the opportunity to reward the degree of accuracy shown by pupils.

Add bonus marks out of 3 as follows:
1 mark – pupil manages to communicate the basic messages, language is often inaccurate but the meaning of most of the messages is there. Substantial help is needed from the teacher.
2 marks – communicates all the messages despite inaccuracies. Some help from the teacher.
3 marks – communicates the messages well. Language often very accurate. Little help needed.

10 marks for communication plus 3 bonus marks. Total 13.

C – Epreuve de lecture

Exercice 1
This test requires only the understanding of recycled subjects presented in short phrases from **Camarades 1**, together with some of the comments on progress in Unit 6 of **Camarades 2**.

This is a test of performance at Level 1. Pupils gaining at least 3 marks are showing some characteristics of performance at Level 1. Total 4.
1 B **2** B **3** A **4** A

Exercice 2
The test focuses on the understanding of directions. Pupils have to show understanding of short texts made up of familiar language. They identify main points and, from a given starting point (make sure that they all understand where this is), they have to identify the correct place on the map. This is a test of performance at Level 3. Pupils gaining 4 marks or more are showing characteristics of performance at Level 3. Total 6.
1 I **2** A **3** H **4** E **5** F **6** C

Exercice 3
Pupils read a short text about a visit to Paris. The language used reflects the structures and vocabulary met in Units 5 and 6 and the narrative here is mainly first person with some third person in the perfect tense. The questions involve following the time-line of the account and pupils are expected to identify and note main points and some detail, including likes, dislikes and feelings. Pupils have to fill in the boxes (following the time-line of the day's events) with the correct letter. The last question is answered by ticking the appropriate box and tests Aline's favourite activity. This is a test of performance at Level 4. Pupils gaining 6 marks or more are showing characteristics of performance at Level 4. Total 8.
7h30 / B (example)   **1** A+H (accept either order)
2 10h / D + I **3** 12h / C **4** 2h / E **5** 3h / F
Aline a préféré visiter la Tour Eiffel.

Exercice 4
Pupils read a longer text, a letter covering past and future events and they have to identify main points and specific details (Level 5). To do this, comprehension of opinions and an ability to distinguish between past, present and future is needed (Level 5). First and third person use of structures is featured and the vocabulary focuses on language met both earlier in the book and in Units 5 and 6. This is a test of performance at Level 5. Pupils gaining 5 marks or more are showing characteristics of performance at Level 5. Total 7.
1 *avec le collège* **2** *en car* **3** *a fait de la marche à pied* **4** *à la campagne* **5** *faire de la lecture* **6** *Destination:* look for *(à la) mer / (à la) plage* – mark for communication. *Raison:* accept any of the following *(peut) / (veut) nager / bronzer / faire des barbecues* (2 marks)

D – Epreuve écrite

Exercice 1

Pupils are required to copy familiar short phrases correctly. They also match the phrases to the appropriate pictures. This therefore tests elements of performance at Level 2.

1 mark for each correctly matched and copied phrase. Ignore accents.

1/2 mark for incorrectly matched but correctly copied phrase.

0 marks if one or more copying errors (apart from accents)

1 mark for each correctly copied sentence. Total 8. Pupils scoring at least 6 marks are showing some characteristics of performance at Level 2. An assessment of the ability to copy words in each sentence could be carried out as a means of testing performance at Level 1.

1 *Je vais pêcher dans le lac.*
2 *Je vais faire du vélo.*
3 *Je vais jouer sur la plage.*
4 *Je vais nager dans la mer.*
5 *Je vais faire des promenades.*
6 *Je vais partir en voiture.*
7 *Je vais faire des barbecues.*
8 *Je vais faire du ski.*
9 *Je vais faire du camping.*

Exercice 2

In this exercise, pupils adapt a model by substituting individual words and phrases. This tests elements of performance at Level 4. Please note that pupils will need to write their answers on a separate sheet of paper.

Award marks out of 8 following the criteria below. Pupils scoring at least 6 marks are showing some characteristics of performance at Level 4.

Award an impression mark out of 8 based on the following criteria:

7/8 marks – correct substitution of all six details. A very good standard of accuracy.

5/6 marks – correct substitution of 4 or 5 details. A good standard of accuracy.

3/4 marks – correct substitution of 3 details. A fair standard of accuracy.

1/2 marks – correct substitution of 1 or 2 details. Rather poor standard of accuracy.

0 marks – no success of substitution of details. Very poor accuracy.

[Note: one or both of the above criteria may apply in each case]

Exercice 3

Pupils are tested on their ability to write sentences in the perfect tense. Their memory of specific activities is tested and they are encouraged (by the example) to include their personal responses simply. This exercise therefore has elements of performance at Level 4, moving towards Level 5. Level 5 performance would be evident in those pupils who write at length and include personal reactions to the events. Please note that pupils will need to write their answers on a separate sheet of paper.

1 mark for each different past tense phrase. Total 9.

Pupils scoring at least 7 marks are showing some characteristics of performance at Level 4.

1 mark – sentence communicates, with reasonable accuracy, the activity depicted. Expect a good mastery of the perfect tense. Expect correct use of acute accent on past participle.

1/2 mark – sentence communicates with fair accuracy the activity depicted. Expect a fair mastery only of the perfect tense. Present tense or infinitives may have been used.

0 marks – the French does not communicate the activity depicted. Accuracy is so poor that communication is severly hindered.

Note: the activities can be described in any order. Do not credit repetition of *j'ai regardé la télévision* but do credit appropriate alternative to this if it describes the picture (e.g. *J'ai vu un programme intéressant.*)

A – Epreuve d'écoute

Exercice I

Two topics are tested in this opening exercise – times and understanding of activities in the past. The passage in full is quite long, but is split into small sections. It is spoken at near normal pace and is repeated. There is no interference. It tests elements of performance at Level 3.

COUNTER

Exemple
– Voici ce que j'ai fait hier. Alors, à sept heures et demie j'ai pris une douche.

1 – Après ça, à huit heures moins le quart, j'ai pris le petit déjeuner. J'ai mangé du pain et j'ai bu du café.

2 – A huit heures, je suis sorti de la maison et je suis allé au travail à pied.

3 – Au travail, j'ai donné quelques coups de téléphone. A midi, j'ai téléphoné à Paris et à Bordeaux.

4 – Après le travail, à cinq heures et quart, j'ai fait une promenade. C'est bien de faire une promenade après le travail!

5 – Le soir, j'étais très fatigué, donc j'ai été au lit à dix heures vingt. J'ai très bien dormi!

1 mark for each correct answer. Total 10. Pupils scoring at least 7 marks are showing some characteristics of performance at Level 3.

1 7.45 F **2** 8.00 E **3** 12.00 C **4** 5.15 G
5 10.20 D

Exercice 2

The topic of jobs is tested, together with opinions about work. The text is slightly more dense than in the previous exercise, the speed of delivery near normal, but there is little interference. This tests elements of performance at Level 4.

COUNTER

Exemple 1 – Philippe
– Mon père travaille dans un restaurant. Il est chef cuisinier. Il adore son travail.

Exemple 2 – Marie
– Ma mère est ménagère. Elle travaille à la maison. Elle a beaucoup de travail à faire. Elle n'aime pas travailler à la maison.

1 – Luc
– Ma mère est infirmière. Elle travaille à l'hôpital dans notre ville. Elle trouve que le travail est formidable.

2 – Catherine
– Mon père est fermier. Il travaille dans une ferme près de notre village. Il commence le travail à cinq heures du matin, mais c'est un travail qu'il aime bien.

3 – Ahmed
– Mon père travaille dans une grande usine de voitures à Billancourt, près de Paris. Il travaille beaucoup et il est toujours très fatigué après l'usine. Pauvre papa! Il déteste son travail.

4 – Julie
– Ma mère travaille à la réception d'un hôtel en ville. Elle reçoit les clients quand ils arrivent à l'hôtel. Elle dit que le travail est très intéressant.

5 – Pierre
– Mon père travaille dans un bureau au centre de Paris. Il est secrétaire dans une grande entreprise. Mais il n'est pas content – il trouve le travail est ennuyeux.

1 mark for each correct answer. Total 10. Pupils scoring at least 7 marks are showing some characteristics of performance at Level 4.

1 D likes **2** H likes **3** F dislikes **4** A likes
5 B dislikes

Exercice 3

In the final exercise, the text is denser and the speed of delivery faster. Candidates are required to pick out particular details from a wide choice given. The speakers use the immediate future tense. This exercise tests elements of performance at Level 5.

COUNTER

Exemple – Nicole
– Pendant les vacances d'été, je vais aller en Angleterre avec ma famille. On va loger à l'auberge de jeunesse de Londres. Pour aller en Angleterre nous allons prendre le bateau de St. Malo à Portsmouth. On va partir le cinq août pour y passer une semaine. Je vais faire beaucoup de choses. J'espère bien aller danser parce qu'il y a de bonnes discothèques en Angleterre.

1 – Marc
– Moi, pendant les vacances d'été cette année je vais aller en Espagne avec la famille. Nous allons passer deux semaines dans un hôtel à Malaga dans le sud de l'Espagne. Ça va être formidable. On va prendre l'avion - ça va être la première fois que je prends l'avion, d'ailleurs! Nous allons partir le premier août et nous allons passer deux semaines en Espagne. Je vais nager chaque jour dans la piscine de l'hôtel.

2 – Lucille
– Alors pendant les grandes vacances, je vais partir avec mes amis au bord de la mer. On va au bord de la mer donc, et on va faire du camping (je n'aime pas les hôtels). Pour arriver au bord de la mer, on va prendre le car. On va partir le 12 août et on va rester là-bas pendant deux semaines. On va beaucoup s'amuser, et j'espère bien faire de la voile.

½ mark for each correct answer. Total 5. Pupils scoring at least 3½ marks are showing some characteristics of performance at Level 5.
1 Marc: E; G; L; O; T. **2** Lucille: A; F; M; R; V.

B – Epreuve orale

Exercice 1
Pupils work in pairs and point out and name four destinations and four means of transport. This is a test of performance at Level 1 or Level 2 depending on the outcome. Pupils responding with single words, e.g. *France + train* are showing characteristics of performance at Level 1. Pupils responding more fully e.g. *Je vais en France en train* are showing some characteristics of performance at Level 2. Allow $^1/_2$ mark per item then round up half marks. Pupils scoring at least 3 marks are showing some characteristics of performance at Level 1 or Level 2 depending on their type of utterance as outlined above. Total 4.

Exercice 2
Pupils use visual cues to help them give and request information. The language used is memorised, no substitution of lexical items is required. Two or three exchanges is characteristic of performance at Level 3. The test is targeted at Level 3 (tasks prepared from brief). However, pupils who are successful in all four tasks, and who are able to display accurate pronunciation and some consistency in intonation, show some characteristics of performance at Level 4. Teachers requiring a test bearing more characteristics of a Level 4 performance could provide pupils with the *métro* map in the Pupil's Book and ask pupils to improvise a conversation in which they show the ability to adapt and substitute single words phrases - working from the two models given in this exercise. Total 4.

Exercice 3
The differentiation in this exercise is related to outcome. The Copymaster is intended to cue utterances which enable pupils to display characteristics of performance at several levels. Total 6.

At Level 3 pupils should be able to use short phrases to express their likes and dislikes using mainly memorised language. Marks are available for giving their age (1 mark), saying they like (playing) tennis, football (1 mark) and (watching) TV (1 mark), saying they prefer cartoons, TV games shows (1 mark), expressing dislike for tidying a room, washing up and giving a reason (1 mark). Teachers should note that some pupils can communicate meaning but need more help from the teacher to cue their response and may not always be able to produce a phrase including a verbal construction, e.g. *le tennis + la télévision* in response to *Qu'est-ce que tu aimes faire comme activité?* These pupils may be showing characteristics of performance more consistent with Level 2. A Level 3 response might include phrases such as *J'aime jouer au tennis – Je déteste ranger ma chambre*. Pupils responding in such a way and who score at least 4 marks are showing characteristics of performance at Level 3.

At Level 4, teachers could ask pupils to provide a further possibility of their own (an extra activity, favourite programme and household task). In this way pupils would adapt and substitute phrases (Level 4). Accurate pronunciation and consistent intonation are expected. Pupils who correctly identify at least four of the given visual cues and who then go on to adapt show some characteristics of performance at Level 4.

Exercice 4
Pupils work in pairs. Pupil **B** is assessed. This type of exercise is intended to elicit characteristics of performance up to Level 5. Pupils are expected to convey information and opinions in simple terms referring to events in the past on the topic of holidays. Cues are used (a characteristic of Level 4) but performance at Level 5 could be assessed if teachers ask Pupil **A** only to use the card and **B** is given the freedom to respond as s/he wishes (no support from cues). 1 mark available for each visual cue and an opinion and reason on the last cue. Total 8.

Pupils scoring more than half marks may well still be responding in short phrases. However, as long as they communicate the information accurately enough to be understood (not necessarily in the appropriate tense) and with consistent pronunciation, they will be showing some characteristics of performance at Level 4.

Pupils scoring at least 6 of the set marks and who can supply their own options and who attempt to communicate in the correct tense are showing some characteristics of performance at Level 5.

Teachers may also wish to add bonus marks as below. These enable the amount of help/support from the teacher to be taken into account. Some pupils may need considerable support in the form of extra questions and may not show great immediacy of response. These marks also give the teacher the opportunity to reward the degree of accuracy.
1 mark – pupil manages to communicate the basic messages - language is often inaccurate but the meaning of the messages is there. Substantial help is needed from the teacher.
2 marks – communicates nearly all the messages despite inaccuracies in short simple responses. Some help from the teacher.
3 marks – communicates messages well. Language often very accurate. Little help needed.

C – Epreuve de lecture

Exercice 1
This test requires understanding of short phrases presented in a familiar context. This is a test of performance at Level 2. Pupils scoring 4 or more marks are showing some characteristics of performance at Level 2. Total 6.

Raphaël = i + e
Emilie= h + b
Alain = g + a

Exercice 2
Pupils are required in this test to show understanding of printed short texts made up of familiar language. Main points are identified including likes and dislikes. This is a test of performance at Level 3. Pupils scoring at least 3 marks are showing some characteristics of performance at Level 3. Total 4.

J'aime parler des langues = Axelle

J'adore faire de la musique et jouer avec mon ordinateur = Pierre

J'aime faire du cheval et regarder des films = Renaud

J'adore lire mais je n'aime pas nager = Mélanie

Exercice 3

Pupils are expected to show understanding of a factual text based on the topic of school and the use of modal verbs. They identify and note main points by ticking a grid alongside statements which they have to indicate are possible, necessary or impossible according to the text. This is a test of performance at Level 4. The final question asks pupils to say whether the school is strict and to justify their decision. Pupils scoring 7 or more marks are showing some characteristics of performance at Level 4. Total 9.

Nécessaire, impossible, nécessaire, impossible, possible, impossible, possible, nécessaire

For the final 'open' question, accept *oui* (1 mark) and any credible reason (1 mark) for the school being strict (eg, *on ne peut pas bavarder en classe*). Only accept *non* if given with *on ne doit pas porter un uniforme / d'uniforme scolaire.*

Exercice 4

Pupils are expected to show understanding of a text which includes past and future events. To answer they need to be able to identify and note main points and specific details, including opinions. This is a test of performance at Level 5. Pupils scoring 4 or more marks are showing some characteristics of performance at Level 5. Pupils identify the true/false statement and are expected to correct false statements to gain the mark (full sentences not expected). No half marks. Total 6.

1 *Faux*, accept *des billets pour un concert.* **2** *Faux*, accept *avec sa sœur.* **3** *Vrai* **4** *Vrai* **5** *Faux*, accept *plus de progrès* or concept *elle a bien travaillé.* **6** *Vrai.*

D – Epreuve écrite

Exercice 1

An exercise containing elements of performance at Level 2, in which pupils are required both to copy short phrases and to write words from memory.

1 mark for each answer. Total 5. Pupils scoring at least 3¹/2 marks are showing some characteristics of performance at Level 2.

Award 1 mark if the phrase is copied correctly and any single item of clothing pictured has been rendered with reasonable accuracy. Gender errors can be ignored.

Award ¹/2 mark if there are a few errors of copying or if the item of clothing is not clearly understandable.

Exercice 2

In this exercise, pupils construct simple sentences based on likes/dislikes and the topic of food. This reflects evidence of performance at Level 3.

Spelling should be reasonably accurate. The intention is that the phrases *j'adore* and *je déteste* should be used for Questions 3 and 5, but do not insist on this.

1 mark for each answer. Total 5. Pupils scoring at least 3¹/2 marks are showing some characteristics of performance at Level 3.

1 mark if phrase communicates clearly, with appropriate phrase for like/dislike and food item. Ignore gender and accent errors.

¹/2 mark if errors impede comprehension in either part of sentence.

Sample correct answers:
1 *J'aime les bonbons.* **2** *J'aime le poisson.* **3** *J'adore les glaces.* **4** *Je n'aime pas les tomates.* **5** *Je déteste le jambon.*

Exercice 3

By adapting a model, substituting words and phrases, pupils are being tested on elements of performance at Level 4. Please note that pupils will need to write their answers on a separate sheet of paper.

¹/2 mark for each correct substitution (written with reasonable accuracy). 10 x ¹/2 = 5 marks. Pupils scoring at least 3¹/2 marks are showing some characteristics of performance at Level 4.

huit heures / sept heures et quart; en autobus; ma sœur; une limonade; fromage; un livre; la boulangerie; du pain; et quart; écouter de la musique / des disques / des CD

Exercice 4

This exercise tests elements of performance up to Level 5, in that pupils are required to produce writing in which they express opinions and refer to past events. Please note that pupils will need to write their answers on a separate sheet of paper.

With a working total of 10 marks, reward up to 2 marks for each of the five elements depicted. Accept a fair degree of error, but award 2 marks only if there is a clear attempt to use the perfect tense. Award 1 mark if the idea is conveyed fairly clearly but without perfect tenses. Use ¹/2 marks if some knowledge of the required vocabulary is shown.

Pupils scoring at least 7 marks out of 10 are showing some characteristics of performance at Level 5.

If pupils fail to express the past tense correctly, their performance can be assessed at Level 3 if they manage to write 2 or 3 sentences.

Sample renderings of each illustration:
a *Je suis allé/e au bord de la mer.* **b** *J'ai passé les vacances dans un hôtel. C'était bien*.* **c** *J'ai fait du vélo avec mes amis.* **d** *J'ai joué au tennis avec ma sœur.* **e** *J'ai nagé dans la mer. Il a fait beau*.*

*there is no obligation to include an opinion, reference to the weather and so on, but inclusion of these, as of extra material, link phrases etc. can be taken into consideration in awarding marks.